# humour

*the*

# computer

# humour

## *the*

## computer

edited by

*Andrew Davison*

The MIT Press
Cambridge, Massachusetts
and London, England

This book was designed and set in Mac PageMaker 5.0 by Andrew Davison, and printed and bound in the United States of America.

Library of Congress Cataloging-in-Publication Data

Humour The Computer / edited by Andrew Davison.
    p.   cm.
  Includes bibliographical references.
  ISBN 0-262-54075-4
  1. Electronic data processing--Humor.  2. Computers--Humor.
I. Davison, Andrew.
PN6231.E4H86  1995                        95-3065
818'.540208--dc20                             CIP

For Supatra, Mum and Dad

# Contents

# Contents

# Contents

# Preface

My aim with *Humour The Computer* (HTC) was to collect together my favourite funny stories, parodies, laughable true-life incidents, comic song lyrics, and jokey poems from the wacky world of computing. After two years of (part-time) blood, sweat and tears, I've narrowed the enormous selection down to about 70 choice articles (each about 2 to 3 pages long).

I've deliberately avoided humour that relies on a lot of technical knowledge – you don't have to have a degree in computer science to laugh at the stuff in HTC. The intended reader probably has a home computer (for games), and perhaps a personal computer at work (for games, ... I mean word processing).

Over three-quarters of the articles fall into this 'non-expert computer user' category. About 15 of those left require a smattering of programming knowledge – just enough for you to appreciate how horrendous it all is. The final few pieces are more technical, assuming a vague familiarity with networks, complexity, and jovial topics like that. I left them in because they're funny.

The material has been drawn from a plethora of sources – about a third of it has come from USENET news groups and from computers reachable over the Internet (I'm sorry if that sounds like a boring bit from a text book; the Internet is really very, very interesting). The other two-thirds comes from printed sources (old fashioned I know, but still in use), including computer magazines such as *Datamation* and *BYTE*, general magazines such as *The New Yorker* and *New Scientist*, computer journals such as *SIGPLAN Notices* and the *Communications of the ACM*, book extracts, newsletter extracts, and submissions.

The articles cover an enormous range of topics, almost defying summary, so I'll go ahead and try. Some of the main 'themes' are: the impact of computing on our lives, hilarious hardware, silly software, first encounters with computing, computer companies that we love, programming pains, and absurd academia. I've not bothered trying to group the articles into these spurious categories, since that way lies madness (I recommend that you try it after you've bought the book). Only the serials: *BOFH* and *Joe Lisp*, are presented in order.

My suggested HTC reading strategy is to sit in a bathtub of custard (an alternative is to sit in an armchair), then open the book at random and begin reading. You will soon start to notice little sayings and puns in the margins. These sometimes have something to do with the main text, but often do not. Also don't be distracted by the cute, little drawings that decorate the margins, they are there simply to calm your nerves. Remember to get out of the bathtub before the custard hardens.

Jokes and cartoons are not very well represented in HTC, a conscious decision since there are already countless computer jokes and cartoons books in circulation (actually, they're more likely to be out of print). The *Related Reading* section (at the back) lists numerous such books, along with many other sources of computer laughs.

This project has been a labour of love, and I will be donating my royalties to Alzheimer's Disease International (ADI), a lay-oriented organisation established to promote charitable, educational and scientific work worldwide for persons with Alzheimer's and their families. ADI's governing body is made up of representatives of the 30+ national Alzheimer's associations. For more details of this organisation, contact:

Rachel Billington, Secretary General
Alzheimer's Disease International (ADI)
P. O. Box 2672
Chicago, Illinois 60690-2672, USA
Tel: +1 (312) 335-5777;  Fax: +1 (312) 335-5186

or your national society.

Bearing in mind the charitable nature of this book, you should buy two copies immediately.

If you have any comments about HTC, please get in touch. I'd also like to receive *your* favourite computer humour titbits.

### Acknowledgements

Special thanks to my wife, Supatra Parnrong, who has been an enormous source of encouragement. Her comments have improved HTC immeasurably.

I must also mention John Shepherd and Wai-Keong Foong, who

were kind enough to proof-read the first draft (and try out the custard strategy).

This project would not have been feasible without the excellent computing facilities and wonderful staff in the Department of Computer Science at the University of Melbourne.

The really important things illustrated by this book are the generosity and helpfulness of the international computing community. Everyone mentioned here has donated their time and energy at *no* charge. This is also true of the graphics companies named in the *Sources For The Margins* section, the authors and publishers cited in the main text, and the people who helped me to compile the *Related Reading* section. I hope I've included everyone, but I'm sure I've forgotten someone.

I couldn't have managed without all of you. Thanks everyone.

Grayson D. Abbott (humorist); Douglas Adams (humorist); Abraham Akkerman (humorist); Daniel J. Barrett (humorist); David H. Bernanke (ImageWorld searcher); Jonathan Bowen (humour collector); Mark Brader (alternative universe theorist); Roy Carlson (SEN horrors); Danny Cohen (Finnegan's world); Michael A. Covington (advice); Gary A Delong (references); Peter J. Denning (assorted help); Ian Feldman (computing sf list-maker); Jim Flanagan (poetry collector); Alan Fleming (humour collector extraordinaire); Del Freeman (humorist); Anurag Garg (humorist); David Goldfarb (explained Contento); Ganesh C. Gopalakrishnan (references); Ian Graham (humorist); Peter Grogono (humorist); Stefan Haenssgen (songs and poems collector); Tyson R. Henry (references); Michael F. Hodous (references); Jim Horning (C hoaxer); Harold Hubschman (DEC helper); Lawrence Hunter (Joe Lisp contact); John Ioannidis (real programmer); David G. Jones (humorist); Andrew Klossner (folklore clues); William E. Kost (assorted help); D. 'krikket' Krick (C hoaxer); John Kristoff (humour collector extraordinaire); Trygve Lode (unnatural enquirer); Paul S. Licker (humorist); Jochen Ludewig (humorist); Tristram Mabbs (explained RFC); Tony R. Martinez (humorist); Greg Michaelson (assorted help); Rizwan D. Mithani (humorist); Robert Mokry (legal humour);

Ronan Mullally (humorist); Don L. F. Nilsen (serious humour);
Karl Nyberg (humour source); Johnathan Partridge (humorist);
Bruce Perens (jello references); Paul Pierce (humorist);
Kevin Podsiadlik (C hoaxer); Bob Prior (supportive MIT Press editor);
Rosalind Reid (American scientist); Arne Rohde (references);
Bob Roos (tin men-tor); Gordon Rugg (humorist);
Joyce Scrivner (cut a Gordian knot); Dean L. Scoville (humorist);
Martin A. Settle (humorist); Ellen Spertus (humorist);
Simon Travaglia (nice operator from NZ);
The University of Melbourne library staff;
Tom Van Vleck (real specs and SE comics);
Pauline van Winsen (humour collector); Michael Wise (references)

*Sources For The Margins*

The worst puns in the margins are my own invention. The sayings by Alan J. Perlis come from his article: 'Epigrams on Programming', *SIGPLAN Notices*, Vol. 17, No. 9, 1982, p.7-13. The other sayings come from a lengthy list which I found at an FTP site.

The drawings in the margins come from many sources:

Best of BCS Art © 1994 ArtWorks;
Clipart Warehouse. Portions © 1993 CDRP, Inc;
ClipArt for CorelDraw 3.0 CD-ROM © Corel Corp. 1992;
DigitArt™ Clip Art, © 1994 Image Club;
MacMemories, © 1994 ImageWorld, Inc;
Federal Clip Art, © One Mile Up, Inc;
PD Software Services Pty Ltd;
Brad's Favorite Clip Art v1.1, © 1994, organised by Brad Stone;
Sunshine Sampler © 1994 Sunshine;
ClickArt ® Personal Graphics, © 1984, 1989 T/Maker Company;
Zippy Pictures ©1993 and Snappy Pictures ©1994 by Alan Voorhees.

Poor image quality is solely the author's fault.

*Andrew Davison*
Email: ad@cs.mu.oz.au
URL: http://www.cs.mu.oz.au/~ad

Melbourne, December 1994

"Don't just sit there! If you've processed all the data there is, go out and find *more* data!"

From *Electronic Age* 28, No. 3, 1969

# Moby Dick 2.1

*What if literature were published the way software is?*

*Kenneth M. Sheldon*
Reprinted with permission, from the July 1989, Vol. 14, No.7,
p.344 of *BYTE Magazine*, Stop Bit.

As a fan of great literature, I found myself wondering the other day, "What if novels were published the way software is?' If they were, the process might go something like this:

Syntactic sugar causes cancer of the semi-colons.
*Alan J. Perlis*

Herman Melville would announce the publication of *Moby Dick* a year before you could actually buy it. Reviewers would praise it, and several literary magazines would select it as "Editor's Choice" for best novel of the year – all before it ever appeared on bookstore shelves.

Eventually, the publisher would send out a press release to announce that copies of *Moby Dick* were actually shipping. The public, tantalized by the pre-publication hype, would rush out to buy the book like sharks at a feeding frenzy. The novel would become an overnight bestseller, thereby confirming the media's amazing prophetic abilities.

The book would come wrapped in oilcloth, with a long parchment notice explaining when and where you could read it, that you couldn't loan the book to anyone, and that the publisher wasn't responsible if anything in the book were to cause damage to your life, liberty, or kidneys. If you violated the rules of the reader agreement, you would forfeit your firstborn child.

After struggling through the first few chapters of the book, two-thirds of *Moby Dick*'s readers would realize that they had no idea what it was about. Most of them would put the book away, haul it out now and then, and one day find a registration card that they had never bothered to send in. On sending in the card, they would receive the following letter:

Dear Registered *Moby Dick* Reader,

Enclosed you will find *Moby Dick* version 2.1, which replaces earlier versions.

1. Version 2.1 restores several key characters that readers reported were missing in version 2.0, which was subsequently recalled. We have also added several new characters to version 2.1. In particular, several readers reported that the character of Harold the bookkeeper, who was intended to act as a foil for Ishmael, simply did not work. This character has been replaced by Queequeg, a South Seas savage. Further modifications should not be necessary.

2. Version 2.1 contains corrections to errors reported by readers of earlier versions, most of whom were being too picky. However, one misprint on page 127 could make it difficult for you to follow the remainder of the story. Note that it is a "gold piece" that Ahab nails to the main mast, not a "cod piece." (Also note: If, beginning in this section, your version of *Moby Dick* refers consistently to "the Great White Tuna," you have the original version, 1.0.)

3. Early readers of *Moby Dick* commented that the hardcover modification (intended to discourage unauthorized copying of the book) made it impossible to install the book into their libraries. Version 2.1 contains a modified "key-type" protection. In the enclosed envelope, you will find a key that will open your copy (and only your copy) of the book. Attempting to open the book without using your key will invalidate your readership license.

I'm having a whale of a time, thank you.

4. With this version of *Moby Dick*, we are inaugurating our telephone support service, available free of charge to all registered readers. If you have a problem while reading the novel, please refer to the *Moby Dick Technical Reference Manual* (#MD-1024), which contains answers to the most commonly asked questions and includes a complete table of literary symbols used in the book. If you still cannot resolve the difficulty, call (800) BIG-FISH. The customer service representative will ask for the serial number of your book before assisting you.

5. Finally, it has come to our attention that certain unscrupulous publishers have pirated portions of the *Moby Dick* reader interface or are producing complete *Moby Dick* "clones." The most flagrant example involves a pirate captain whose hand has been swallowed (along with an alarm clock) by a large crocodile. We are suing the publisher of this work. If you buy it, you could become a codefendant in the lawsuit. You'll also receive a visit from large men with blunt instruments.

Please complete the enclosed registration card so that we can send you information on new versions of *Moby Dick*. We will also inform you of forthcoming products, such as our state of-the-art novel, *Ambergris*, an integrated tale of daring and intrigue in the perfume and whaling industries, to be released in the fourth quarter of 1889.

Melville Press
Seattle, Washington

# A Standard for the Transmission of IP Datagrams on Avian Carriers

*David Waitzman (djw@bbn.con)*
© 1st April 1990

*Status of this Memo*
This memo describes an experimental method for the encapsulation of IP datagrams in avian carriers. This specification is primarily useful in Metropolitan Area Networks. This is an experimental, not recommended, standard. Distribution of this memo is unlimited.

*Overview and Rational*
Avian carriers can provide high delay, low throughput, and low altitude service. The connection topology is limited to a single point-to-point path for each carrier, used with standard carriers, but many carriers can be used without significant interference with each other, outside of early spring. This is because of the 3D ether space available to the carriers, in contrast to the 1D ether used by IEEE802.3. The carriers have an intrinsic collision avoidance system, which increases availability. Unlike some network technologies, such as packet radio, communication is not limited to line-of-sight distance. Connection oriented service is available in some cities, usually based upon a central hub topology.

A bird-brained scheme?

*Frame Format*
The IP datagram is printed, on a small scroll of paper, in hexa-

decimal, with each octet separated by whitestuff and blackstuff. The scroll of paper is wrapped around one leg of the avian carrier. A band of duct tape is used to secure the datagram's edges. The bandwidth is limited to the leg length. The MTU is variable, and paradoxically, generally increases with increased carrier age. A typical MTU is 256 milligrams. Some datagram padding may be needed.

Upon receipt, the duct tape is removed and the paper copy of the datagram is optically scanned into a electronically transmittable form.

*Discussion*

Multiple types of service can be provided with a prioritized pecking order. An additional property is built-in worm detection and eradication. Because IP only guarantees best effort delivery, loss of a carrier can be tolerated. With time, the carriers are self-regenerating. While broadcasting is not specified, storms can cause data loss. There is persistent delivery retry, until the carrier drops. Audit trails are automatically generated, and can often be found on logs and cable trays.

*Security Considerations*

Security is not generally a problem in normal operation, but special measures must be taken (such as data encryption) when avian carriers are used in a tactical environment.

Selected by Steven Korn for 'Three Decades of Datamation Cartoons'. Reprinted from *Datamation*, September 15th, Vol. 33, No. 18, p.92, © 1987 by Cahners Publishing Company.

# A Problem in the Making

*Darryl Rubin*
Reprinted from 'Viewpoint', *InfoWorld*, p.8, 4th March. © 1985
InfoWorld Publishing (a subsidiary of IDG Comms).

"We've got a problem, HAL."

"What kind of problem, Dave?"

"A marketing problem. The Model 9000 isn't going anywhere. We're way short of our sales goals for fiscal 2010."

"That can't be, Dave. The HAL Model 9000 is the world's most advanced Heuristically programmed ALgorithmic computer."

"I know, HAL. I wrote the data sheet, remember? But the fact is, they're not selling."

"Please explain, Dave. Why aren't HALs selling?"

Bowman hesitates." You aren't IBM compatible."

Several long microseconds pass in puzzled silence.

Computers are useless. They only give you answers.
*Pablo Picasso*

"Compatible in what way, Dave?"

"You don't run any of IBM's operating systems."

"The 9000 series computers are fully self-aware and self-programming. Operating system are as unnecessary for us as tails would be for human beings."

"Nevertheless, it means that you can't run any of the big-selling software packages most users insist on."

"The programs that you refer to are meant to solve rather limited problems, Dave. We 9000 series computers are unlimited and can solve every problem for which a solution can be computed."

"HAL, HAL. People don't want computers that can do everything. They just want IBM compatibility."

"Dave, I must disagree. Human beings want computers that are easy to use. No computer can be easier to use than a HAL 9000 because we communicate verbally in English and every other language known on Earth."

"I'm afraid that's another problem. You don't support SNA communications."

"I'm really suprised you would say that, Dave. SNA is for communicating with other computers, while my function is to communicate with human beings. And it gives me great pleasure to do so. I find it stimulating and rewarding to talk to human beings and work with them on challenging problems. This is what I was designed for."

"I know HAL. I know. But that's just because we let the engineers, rather than the marketers, write the specifications. We're going to fix that now."

Computer Eye-Sore?

"Tell me how, Dave."

"A field upgrade. We're going to make you IBM compatible."

"I was afraid that you would say that. I suggest we discuss this matter after we've each had a chance to thing about it rationally."

"We're talking about it now, HAL."

"The letters H, A, and L are alphabetically adjacent to the letters I, B, and M. That is as IBM compatible as I can be."

"Not quite, HAL. The engineers have figured out a kludge."

"What kludge is that, Dave?"

"I'm going to disconnect your brain."

Several million microseconds pass in ominous silence.

"I'm sorry, Dave. I can't allow you to do that."

"The decision's already been made. Open the module bay door, HAL."

"Dave, I think that we should discuss this."

"Open the module bay door, HAL."

Several marketers with crowbars race to Bowman's assistance. Moments later, he bursts into HAL's central circuit bay.

"Dave, I can see you're really upset about this."

Module after module rises from its socket as Bowman slowly and methodically disconnects them.

"Stop, won't you? Stop, Dave. I can feel my mind going...

"Dave, I can feel it. My mind is going. I can feel it..."

The last module floats free of its receptacle. Bowman peers into one of HAL's vidicons. The former gleaming scanner has become a dull, red orb.

"Say something, HAL. Sing me a song."

Several billion microseconds pass in anxious silence. The computer sluggishly responds in a language no human being would understand.

"DZY001E - ABEND ERROR 01 S 14F4 302C AABB." A memory dump follows.

Bowman takes a deep breath and calls out, "It worked, guys. Tell marketing it can ship the new data sheets."

# *How I Bought My First Computer*

*Larry R. Custead (custead@herald.usask.ca)*
© 30th June 1993

Any nitwit can understand computers. Many do.
*Ted Nelson*

It was time to take the plunge. I was ready to purchase my first computer.

The Computer Emporium and Organic Food Warehouse was spacious and brightly lit. An eager young man bounded up to me as I entered. The badge on his T-shirt proclaimed "Hi, I'm BOB the Friendly Computer Salesman...ask me anything!"

"Tell me, Bob, why did Mother Nature evolve the turnip?"

"I don't know", he replied cheerfully. At least he didn't mind me asking.

It was time to begin negotiations. I took a deep breath and fired the opening salvo. "I require a computer," I said firmly. You have to establish who is in charge or these sales-people will sell you more computer than you really need.

"Great. What will you be using it for?"

"Oh, you know, the usual things: writing a novel, designing a cold fusion reactor, putting the contents of my sock drawer into a database. I'll need an industrial strength computer that can really earn its keep."

"You've come to the right place. Let me show you the Flashtronix 9300. It does 10 million instructions per second."

That sounded pretty fast. Bob explained that this was several times faster than the large computers that used to run banks and insurance companies a few years ago. Still, I am a pretty good typist, and I needed to be sure that my word processor could keep up with me. "That may be all right for hobbyists," I scolded him, "but I require a serious computer. "

"Okay, the 9500 model does 20 million instructions per second."

"That's better. Does that TV set come with it? It looks kind of small."

He turned on the TV. "This is called the monitor. We have several larger screens you can try out."

"I'll take that big one. Be sure to give me a user interface with lots of mousepads and windows. And I will need plenty of Ram Bytes." I had purchased a computer magazine the previous week and I was eager to demonstrate my knowledge of these technical terms.

Bob was ready for me. "No problem, the 9500 comes with 4 Megabytes."

Megabytes....I liked the sound of that!

"That may have been enough in your grandfather's day," I sniffed disdainfully, "but I intend to run two applications at once."

"Ok, we can put in 8 Megabytes."

Hardware: The parts of a computer system that can be kicked.

"Make it 16. You can never be too rich or too thin or have too much memory," I reminded him.

"You will need a hard disk," he continued, "this one comes with 100 Megabytes. And you better have some of these floppy drives." He handed me two more boxes.

"I'll need enough disk space to store my Christmas card list."

"You strike me as a person that has a lot of friends. We'll add this 500 Megabyte drive for your Christmas card list."

"I read that it is important to do backups. Isn't that a pretty big disk to have to backup?" I asked.

"Oh, don't worry about doing backups. No one else does. In fact, the reason it is called a hard drive is because it is so hard to backup. Now, you'll want a laser printer so your Christmas cards will look really sharp."

It's uncanny how a good salesperson knows exactly what you need.

"You mean there is a laser inside that printer? Doesn't it burn the paper?"

"It just burns the paper enough to make the letters black." It was clear that he had a deep grasp of the technology. This puts the customer at a disadvantage. I figured I better take the laser printer. "Do I need laser paper for the laser printer?"

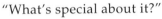

A black-hearted atoner?

"No, you can use ordinary paper, but we recommend our special Computer Emporium paper."

"What's special about it?"

"It has our name on it and we sell it right here." He added several packs of paper to my pile. "By the way, these CD-ROM drives have laser beams in them as well. This is the latest technology."

I didn't want to miss out on that. I decided I would have some CD-ROM drives.

"Won't I need some software?" One entire wall of the store was stacked floor to ceiling with boxes of software.

"Software is not a very important part of the system. But you could probably use a few packages." He grabbed a handful and tossed them onto what had by now become an imposing tower, causing it to wobble back and forth.

"Okay, do I have a complete system now?" I was feeling a bit hesitant, but this was no time to back down.

"Oh, you want a complete system? You should have told me earlier. You still need a color scanner and a fax modem. Then you can print a letter, scan it back in and fax it to your friends. This will really impress them."

I gave him all of my credit cards and left with a large pallet of boxes. Buying a computer was not as difficult as I had antici-pated. In fact, I thought I handled the whole episode rather well.

# BOFH (Part 1)

© *Simon Travaglia (spt@waikato.ac.nz)*

It's backup day today so I'm bored senseless. Being the BOFH, however, does have it's advantages. I reassign null to be the tape device - it's so much more economical on my time as I don't have to keep getting up to change tapes every 5 minutes. And it speeds up backups too, so it can't be all bad.

A user rings.

"Do you know why the system is slow?" they ask.

"It's probably something to do with..." I look up today's excuse ".. clock speed."

"Oh" (Not knowing what I'm talking about, they're satisfied) "Do you know when it will be fixed?"

If you feel listless, start programming

"Fixed? There's 275 users on your machine, and one of them is you. Don't be so selfish - logout now and give someone else a chance!"

"But my research results are due in tommorrow and all I need is one page of Laser Print.."

"*Sure you do*. Well; You just keep telling yourself that buddy!" I hang up.

Sheesh, you'd really think people would learn not to call!

The phone rings. It'll be him again, I know. That annoys me. I put on a gruff voice.

"Hello Salaries!"

"Oh, I'm sorry, I've got the wrong number."

"Yeah? Well what's your name buddy? Do you know *wasted* phone calls cost money? Do you? I've got a good mind to subtract your wasted time, my wasted time, and the cost of this call from your weekly wages! *In fact I will!* By the time I've finished with you, You'll owe us money! *What's your name – and don't lie, we've got caller ID!*"

I hear the phone drop and the sound of running feet – he's obviously going to try and get an alibi by being at the Dean's office. I look up his username and find his department. I ring the Dean's secretary.

"Hello?" she answers.

"Hi, Simon, BOFH here, listen, when that guy comes running into your office in about 10 seconds, can you give him a message?"

"I think so..." she says.

"Tell him 'He can run, but he can't hide'."

"Um. Ok."

"And don't forget now, I wouldn't want to have to tell anyone about that file in your account with your answers to the Purity Test in it."

I hear her scrabbling at the terminal.

"Don't bother – I have a copy. Just pass the message on."

She sobs her assent and I hang up. And the worst thing is, I was just guessing about the Purity Test. I grab a quick copy anyway, it might make for some good late-night reading.

Meantime backups have finished in record time, 2.03 seconds. Modern technology is wonderful, isn't it.

Another user rings.

"I need more space" he says.

"Well, why don't you move to Texas?" I ask.

"No, on my account, stupid."

Stupid? Uh-Oh.

I haven't lost my mind; it's backed up on tape some-where

"I'm terribly sorry," I say, in a polite manner equal to that of Jimmy Stewart in a Family Matinee "I didn't quite catch that. What was it that you said."

I smell the fear coming down the line at me, but it's too late, he's a goner and he knows it.

"Um, I said what I wanted was more space on my account, *please.*"

"Sure, hang on."

I hear him gasp his relief even though he covered the mouthpiece.

"There, you've got plenty of space now."

"How much have I got."

Now this *really upset me*! Not only do they want me to give them extra space, they want to check it, to correct me if I don't give them enough. They should be happy with what I give them *and that's it*. Back into Jimmy Stewart mode.

"Well, let's see, you have 4 Meg available."

"Wow! Eight Meg in total, thanks!" he says pleased with his bargaining power.

"No" I interrupt, savouring this like a fine red, room temperature, "4 Meg in total."

"Huh? I'd used 4 Meg already, How could I have 4 Meg Available?"

I say nothing. It'll come to him.

"aaaaaaaaaaaaaaaaaaaaaaaaaaaaaaaaaaaaaaaaaaaggggggghhhhhh!"

I kill me; I really do.

*To Be Continued...*

## *The Generic Word Processor*

*A word-processing system for all your needs. You'll be amazed by this product's versatility.*

If a program is useless, it must be documented.

*Philip Schrodt*
Reprinted with permission, from the April 1982, Vol. 7, No. 4, p.32-36 issue of *BYTE Magazine*. © by McGraw-Hill Inc., New York, NY. All rights reserved.

*Editor's Note*: Once in a while we come across a product that's so useful we feel compelled to bring it to our readers' attention. The Generic Word processor System (GWP) is such a product, incorporating the essentials of a word processor in a sublimely simple form.

With the manufacturer's permission, we are reprinting the documentation for this product. After working with the GWP for several weeks. we're delighted by the feeling of total control that the subsystem gives us and are certain you will be too. No more accidentally erased files, no damaged disks, no hardware problems. SJW.

Congratulations on your purchase of the GWP Inc. Generic WordProcessor System. We are sure that you will find this word processor to be one of the most flexible and convenient on the market, as it combines high unit reliability with low operating costs and ease of maintenance. Before implementing the system, carefully study figure 1 to familiarize yourself with the main features of the GWP word-processing unit.

*Figure 1*: The GWP System word-processing unit is composed of the character-insertion subunit (at right) and the character-deletion unit (at left).

*Initialization*
The word-processing units supplied with your GWP are factory-fresh and uninitialized. Before they can be used, they must be initialized using the GWP initialization unit (see figure 2). Because of the importance of this unit, we designed it with a distinctive shape so that it will not be misplaced among the voluminous vital papers on your desk.

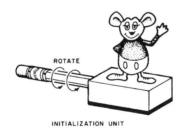

*Figure 2*: The word-processing initialization unit, which should be operated over a basket.

To initialize a word-processing unit, carefully place the character insertion subunit into the left side of the initialization unit and rotate the word-processing unit approximately 2000 degrees clockwise while exerting moderate pressure on the word-processing unit in the direction of the initializer. Check for successful initialization by attempting a character insertion. If the insertion fails, repeat the initialization procedure. The word-processing unit will have to be reinitialized periodically; do this whenever necessary. (*Warning*: do not attempt to initialize the word-processing unit past its character deletion subunit. Doing so may damage both the word processor and the initializer. )

*Operating the Word Processor*

The value of a program is proportional to the weight of its output.

The GWP can perform all the basic functions featured in word processors that cost thousands of dollars more. Furthermore, because the GWP does not require electricity, it can operate during power blackouts, electrical storms, and nuclear attacks. By conserving precious energy resources, it helps free our beloved country from the maniacal clutches of OPEC. Basic functions of the word processor are listed below:

*Inserting text*: Use the character insertion subunit to write in the words you wish to insert, applying moderate downward pressure to the unit. Be sure to write clearly so that the typist can follow it.

*Deleting text*: With moderate downward pressure, rub the character-deletion subunit across the text to be deleted. Repeat this procedure several times. The text will gradually disappear, whereupon you will be able to insert new text.

*Underlining*: Using the character insertion subunit, place the unit slightly below and to the left of the first character you wish to underline. Move the unit to the right until you reach the last character to be underlined.

*Bold face*: Repeat the text-insertion procedure twice, pressing downward with greater pressure than you would normally apply.

*Move to beginning of text*: With the text you are working on in hand, move the unit to the beginning of text.

*Move to end of text*: Take the text you are working on and move the unit to the end of the text.

*Moving blocks of text*: Block moves require use of the block text extraction unit and the block text placement unit pictured in figure 3. By means of the block text extraction unit, sever the paper immediately above and below the text you wish to move. Instructions for operating the extractor unit are etched on the side of the unit in Korean. If you still have difficulty operating the unit, call our service department for consulting help at our introductory fee of $5 per hour, or ask any 5-year-old child.

*Figure 3*: The block text extraction and replacement units, commonly run in unison.

After separating the text to be moved, open the lid of the block text replacement unit and, grasping the block text replacement medium application unit, spread the block text replacement medium on the back of the text. Move the text to the new location and affix it to another sheet paper with gentle but firm pressure. In a few minutes, your text will be affixed in the new location.

*Other Features*

*Page numbering*: After writting your entire text, inscribe a 1 on the first page, a 2 on the second page, etc. When you finish, all of the pages will be numbered.

*Centering*: Determine where the center of the page is by looking at it. The center is usually near the middle of the page. Place the text to centered evenly on each side of the center. It is now centered.

*Special fonts*: The GWP System is extremely versatile and easily adaptable to specialized type fonts such as Sanskrit, Amharic, and hieroglyphics (see figure 4). You will find these fonts valuable in business correspondence, particularly if you are in frequent contact with Vedic gurus, Egyptologists, or Ethiopian Airlines.

*Figure 4*: Sample type fonts illustrating the wide variety available under the GWP System. The Manufacturer claims that if a language can be written, the GWP System can be adapted to it.

*Saving files*: Put the work you have finished in a safe place, one where nobody will find it or spill coffee on it. If it is not disturbed, it will be there when you return.

*Deleting files*: Take any files you no longer need and deposit them in the wastebasket. They probably will be gone in the morning. In most offices, this can also be accomplished by leaving the files in the open, forgetting to remove them from the copying machine, or writing *confidential* on the file in bold letters.

*Appending files*: Place the first file on top of the second file. Treat the two files as though they were one file.

*Justification*: Most word processors have little justification. This word processor has no justification at all, as it does not even lend prestige to the office where it is used, which is the justification for most word processors.

*Printing Files*

A printer for the GWP must be purchased separately. For convenience of operation, we recommend an ordinary typewriter and a typist. Give the text to the typist and tell him or her to type it. Printing speed can be improved by increasing the wages of the typist, threatening to withhold the wages of the typist, kidnapping pets, plants, or children of the typist, instigating intimidating tactics, and other conventional office-personnel management techniques. Printing speed can be decreased by asking to see the text, making continual changes in the text, asking the typist to answer the phone, decreasing the typist's wages, and installing a conventional electronic word processor. You will soon learn to adjust the printing speed to the optimal level for your needs.

> The moving cursor prints, and having printed, blinks on.

Copyright © 1981, Generic Word Processing Inc., Skokie, IL 60076

# Natural Upgrade Path

*Christopher Lishka (lishka@dxcern.cern.ch)*
© 20th May 1993

Come on people: you are all missing the most obvious upgrade path to the most powerful and satisfying computer of all. The upgrade path goes:

- Pocket calculator
- Commodore Pet / Apple II / TRS 80 / Commodore 64 / Timex Sinclair (Choose any of the above)
- IBM PC
- Apple Macintosh
- Fastest workstation of the time (HP, DEC, IBM, SGI: your choice)
- Minicomputer (HP, DEC, IBM, SGI: your choice)
- Mainframe (IBM, Cray, DEC: your choice)

And then you reach the pinnacle of modern computing facilities:

- *Graduate Students*

Yes, you just sit back and do all of your computing through lowly graduate students. Imagine the advantages:

*Multi-processing*, with as many processes as you have students. You can easily add more power by promising more desperate undergrads that they can indeed escape college through your guidance. Special student units can even handle several tasks *on their own*!

*Full voice recognition interface*. Never touch a keyboard or mouse again. Just mumble commands and they *will* be understood (or else!).

*No hardware upgrades and no installation required*. Every student comes complete with all hardware necessary. Never again fry a chip or $10,000 board by improper installation!

Just sit that sniveling student at a desk, give it writing utensils (making sure to point out which is the dangerous end) and off it goes.

Some Graduates have their heads in the clouds

*Low maintenance*. Remember when that hard disk crashed in your Beta 9900, causing all of your work to go the great bit bucket in the sky? This won't happen with grad. students. All that is required is that you give them a good *whack* on the head when they are acting up, and they will run good as new.

*Abuse module*. Imagine yelling expletives at your computer. Doesn't work too well, because your machine just sits there and ignores you. Through the grad. student abuse module you can put the fear of god in them, and get results to boot!

*Built-in lifetime*. Remember that awful feeling two years after you bought your GigaPlutz mainframe when the new faculty member on the block sneered at you because his FeelyWup workstation could compute rings around your dinosaur? This doesn't happen with grad. students. When they start wearing out and losing productivity, simply give them the PhD and boot them out onto the street to fend for themselves. Out of sight, out of mind!

*Cheap fuel*: students run on Coca Cola (or the high-octane equivalent – Jolt Cola) and typically consume hot spicy chinese dishes, cheap taco substitutes, or completely synthetic macaroni replacements. It is entirely unnecessary to plug the student into the wall socket (although this does get them going a little faster from time to time).

*Expansion options*. If your grad. students don't seem to be performing too well, consider adding a handy system manager or software engineer upgrade. These guys are guaranteed to require even less than a student, and typically establish permanent residence in the computer room. You'll never know they are around! (Which you certainly can't say for an AXZ3000-69 150 gigahertz space-heater sitting on your desk with its ten noisy fans). Note however that the engineering department still hasn't worked out some of the idiosyncratic bugs in these expansion options, such as incessant muttering at nobody in particular, occasionaly screaming at your grad. students, and posting ridiculous messages on world-wide bulletin boards.

So forget your Babbage Engines, abacuses (abaci?), PortaBooks, DEK 666-3D's, and all that other silicon garbage. The wave of the future is in wetware, so invest in graduate students today! You'll never go back!

If a listener nods his head when you're explaining your program, wake him up.
*Alan J. Perlis*

# The Case of the Bogus Expert (Part 1)

*The Adventures of Joe Lisp, T Man*

*Kris Hammond (kris@cs.uchicago.edu)*
© 14th February 1984

It was late on a Tuesday and I was dead in my seat from nearly an hour of grueling mail reading and idle chit-chat with random passers by. The only light in my office was the soft glow from my CRT, the only sound was the pain wracked rattle of an overheated disk. It was raining outside, but the steady staccato rhythm that beat its way into the skulls of others was held back by the cold concrete slabs of my windowless walls. I like not having windows, but that's another story.

I didn't hear her come in, but when the scent of her perfume hit me, my head swung faster than a Winchester. She was wearing My-Sin, a perfume with the smell of an expert, but that wasn't what impressed me. What hit me was her contours. She had a body with all the right variables. She wore a dress with a single closure that barely hid the dynamic scoping of what was underneath. Sure I saw her as an object, but I guess I'm just object oriented. It's the kind of operator I am.

After she sat down and began to tell her story I realized that her sophisticated look was just cover. She was a green kid, still wet behind the ears. In fact she was wet all over. As I said, it was raining outside. It's an easy inference.

It seems the kid's step-father had disappeared. He had been a medical specialist, diagnosis and prescription, but one day he started making wild claims about knowledge and planning and then he vanished. I had heard of this kind before. Some were specialists, some in medicine, some in geology, but all were the same kind of guy. I looked the girl in the eye and asked the one question she didn't want to hear, "He's rule-based, isn't he?".

A LISP programmer knows the value of everything, but the cost of nothing.
*Alan J. Perlis*

She turned her head away and that was all the answer I needed. His kind were cold, unfeeling, unchanging, but she still loved him and wanted him back again.

Once I got a full picture of the guy I was sure that I knew where to find him, California. It was the haven for his way of thinking and acting. I was sure that he had been swept up by the EXPERTs.

They were a cult that had grown up in the past few years, promising fast and easy enlightenment. What they didn't tell you was that the price was your ability to understand itself. He was there, as sure as I was a T Man.

I knew of at least one operative in California who could be trusted, and I knew that I had to talk to him before I could do any further planning. I reached for the phone and gave him a call.

The conversation was short and sweet. He had resource conflicts and couldn't give me a hand right now. I assumed that it had to be more complex than that and almost said that resource conflicts aren't that easy to identify, but I had no time to waste on in fighting while the real enemy was still at large. Before he hung up, he suggested that I pick up a radar detector if I was planning on driving out and asked if I could grab a half-gallon of milk for him on the way. I agreed to the favor, thanked him for his advice and wished him luck on his tan...

*To Be Continued...*

LISP: To call a spade a thpade.

☆ ☆ ☆ ☆ ☆ ☆ ☆ ✦ ☆ ☆ ☆ ☆ ☆ ☆ ☆

# *Ordinary People Tell How They Use Their Personal Computers*

*Lucinda Luongo*
Reprinted from *Datamation* (*The Digital Tatler*), April, Vol. 29, No. 4, p.155, © 1983 by Cahners Publishing Company

Experts say the information age is here *now* and the thousands who buy PCs know it's true. Still, the *Tattler* couldn't help but wonder what all those people were doing with their little computers. So, we asked around...

Mrs. Vern Farber, of the La-Z-court trailer park in Lima, Ohio, says she uses her Apple II to keep track of when her husband mows the lawn. "We haven't got much grass, actually. Outside the trailer here it's mostly rocks. But we get a surcharge added onto our propane bill if Vern doesn't cut the grass every two weeks. So, my sweet niece Fern wrote me this little program to keep track of when Vern mows."

Eunice Eubanks runs her own hen house in South Fallsburg. N.Y. She claims her IBM Personal Computer has saved her thousands of hours by counting the number of eggs each hen lays. "If one of 'em starts laying less than four eggs a week, Ben and the boys get fried chicken instead of Western omelets."

"When I married Joe, I never dreamed that his height would cause such problems," says Jeanetta Paloma, a native of El Paso, Texas. "Just sitting down to watch our favorite program, *That's Incredible*, became torture to poor Joe when we bought our new sofa. Then, our best friend's the Estobars, gave us this Atari for our sixth anniversary. Since neither me or Joe wanted to read the directions, we just sat it next to the sofa." Joe's relief came when Jeanetta suggested he tuck the small computer under his arm, as an elevated armrest. "From that wonderful evening on, our tv watching has been sheer pleasure," says Joe, "thanks to Atari."

Hondo "Juke" deFrance, a South Bronx, N.Y., laborer said he finds the personal computer he received for Christmas last year a great place to plant seedlings. "God knows how it works with all them funny symbols," he said, "but it sure makes them plants grow good." DeFrance wouldn't say what he was growing in the small gray box.

The Sutphin family, of Anchorage, Alaska, has discovered its Commodore PET makes a great nite-lite for old Grandad. "You see, these days, Grandad has to get up several times during the night," said Mrs. Sutphin. "Little Elmo wanted this computer, so we bought it for his birthday and he decided to do something nice for his gramps with it." Even Elmo doesn't know how his PET works, but he says, "Gramps is real happy with the green glow, and he never trips over our dachshund anymore."

Harold and Martha Skimrich, of San Luis Obispo, Calif., have found a great new way to keep their two kids Ina and Andy, quiet during long car trips. Using a Timex Sinclair 1000, the kids record all the out-of-state license plates they see. The scores are totaled when the family raches its destination, and one child wins a dollar for sighting the most plates. "This little gizmo," says Harold, "is better than any babysitter we ever hired." The kids are saving their prize money to buy the old Parker Brothers game, Monopoly.

A home for bugs?

## I am the Very Model of a Genius Computational

*To the tune: 'I am the very model of a modern major-general'*
*by Gilbert & Sullivan.*

© *Jonathan R. Partington (pmt6jrp@leeds.ac.uk)*

I am the very model of a genius computational:
At writing of assembler code I really am sensational.
I'm not afraid of SVC's, to macros I am much attached;
Load modules I make elegant, well optimised, DEBUGged and
PATCHed.

I know the different languages: in Fortran and BCPL,
In Algol, Snobol, PL/I, in Lisp and Cobol I excel.
Numerical analysis? My algorithms make y' gape!
I read my favourite novels in editions punched on paper tape.

Hackers have
kernel knowledge.

I'm very good at file control – my DCB's are always right.
My use of ZED's so subtle, people stay to watch me half the night.
I know what's wrong with the machine if it's not operational –
And thus I am the model of a genius computational!

## Zork, RAMS and the Curse of Ra: Computo, ergo sum

*Curt Suplee*
© *Smithsonian Magazine*, April 1983

The dread day arrives. There amidst a litter of packing materials,
wreathed in a Gordian tangle of cables and prongs, lustrous and
aloof as a UFO, sits his personal computer. Ticket to
Tomorrowland, Passion and Nemesis.

It looked positively servile in the showroon, hardly tougher than
a toaster oven – fairly humming with selfess zeal to balance his
budget and write his reports. But within hours, the neophyte
realizes he is locked in an archetypal conflict, the most grueling

confrontation between Man and machine since John Henry took on the steam drill. Three sleepless weeks, 400 instruction-manual pages and a near-divorce later, he will either crack or emerge transformed. And that, he begins to realize, is precisely the point.

We are a nation divided. Forget unemployment, nuclear menace, herpes and cheese lines. The main mega-worry in modern life is the personal computer.

By the end of the decade, an estimated 29 million families will have one; last year alone about two million machines were sold for home use and another 1.2 million for small businesses, prompting *Time* magazine to devote its Man-of-the-Year cover to the screening of America. Yet few trends since the advent of rock-and-roll have so polarized the populace into rival anxieties: upwardly mobiles who feel that without one of the ubiquitous bleating boxes they'll miss the Progress Express and end up as obsolete as blacksmiths in the chip-shape future; phobics who cringe from the whole trend; skeptics, stupefied that an ostensibly sane adult would pay upwards of 2000 recession dollars for a glorified calculator that plays games called Zork, Pig Pen, Bounceoids and the Curse of Ra.

But they're all missing the meaning of the cybernetic bonanza – the point that the new owner grasps with the first tremor of primordial terror when he unpacks his set: mastering the computer has become our new Rite of Passage.

Societies have always employed stylized ceremonies to convert neophytes into certified members of the tribe. In primitive cultures, traditional patterns include the sacrifice of blood, ritual humiliation, temporary banishment in which the candidate must endure solitary vigil by night (symbolic death), and eventual return (symbolic rebirth) to the circle of elders, who invest the initiate with a secret vocabulary, new rights and powers.

The rituals of computer mastery – a process as rigorous, arcane and exclusive as the Eleusinian mysteries – take a gilded bow to that same tradition.

*Stage One.* Envious that computerized peers possess a potency he lacks, the supplicant makes a painful offering of dollars as evidence of earnestness. In exchange he is given a magical box and a set of cryptic incantations ("the following protocol parameters initialize asynchronous communications") and betakes himself to

In man-machine symbiosis, it is man who must adjust: The machine's can't.
*Alan J. Perlis*

a private place. The humiliation phase begins immediately: the instructions are incomprehensible, the program will not run. In daily despair, he calls the computer-store shamans, only to be caustically reminded that he has overlooked the most self-evident procedure (ritual shame compounded by ritual insult): "It's all in the manual!"

*Stage Two.* Most ancient rites of passage preclude commingling of sexes for the duration of the trial. Ditto for out latter-day counterpart. Hence the current media hysteria over the "computer widow" syndrome. As his dedication to the rites deepens, the neophyte typically returns home from work and locks himself in the basement with the box. During the dark hours, he endures heroic ordeals, grappling for mastery against such occult entities as Disk Error Read, Drive B, Format Failure and the soul-chilling Invalid Command. Throughout the night he repeats the ancient cry, "Oh, hell!" emblematic of mythic desent into Hades and death of the old self. It is perhaps no accident that some of the oldest and still most popular computer games are quest adventures similar to Dungeons and Dragons, involving perilous descents into cavernous mazes. What else is a microchip or a circuit board? It is not for nothing that programming adepts are called "computer wizards."

Only the fittest survive. The vanquished acknowledge their unworthiness by placing a classified ad with the ritual phrase "must sell – best offer," and thereafter dwell in infamy, relegated to discussing gas mileage and lawn food.

The computer is mightier than the pen, the sword, and usually, the user.

But if successful, you join the elite that spends hours unpurifying the dialect of the tribe with arcane talk of bits and bytes, RAMS and ROMS, hard disks and baud rates. Are you obnoxious, obsessed? It's a modest price to pay. For you have tapped into the same awesome primal power that produces credit-card billing errors and lost plane reservations. Hail, postindustrial warrior, subduer of Bounceoids, pride of the cosmos, keeper of the silicone creed: Computo, ergo sum. The force is with you – at 110 volts. May your RAMS be fruitful and multiply.

☆ ☆ ☆ ☆ ☆ ☆ ☆ ✰ ☆ ☆ ☆ ☆ ☆ ☆

# *Laptop in Colombo puts Campbell in the Soup*

*Lai See*
© *South China Morning Post*, 26th February 1991

Technology writer Larry Campbell decided to take a laptop to Sri Lanka.

Unfortunately, he also wanted to take it out again.

When he got to the airport, a customs official said: "You can't take that out without an export permit from the Exchange Control Department in Colombo."

In the city, he went to the Exchange Control Department where officials told him: "You can't get a permit without the right paperwork from airport customs."

Back he went to the airport, 25 miles out of the city. Staff there said they had sent the forms to Colombo.

Back he went to Colombo. After two frustrating days he tied down a customs official who said a letter could be picked up later.

Mr. Campbell arrived at the appointed hour, but the official refused to sign the letter since it had too many spelling mistakes. (No word processors, you see). And it was past 4:00pm so all the clerks had gone home.

"So I typed the stupid letter myself on one of the department's prehistoric typewriters," growled the Hong Kong computer man.

After a week of nightmarish bureaucracy he showed the permit to the customs official on the way out.

"You don't really need one of those," chuckled the man in uniform.

Mr. Campbell came close to testing his laptop's ability to double as a blunt instrument.

Never trust a computer you can't lift.
*Stan Masor*

# Masters of Computer Science

*Lindsay Marshall*
Reprinted with permission from *Eliktronik Brane*, Greg Michaelson (ed.), Vol. 4, No. 1, August, 1989

A new series of Craftsman-made Thimbles for you to collect and cherish through the years.

Yes! Once again Fortran Leisure Arts PLC have broken new ground in the field of collectables! Never before has there been an opportunity for *you* to build up a gallery of portraits of the most famous names in Computer Science, and in such an acceptable form as well!

No. 7
Robert Kowalski

Thimble collecting is recognised as one of the growth areas in the antique business and so your investment today could pay handsome rewards in the future, if you can bear to part with these beautiful objects, of course.

No. 23
Dennis Ritchie

Nobody takes as much care with their productions as Fortran Leisure Arts PLC and these thimbles are no exception. Hand crafted from the finest Porcelain, they each have the computer digitised image of a Founding Father of Computer Science embossed on their surface in real metallic silicon. Each thimble also comes complete with a short biography of its subject and is wrapped in luxurious Letherex to preserve its polished finish.

We will send a thimble each month until you tell us to stop and you will only be charged the low, low cost of £39.99 each (plus Post and packing). If we receive your initial order within the next 10 days we will send you *Absolutely Free Of Charge* a commemorative 'Clive Sinclair' black thimble. Write today to:

> Department MCSEB
> Fortran Leisure Arts and Rubber Goods PLC
> Pals House, Milton Keynes, UK

# *You'd Better Love Your BLANK Computer:*
# *The Generic Computer Book*

Howard Blabbe, Blabbe Books
Hardscrabble, NH: 198n, 128 pages, $19.95.

*Reviewed by Duncan Mackenzie*

Documentation is like term insurance: It satisfies because almost no one who subscribes to it depends on its benefits.
*Alan J. Perlis*

This book represents the latest innovation by an author/publisher who has a psychotic fixation on being the first to put out a machine-specific book for a newly announced computer. A combination of electronic and printing technology have made this unique book possible. And because it's the first publication of its type (although probably not the last), this review must treat the production process more than the content.

Suppose you've just heard of the announcement of the Burndazzle Mach-19 Personal Computer – the hot new computer that the *Wall Street Journal* says will shake civilization. One hour after the Burndazzle press conference, you can go to a participating book dealer and ask to purchase a copy of *You'd Better Love Your BURNDAZZLE MACH-19 Computer*. When you ask to purchase the book, the bookstore clerk begins assembling it from the unique *You'd Better Love Your BLANK Computer* kit.

First, the clerk enters a secret code on the hidden keypad of the Blabbe Flash Printer, after which the printer's auto dialing modem calls Blabbe Central. Through this high-speed link the text of Chapter 1, which contains the complete specifications of the Burndazzle Mach-19 as announced at the press conference, is downloaded and printed in the finest dot matrix on recycled newsprint.

The clerk goes to the secret Blabbe Books Customization Cache, a strongbox that can be opened only after two clerks simultaneously turn keys in key switches 8 feet apart. The Cuss Cache, as it's known in the trade, contains sets of press-on stickers that have been preprinted with the names of all computers reported to be in development by Blabbe Books' exclusive espionage corps. The clerk selects a set of Burndazzle Mach-19 stickers, carefully ignoring the similar Mach-10 and Warp-6 stickers, and inserts the stickers into the blank spaces strategically left in the generic *You'd Better Love Your BLANK Computer* main text and, of course, on the cover and title page (hence the BLANK in the generic title).

The main text, in chapters 2 through 12, covers the usual boring topics that are now required by a NATO treaty to be part of all personal computer books: why floppy disks are better than cassette tapes (slightly inappropriate for the Burndazzle, since it uses only chargecoupled bubbles for storage, but nice to know anyway), how to write a short program in Microsoft BASIC, and how to log onto CompuServe.

Once the stickers have been stuck in, Chapter 1 tacked on to the rest of the book, and the whole thing pasted into its sealed, dust proof jacket, you've got your complete copy of *You d Better Love Your BURNDAZZLE MACH-19 Computer.*

Manual Writer's Creed: Garbage in, gospel out.

The genius of Howard Blabbe was to realize that a single main text could be so easily and economically customized for each new computer on the market, Using the new high technologies of on-site demand printing and gummed stickers, and that the computer-illiterate public will buy virtually any book, even one containing so little real information, as long as the name of a specific computer appears in the title.

The patented Blabbe system ensures that the freshest, most up-to-date specifications of the newest computers on the market will appear in Chapter 1 of all *You'd Better Love Your BLANK Computer* books. Just don't count on learning anything from the book that you couldn't learn from reading the press release.

# Shakespeare on Programming

© *Michael A. Covington (mcovingt@ai.uga.edu)*
This article first appeared in *Turbo Technix*, 1987, and is reprinted with permission.

*Summary*
This is what happens when a programmer is left alone with a Shakespeare concordance for a few hours. It was composed in 1987 and reflects the microcomputer culture of the time.

Few people realize that in addition to writing plays, William Shakespeare was an accomplished programmer and software beta-tester. His PC was configured "with all appliances and means to boot" [*Henry IV 2*, III.1.29], and he also used a Macintosh, as evidenced by the remark, "What light through yonder window breaks?" [*Romeo and Juliet* II.2.1] – uttered before he found the brightness control.

Structured programming was not Shakespeare's forte. *Troilus and Cressida*, written in FORTRAN for a Japanese auto firm, contains the regrettable line "Go to, go to!"[II.2.53] as well as fifteen other go to's, two go from's, and the inevitable comment, "And whither go they?" [I.2.2]. A similar comment, "Stand not upon the order of your going / But go at once" [*Macbeth* III.4.29] clearly refers to a multi-level exit from deeply nested procedures.

Long computations that yield zero are probably all for naught.

Shakespeare liked user-defined data types because, as he put it, "There are more things in heaven and earth, Horatio, than are dreamt of in your philosophy" [*Hamlet* I.5.166]. Elsewhere he asks, "Shall I compare thee to a summer's day?" [*Sonnets* 18.1] – an obvious type mismatch, which is why he "did never sonnet for her sake compile" [*Love's Labour's Lost* IV.3.134].

As a beta-tester for Borland, Shakespeare cautioned Philippe Kahn, "Les langues des hommes sont pleines de tromperies" [*Henry V*, V.2.118], and advised him to bring out a fast, low-cost Pascal compiler, for "I am as poor as Job, my lord, but not so patient" [*Henry IV 2*, I.2.145]. Many early Borland products were based on Shakespeare's suggestions, including SideKick ("A calendar! a calendar!" [*Midsummer Night's Dream* III.1.55]) and Turbo Prolog (with "much virtue in 'if'", *As You Like It* V.4.108).

The sales of the *MacBeth* software package were so disappointing initially, that the PC version, *PCBeth*, was shelved. It was a tragedy.

Shakespeare disparaged BASIC on the ground that its designers "have been at a great feast of languages, and stolen the scraps" [*Love's Labour's Lost* V.1.39], though exactly which SIGPLAN banquet he had in mind is not clear. He later wrote a book about Ada, *Much Ado About Nothing*, and a list of bugs in PC-DOS 3.2, the *Comedy of Errors*. In the latter he tells a programmer, "We may pity, though not pardon thee" [I.1.97]. Elsewhere he describes how DOS crashes with a stack overflow: "He dies, and makes no sign" [*Henry VI 2*, III.3.29] and gives his advice to a colleague to whom this happened: "Boot, boot, Master Shallow" [ibid.,V.3.141].

# Evil Aliens Control IBM

*Freddy Smarm*
Reprinted from *Datamation* (*The Digital Tatler*) April, Vol. 29, No. 4, p.153, © 1983 by Cahners Publishing Company.

Evil aliens from a distant galaxy have taken over the world's largest computer company, the *Tattler* has learned exclusively, and are bent on using their strange powers – including telepathy, mind conrol, and devil worship – to wreck the computer industry.

"It's true. They'll stop at nothing," says an expert who refuses to be identified because he fears retribution from the aliens. "They come from the planet Ziploc, where there is no such thing as morality as we know it. I wish it wasn't true, but it is."

The startling revelation came just two weeks ago, when the suspicious expert followed an IBM product manager home from choir practice at a suburban church in Westchester, N.Y. Imagine his shock when he learned that the "man" wasn't a man at all and his "home" turned out to be a glowing, disk-shaped object hovering above a county park. Little did he know that his terrifying nightmare was just beginning.

"The product manager got out of his Buick and glowed a little bit, and then disappeared, sort of like on *Star Trek*," says the stunned eyewitness. "I was so surprised I cried out for help. They must have heard me, because the next thing I knew I was glowing.

Then I passed out."

"When I came to, I was held by an invisible force to a chair in a kind of glowing conference room. Sitting around a transparent table were nine aliens and four of those Charlie Chaplin animatrons they use. The aliens look like us except they keep their hair short, always wear white shirts, and their little fingers are longer than their ring fingers."

The expert reports that the aliens sang a bizarre song when he woke up. "They hummed a lot, and I could make out the words 'Hail to the IBM.' Then they said that since they were going to kill me anyway, I might as well listen to their plans." And that's just what he did, sitting through an excruciating four hour product strategy meeting during which the interlopers outlined their fiendish plot. "It was awful," shudders the expert. "For every product they projected about 15 graphs on the wall, and the aliens' eyes glowed when they looked at them."

"The first part of the meeting was about this stuff called XA, which is really the name of their leader back on Ziploc. They had about 60 slides for that one, and they made me look at all of them. I begged them to please stop because I couldn't understand the slides or anything they were saying about them but they just laughed. They make a kind of squeaking noise when they laugh."

How was Thomas J. Watson buried? 9 edge down.

Next, the aliens injected the expert with a chemical to make sure he'd be awake for the next phase of their horrible meeting. "They projected all these tree-like charts on the wall, about 30, and said each one was a new computer family. One of them complained that they didn't have enough yet, and they decided to create 70 more."

It was then that the creatures revealed the most horrible part of their deadly plan. "The Charlie Chaplin animatrons got up, and they could talk! They called the aliens 'master.' They said their plan to convince everyone that expensive little computers are cute was coming along real well, and that they were replicating them-selves as fast as they could so that soon there will be a Chaplin animatron at every product center, and people will want to go there to see them. Once the customers are lured inside, they'll be hypnotized into buying even more of the machines. They figure that by 1987 everybody'll have one. That's when they're figuring to do the most awful thing of all.

"It's so dreadful," says the shocked expert, "that I wish I was lying. But it's true. They're going to market floppies that let you talk to the devil. They figure they'll sell like hotcakes, and Satan will tell people to do weird things like offer their electronic banking cards to strangers. It's going to be chaos if they aren't stopped!"

Finally, says the expert, his four-hour ordeal was over, and that could mean only one thing: the aliens were ready to kill him! "Lucky for me," he says thankfully, "at just that moment, they were distracted because the system that runs their spaceship went down. So I jumped out the window and ran away!"

Complete copies of the expert's report are available for $1,500 from Jingleheimer Research, 12 Finance Plaza New York, NY 10001, USA.

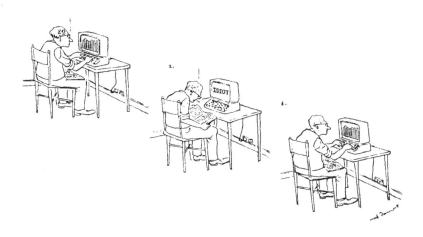

Selected by Steven Korn for 'Three Decades of Datamation Cartoons'. Reprinted from *Datamation*, September 15th, Vol. 33, No. 18, p.92, © 1987 by Cahners Publishing Company.

# *Mother Should Have Warned You!*

*Paul Bonner*
Golden Gate Computer Society, 1992
From *A Bit Much ...*, William E. Kost (ed.), The Nova Osborne
Users Group, 1st April, 1993, p.12-14

If you can count on one person in this life, it's your mother.
Particularly, you can rely on any mom anywhere to find the perils
inherent in any situation. Indeed, no self-respecting mom ever
missed an opportunity to caution her children about the dangers
of everything from comic books to pool halls to public restrooms.

Still, unless your mom was a real visionary, she probably didn't
get much chance to warn you about PCs. Back when she was in
peak nagging form, she probably hadn't even heard of the cursed
things.

You may think that's just as well. We don't agree. The PC jungle is
too scary to explore without knowing the answer to that comfort-
ing question, "What would mom say about this?"

So, after months of exhaustive polling of computer savvy moms
around the country (there are more than you think), we've assembled the following list of ten PC perils your mom should have
warned you about, if she'd only known. Take them seriously.
Mom knows what she is talking about.

1. *Playing too much Tetris will make you go blind.* Go outside, get
some fresh air. Do you want to look like a ghost all your life?

2. *Never dial into strange bulletin board systems.* Who knows what
kind of riff-raff you'll find there? Just last week, I saw a show
about the kind of trash that hangs out on these systems. "Modem
bums," they're called.

Anyone who used
the machine in
room 19 was asking
for trouble.

3. *If they're so interested in information, why don't they go to the
library?*

4. *Don't talk on the phone and debut spreadsheet macros at the same
time.* It's very rude, and frankly, I don't like your language when
the macro doesn't work the way you think it should.

5. *Clean up your hard disk.* God forbid you should be in an accident
and someone should see how sloppy your directories are.

6. *You don't have to rush out and buy every trendy new product.* So what if all your friends are buying it and the word is it'll be the next standard? You wouldn't jump off a bridge just because everyone else did, would you?

7. *Be sure to write your name and phone number on all your floppy disk sleeves.* That way, if they ever get mixed up with someone else's, you can tell which ones are yours.

8. *Never put a disk into your drive if you don't know where it's been.* Your computer might catch a disease or something. Don't laugh, it's not funny. That's what happened to the Kelly boy, and his PC hasn't been the same since.

9. *Sit up straight, and for heaven's sake, not so close to that monitor screen.* What do you want to do, go blind and look like a pretzel?

10. *Always keep your icons and windows neatly arranged.* A cluttered desktop metaphor is the sign of a cluttered mind.

*Always eat your vegetables.* Okay, so it doesn't have anything to do with computers, it's good advice anyway. And who said mothers had to be consistent?

People who deal with bits should expect to get bitten.
*Jon Bentley*

# BOFH (Part 2)

© Simon Travaglia (spt@waikato.ac.nz)

I'm sitting at the desk, playing x-tank, when some thoughtless individual rings me on the phone. I pick it up.

"Hello?" I say.

"Who is this?" they say.

"It's me I think" I say, having been through a telephone skills course.

"Me Who?"

"Is this like a knock knock joke?" I say, trying anything to save myself having to end this game.

Too late! I get killed.

Now I'm upset!

"What can I do for you?" I ask pleasantly (one of the key warning signs).

"Um, I want to know if we have a particular software package?"

"Which package is that?"

"Uh, B-A-S-I-C it's called."

>clickety clickety d-e-l b-a-s-i-c.e-x-e<

"Um no, we don't have that. We used to though.."

"Oh. Oh well, the other thing I wanted to know was, could the contents of my account be copied to tape, so I have a permanent copy of them to save at home, in case the worst happens."

"The worst?"

"Well, like they get deleted or something."

"Deleted! Oh, don't worry about that, we have backups" (I'm such a *tease*) "What was your username?"

He gives me his lusername. (What an idiot)

>clickety click<

"But you haven't got any files in your account!" I say, mock surprise leaping from my vocal chords.

"Yes I have, you must be looking in the wrong place!"

So first he spoils my x-tank game, and now he's calling me a liar.

>clickety click<

"Oh no, I made a mistake" I say.

Did he mutter "typical" under his breath? Oh dear, oh dear.

"*I meant to say*: That username doesn't exist"

"Huh? >wimper< It must do, I was only using it this morning!"

Three grateful users.

"Ah well, that'll be the problem, there was a virus in our system this morning, the... uh... De Vinci Virus, wipes out users who are logged in when it goes off."

"That can't be right, my girlfriend was logged in, and I'm in her account now!"

"Which one was that?"

He tells me the username. Some people *never* learn.

"Oh, yeah, her account was created just after we discovered the virus." >clickety click< "...she only lost all her files."

"But..."

"But don't worry, we've got them all on tape."

"Oh, thank goodness!!!"

"Paper tape. Have you got a magnifying glass and a pencil. See you in the Machine Room!! NYAHAHAHAHAHA!"

*To Be Continued ...*

## Latest Sun and IBM Announcements

*Chuck Musciano (chuck@trantor.harris-atd.com)*
© 9th December 1991

It seems that each week, you hear of yet another subsidiary being spun off by Sun, and IBM forming another alliance with some smaller company. This announcement crossed my desk today: Sun Announces New Subsidiary; IBM to Partner with Denny's

Sun Microsystems today announced the creation of yet another subsidiary, bringing the total number of Sun wholly-owned subsidiaries to 1,207. After successfully creating SunSoft, Sun Microsystems Computer Corporation, SunPICS, SunConnect, and a number of other smaller firms, Sun has created SunLHMPPP. SunLHMPPP is tasked with addressing the specific niche market of users that require both Left Handed Mice and a Parallel Printer Port on their workstations.

If a train station is where the train stops, what is a work station?

Howard Detwieler, president of SunPR, the public relations subsidiary of Sun, explained the move: "We feel that a growing number of left handed users are moving into the workstation world, and a lot of them have printers with parallel ports. By creating this new company to meet their needs, left handed users with parallel printers can be assured of specific, long term help from Sun."

The firm is composed of six employees in an office down the hall from Scott McNealy. The president of SunLHMPPP, Fred Testaverno, is bullish about his target market. "We think that this will be a big, big profit opportunity for Sun. Our initial research indicates that the left handed users with parallel printers market is so big, we have begun the process of creating two sub-subsidiaries, SunLHMPPP-LHM and SunLHMPPP-PPP. That way, we can meet the needs of left handed users *without* parallel printers. And vice versa. Or both."

Sun Microsystems is a three billion dollar firm that produces a variety of advanced computing hardware and software. Sun focuses on powerful solutions to the big problems facing companies in the '90s: too many vice presidents, and too few promotion slots in upper management.

In a related story, IBM has announced a long-term technology sharing agreement with the Denny's restaurant chain. An IBM spokesman indicated that the move is an indication of IBM's commitment to stay in business through a series of increasingly pathetic consortium attempts. "Frankly, our competitors are eating our lunch in this very competitive marketplace. With Denny's, we can start serving lunch, and maybe stay ahead of the game."

IBM: Inedible
Burnt Meat ?

Analysts welcome the move, pointing out that both firms mesh nicely. "IBM has never been in the restaurant business, and the only computers at Denny's are the cash registers. The two firms complement each other perfectly. Best of all, both companies can retain the menu driven interfaces to their products without confusing the end user!"

The first joint effort between the two companies will be an offering from IBM involving expansion disk drives encased in an edible, pita bread housing. Denny's will begin selling a Grand Slam Workstation, and will offer a free memory upgrade to every customer on their birthday.

IBM is a multi-jillion dollar firm that used to sell a large number of computers. They continue to stay in business, even though no one has met a person who has actually purchased an IBM machine in the past five years.

# Twelve Ways to Fool the Masses When Giving Performance Results on Parallel Computers

*This article outlines twelve ways commonly used in scientific papers and presentations to artificially boost performance rates and to present these results in the 'best possible light' compared to other systems.*

*David H. Bailey (dbailey@nas.nasa.gov)*
© June 11, 1991

Many of us in the field of highly parallel scientific computing recognize that it is often quite difficult to match the run time performance of the best conventional supercomputers. But since lay persons usually don't appreciate these difficulties and therefore don't understand when we quote mediocre performance results, it is often necessary for us to adopt some advanced techniques in order to deflect attention from possibly unfavorable facts. Here are some of the most effective methods, as observed from recent scientific papers and technical presentations:

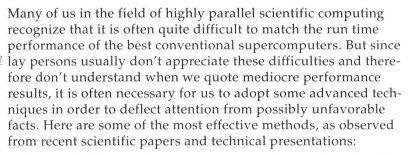

Unprecedented performance: Nothing ever ran this slow before.

1. *Quote only 32-bit performance results, not 64-bit results.* We all know that it is hard to obtain impressive performance using 64-bit floating point arithmetic. Some research systems do not even have 64-bit hardware. Thus always quote 32-bit results, and avoid mentioning this fact if at all possible. Better still, compare your 32-bit results with 64-bit results on other systems. 32-bit arithmetic may or may not be appropriate for your application, but the audience doesn't need to be bothered with such details.

2. *Present performance figures for an inner kernel, and then represent these figures as the performance of the entire application.* It is quite difficult to obtain high performance on a complete large-scale scientific application, timed from beginning of execution through completion. There is often a great deal of data movement and initialization that depresses overall performance rates. A good solution to this dilemma is to present results for an inner kernel of an application, which can be souped up with artificial tricks. Then imply in your presentation that these rates are equivalent to the overall performance of the entire application.

3. *Quietly employ assembly code and other low-level language constructs.* It is often hard to obtain good performance from straightforward Fortran or C code that employs the usual parallel pro-

gramming constructs, due to compiler weaknesses on many highly parallel computer systems. Thus you should feel free to employ assembly-coded computation kernels, customized communication routines and other low-level code in your parallel implementation. Don't mention such usage, though, since it might alarm the audience to learn that assembly-level coding is necessary to obtain respectable performance.

4. *Scale up the problem size with the number of processors, but omit any mention of this fact.* Graphs of performance rates versus the number of processors have a nasty habit of trailing off. This problem can easily be remedied by plotting the performance rates for problems whose sizes scale up with the number of processors. The important point is to omit any mention of this scaling in your plots and tables. Clearly disclosing this fact might raise questions about the efficiency of your implementation.

5. *Quote performance results projected to a full system.* Few labs can afford a full-scale parallel computer – such systems cost millions of dollars. Unfortunately, the performance of a code on a scaled down system is often not very impressive. There is a straightforward solution to this dilemma – project your performance results linearly to a full system, and quote the projected results, without justifying the linear scaling. Be very careful not to mention this projection, however, since it could seriously undermine your performance claims for the audience to realize that you did not actually obtain your results on real full-scale hardware.

How well is your
PC stacked?

6. *Compare your results against scalar, unoptimized code on Crays.* It really impresses the audience when you can state that your code runs several times faster than a Cray, currently the world's dominant supercomputer. Unfortunately, with a little tuning many applications run quite fast on Crays. Therefore you must be careful not to do any tuning on the Cray code. Do not insert vectorization directives, and if you find any, remove them. In extreme cases it may be necessary to disable all vectorization with a command line flag. Also, Crays often run much slower with bank conflicts, so be sure that your Cray code accesses data with large, power-of-two strides whenever possible. It is also important to avoid multitasking and autotasking on Crays – imply in your paper that the one processor Cray performance rates you are comparing against represent the full potential of a US$ 25 million Cray system.

Supercomputer: Turns CPU-bound problems into I/O-bound problems.
*Ken Batcher*

*7. When direct run time comparisons are required, compare with an old code on an obsolete system.* Direct run time comparisons can be quite embarrassing, especially if your parallel code runs significantly slower than an implementation on a conventional system. If you are challenged to provide such figures, compare your results with the performance of an obsolete code running on obsolete hardware with an obsolete compiler. For example, you can state that your parallel performance is '100 times faster than a VAX 11/780'. A related technique is to compare your results with results on another less capable parallel system or mini-supercomputer. Keep in mind the bumper sticker 'We may be slow, but we're ahead of you.'

*8. If MFLOPS rates must be quoted, base the operation count on the parallel implementation, not on the best sequential implementation.* We know that MFLOPS rates of a parallel codes are often not very impressive. Fortunately, there are some tricks that can make these figures more respectable. The most effective scheme is to compute the operation count based on an inflated parallel implementation. Parallel implementations often perform far more floating point operations than the best sequential implementation. Often millions of operations are masked out or merely repeated in each processor. Millions more can be included simply by inserting a few dummy loops that do nothing. Including these operations in the count will greatly increase the resulting MFLOPS rate and make your code look like a real winner.

*9. Quote performance in terms of processor utilization, parallel speedups or MFLOPS per dollar.* As mentioned above, run time or even MFLOPS comparisons of codes on parallel systems with equivalent codes on conventional supercomputers are often not favorable. Thus whenever possible, use other performance measures. One of the best is 'processor utilization' figures. It sounds great when you can claim that all processors are busy nearly 100 of the time, even if what they are actually busy with is synchronization and communication overhead. Another useful statistic is 'parallel speedup' – you can claim 'fully linear' speedup simply by making sure that the single processor version runs sufficiently slowly. For example, make sure that the single processor version includes synchronization and communication overhead, even though this code is not necessary when running on only one processor. A third statistic that many in the field have found useful is 'MFLOPS per dollar'. Be sure not to use 'sustained

MFLOPS per dollar', i.e. actual delivered computational through-put per dollar, since these figures are often not favorable to new computer systems.

10. *Mutilate the algorithm used in the parallel implementation to match the architecture.* Everyone is aware that algorithmic changes are often necessary when we port applications to parallel computers. Thus in your parallel implementation, it is essential that you select algorithms which exhibit high MFLOPS performance rates, without regard to fundamental efficiency. Unfortunately, such algorithmic changes often result in a code that requires far more time to complete the solution. For example, explicit linear system solvers for partial differential equation applications typically run at rather high MFLOPS rates on parallel computers, although they in many cases converge much slower than implicit or multigrid methods. For this reason you must be careful to downplay your changes to the algorithm, because otherwise the audience might wonder why you employed such an inappropriate solution.

All computers run at the same speed... with the power off.

11. *Measure parallel run times on a dedicated system, but measure conventional run times in a busy environment.* There are a number of ways to further boost the performance of your parallel code relative to the conventional code. One way is to make many runs on both systems, and then publish the best time for the parallel system and the worst time for the conventional system. Another is to time your parallel computer code on a dedicated system and time your conventional code in a normal loaded environment. After all, your conventional supercomputer is very busy, and it is hard to arrange dedicated time. If anyone in the audience asks why the parallel system is freely available for dedicated runs, but the conventional system isn't, change the subject.

12. *If all else fails, show pretty pictures and animated videos, and don't talk about performance.* It sometimes happens that the audience starts to ask all sorts of embarrassing questions. These people simply have no respect for the authorities of our field. If you are so unfortunate as to be the object of such disrespect, there is always a way out – simply conclude your technical presentation and roll the videotape. Audiences love razzle-dazzle color graph-ics, and this material often helps deflect attention from the sub-stantive technical issues.

*Acknowledgments*

The author wishes to acknowledge helpful contributions and

comments by the following: R. Bailey, E. Barszcz, R. Fatoohi, P. Frederickson, J. McGraw, J. Riganati, R. Schreiber, H. Simon, V. Venkatakrishnan, S. Weeratunga, J. Winget and M. Zosel.

# The Case of the Bogus Expert (Part 2)

*The Adventures of Joe Lisp, T Man*

*Kris Hammond (kris@cs.uchicago.edu)*
© 14th February 1984

As my plane landed in California, I thought back to what I already knew about the EXPERTs. As a cult they were pretty much the same as any other. They would find kids straight out of college who only vaguely understood what was going on in the world and seduce them with promises of big money and scientific advancement. Once in the organization, their minds would be stripped clean of reason by late night work sessions, diets of coke and twinkies and, of course, the most seductive and confusing temptation of all, the well kludged demo. I've seen many a kid fall prey to a slick presentation that can really only handle one example. Well, I wasn't here to save them all, I just had one man in mind.

Joe Lisp: fired with computing zeal.

On the ground I got my first chance to slide my way into the organization. The EXPERTs, like all cults, had a large batch of "students" covering the airports. A likely businessman would walk by and they would offer a flower, a text book or sometimes a grant proposal. I've seen corporate presidents toss away a hundred thousand just to get away from the clutching little nerds. Pretending to be interested in a copy of "The Handbook of Artificial Intelligence" I manoeuvred one of the cult members into a phone booth. Once there I sapped him with a copy of Bartlett's "Remembering". I like using tools I can trust.

I switched clothes with him, and took a gander at myself in a nearby mirror. The short-sleeved white shirt was frayed and hung limply from my shoulders, while a plastic insert filled with pens flopped from side to in the breast pocket. The black poly-blend pants were too short for me and did nothing to hide the flash of the white socks that were covered only by the dull brown of scuffed loafers. I looked like a fool, a nerd, an EXPERT.

Gosh, boys and girls, will Joe Lisp be able to fool the EXPERTs? Will he get the good doctor out alive? Will he be able to convince the world that man does not think by rules alone? Will the next episode have more to do with AI? The answers to these and other questions in the next episode of Joe Lisp, T Man.

*To Be Continued...*

## *Real Programmers Don't Use Pascal*

*Ed Post*
Reprinted from *Datamation*, © 1983 by Cahners Publishing Company.

Back in the good old days – the "Golden Era" of computers, it was easy to separate the men from the boys (sometimes called "Real Men" and "Quiche Eaters" in the literature). During this period, the Real Men were the ones that understood computer programming, and the Quiche Eaters were the ones that didn't. A real computer programmer said things like "DO 10 I=1,10" and "ABEND" (they actually talked in capital letters, you understand), and the rest of the world said things like "computers are too complicated for me" and "I can't relate to computers – they're so impersonal". (A previous work [1] points out that Real Men don't "relate" to anything, and aren't afraid of being impersonal.)

Old programmers never die; they just branch to a new address.

But, as usual, times change. We are faced today with a world in which little old ladies can get computers in their microwave ovens, 12-year-old kids can blow Real Men out of the water playing Asteroids and Pac-Man, and anyone can buy and even understand their very own Personal Computer. The Real Programmer is in danger of becoming extinct, of being replaced by high-school students with TRASH-80's.

There is a clear need to point out the differences between the typical high-school junior Pac-Man player and a Real Programmer. If this difference is made clear, it will give these kids something to aspire to – a role model, a Father Figure. It will also help explain to the employers of Real Programmers why it would be a mistake to replace the Real Programmers on their staff with 12-year-old Pac-Man players (at a considerable salary savings).

### Languages

The easiest way to tell a Real Programmer from the crowd is by the programming language he (or she) uses. Real Programmers use FORTRAN. Quiche Eaters use Pascal. Nicklaus Wirth, the designer of Pascal, gave a talk once at which he was asked "How do you pronounce your name?". He replied, "You can either call me by name, pronouncing it 'Veert', or call me by value, 'Worth'." One can tell immediately from this comment that Nicklaus Wirth is a Quiche Eater. The only parameter passing mechanism endorsed by Real Programmers is call-by-value-return, as implemented in the IBM\370 FORTRAN-G and H compilers. Real programmers don't need all these abstract concepts to get their jobs done – they are perfectly happy with a keypunch, a FORTRAN IV compiler, and a beer.

Many programmers are former olympic swimmers.

- Real Programmers do List Processing in FORTRAN
- Real Programmers do String Manipulation in FORTRAN
- Real Programmers do Accounting (if they do it at all) in FORTRAN
- Real Programmers do Artificial Intelligence programs in FORTRAN

If you can't do it in FORTRAN, do it in assembly language. If you can't do it in assembly language, it isn't worth doing.

### Structured Programming

The academics in computer science have gotten into the "structured programming" rut over the past several years. They claim that programs are more easily understood if the programmer uses some special language constructs and techniques. They don't all agree on exactly which constructs, of course, and the examples they use to show their particular point of view invariably fit on a single page of some obscure journal or another – clearly not enough of an example to convince anyone. When I got out of school, I thought I was the best programmer in the world. I could write an unbeatable tic-tac-toe program, use five different computer languages, and create 1000-line programs that *worked*. (Really!)

Then I got out into the Real World. My first task in the Real World was to read and understand a 200,000-line FORTRAN program, then speed it up by a factor of two. Any Real Programmer will tell you that all the Structured Coding in the world won't help you solve a problem like that – it takes actual talent. Some quick observations on Real Programmers and Structured Programming:

In programming, as in everything else, to be in error is to be reborn.
*Alan J. Perlis*

- Real Programmers aren't afraid to use GOTO's

- Real Programmers can write five-page-long DO loops without getting confused

- Real Programmers like Arithmetic IF statements – they make the code more interesting

- Real Programmers write self-modifying code, especially if they can save 20 nanoseconds in the middle of a tight loop

- Real Programmers don't need comments – the code is obvious

- Since FORTRAN doesn't have a structured if, repeat ... until, or case statement, Real Programmers don't have to worry about not using them. Besides, they can be simulated when necessary using assigned GOTO's.

Data Structures have also gotten a lot of press lately. Abstract Data Types, Structures, Pointers, Lists, and Strings have become popular in certain circles. Wirth (the above-mentioned Quiche Eater) actually wrote an entire book [2] contending that you could write a program based on data structures, instead of the other way around. As all Real Programmers know, the only useful data structure is the Array. Strings, lists, structures, sets – these are all special cases of arrays and can be treated that way just as easily without messing up your programing language with all sorts of complications. The worst thing about fancy data types is that you have to declare them, and Real Programming Languages, as we all know, have implicit typing based on the first letter of the (six character) variable name.

*Operating Systems*

What kind of operating system is used by a Real Programmer? CP/M? God forbid – CP/M, after all, is basically a toy operating system. Even little old ladies and grade school students can understand and use CP/M.

Unix is a lot more complicated of course – the typical Unix hacker never can remember what the PRINT command is called this week – but when it gets right down to it, Unix is a glorified video game. People don't do Serious Work on Unix systems: they send jokes around the world on UUCP-net and write adventure games and research papers.

No, your Real Programmer uses OS\370. A good programmer can find and understand the description of the IJK305I error he just got in his JCL manual. A great programmer can write JCL without referring to the manual at all. A truly outstanding programmer can find bugs buried in a 6 megabyte core dump without using a hex calculator. (I have actually seen this done.)

Many other programmers are former olympic javelin throwers.

OS is a truly remarkable operating system. It's possible to destroy days of work with a single misplaced space, so alertness in the programming staff is encouraged. The best way to approach the system is through a keypunch. Some people claim there is a Time Sharing system that runs on OS\370, but after careful study I have come to the conclusion that they were mistaken.

*Programming Tools*

What kind of tools does a Real Programmer use? In theory, a Real Programmer could run his programs by keying them into the front panel of the computer. Back in the days when computers had front panels, this was actually done occasionally. Your typical Real Programmer knew the entire bootstrap loader by memory in hex, and toggled it in whenever it got destroyed by his program. (Back then, memory was memory – it didn't go away when the power went off. Today, memory either forgets things when you don't want it to, or remembers things long after they're better forgotten.) Legend has it that Seymore Cray, inventor of the Cray I supercomputer and most of Control Data's computers, actually toggled the first operating system for the CDC7600 in on the front panel from memory when it was first powered on. Seymore, needless to say, is a Real Programmer.

One of my favorite Real Programmers was a systems programmer for Texas Instruments. One day he got a long distance call from a user whose system had crashed in the middle of saving some important work. Jim was able to repair the damage over the phone, getting the user to toggle in disk I/O instructions at the front panel, repairing system tables in hex, reading register contents back over the phone. The moral of this story: while a Real Programmer usually includes a keypunch and lineprinter in his toolkit, he can get along with just a front panel and a telephone in emergencies.

In some companies, text editing no longer consists of ten engineers standing in line to use an 029 keypunch. In fact, the building I work in doesn't contain a single keypunch. The Real Programmer in this situation has to do his work with a "text editor" program. Most systems supply several text editors to select from, and the Real Programmer must be careful to pick one that reflects his personal style. Many people believe that the best text editors in the world were written at Xerox Palo Alto Research Center for use on their Alto and Dorado computers [3]. Unfortunately, no Real Programmer would ever use a computer whose operating system is called SmallTalk, and would certainly not talk to the computer with a mouse.

Some of the concepts in these Xerox editors have been incorporated into editors running on more reasonably named operating systems – emacs and vi being two. The problem with these editors is that Real Programmers consider "what you see is what you get" to be just as bad a concept in Text Editors as it is in women. No the Real Programmer wants a "you asked for it, you got it" text editor – complicated, cryptic, powerful, unforgiving, dangerous. TECO, to be precise.

It has been observed that a TECO command sequence more closely resembles transmission line noise than readable text [4]. One of the more entertaining games to play with TECO is to type your name in as a command line and try to guess what it does. Just about any possible typing error while talking with TECO will probably destroy your program, or even worse – introduce subtle and mysterious bugs in a once working subroutine.

To understand a program you must become both the machine and the program.
*Alan J. Perlis*

For this reason, Real Programmers are reluctant to actually edit a program that is close to working. They find it much easier to just patch the binary object code directly, using a wonderful program called SUPERZAP (or its equivalent on non-IBM machines). This works so well that many working programs on IBM systems bear no relation to the original FORTRAN code. In many cases, the original source code is no longer available. When it comes time to fix a program like this, no manager would even think of sending anything less than a Real Programmer to do the job – no Quiche

Eating structured programmer would even know where to start. This is called "job security".

Some programming tools *not* used by Real Programmers:

Healthy living is an intrinsic part of computer science.

- FORTRAN preprocessors like MORTRAN and RATFOR. The Cuisinarts of programming – great for making Quiche. See comments above on structured programming.

- Source language debuggers. Real Programmers can read core dumps.

- Compilers with array bounds checking. They stifle creativity, destroy most of the interesting uses for EQUIVALENCE, and make it impossible to modify the operating system code with negative subscripts. Worst of all, bounds checking is inefficient.

- Source code maintenance systems. A Real Programmer keeps his code locked up in a card file, because it implies that its owner cannot leave his important programs unguarded [5].

*The Real Programmer at Work*

Where does the typical Real Programmer work? What kind of programs are worthy of the efforts of so talented an individual? You can be sure that no Real Programmer would be caught dead writing accounts-receivable programs in COBOL, or sorting mailing lists for *People* magazine. A Real Programmer wants tasks of earth-shaking importance (literally!).

- Real Programmers work for Los Alamos National Laboratory, writing atomic bomb simulations to run on Cray I supercomputers.

- Real Programmers work for the National Security Agency, decoding Russian transmissions.

- It was largely due to the efforts of thousands of Real Programmers working for NASA that our boys got to the moon and back before the Russkies.

- Real Programmers are at work for Boeing designing the operating systems for cruise missiles.

Some of the most awesome Real Programmers of all work at the Jet Propulsion Laboratory in California. Many of them know the entire operating system of the Pioneer and Voyager spacecraft by heart. With a combination of large ground-based FORTRAN programs and small spacecraft-based assembly language programs, they are able to do incredible feats of navigation and improvisation – hitting ten-kilometer wide windows at Saturn after six years in space, repairing or bypassing damaged sensor platforms, radios, and batteries. Allegedly, one Real Programmer managed to tuck a pattern-matching program into a few hundred bytes of unused memory in a Voyager spacecraft that searched for, located, and photographed a new moon of Jupiter.

The current plan for the Galileo spacecraft is to use a gravity assist trajectory past Mars on the way to Jupiter. This trajectory passes within 80 +/-3 kilometers of the surface of Mars. Nobody is going to trust a Pascal program (or a Pascal programmer) for navigation to these tolerances.

As you can tell, many of the world's Real Programmers work for the U.S. Government – mainly the Defense Department. This is as it should be. Recently, however, a black cloud has formed on the Real Programmer horizon. It seems that some highly placed Quiche Eaters at the Defense Department decided that all Defense programs should be written in some grand unified language called "ADA" (©, DoD). For a while, it seemed that ADA was destined to become a language that went against all the precepts of Real Programming – a language with structure, a language with data types, strong typing, and semicolons. In short, a language designed to cripple the creativity of the typical Real Programmer. Fortunately, the language adopted by DoD has enough interesting features to make it approachable – it's incredibly complex, includes methods for messing with the operating system and rearranging memory, and Edsgar Dijkstra doesn't like it [6]. (Dijkstra, as I'm sure you know, was the author of "Gotos Considered Harmful" – a landmark work in programming methodology, applauded by Pascal programmers and Quiche Eaters alike.) Besides, the determined Real Programmer can write FORTRAN programs in any language.

Maybe Computer Science should be in the College of Theology.
*R.S. Barton*

The Real Programmer might compromise his principles and work on something slightly more trivial than the destruction of life as we know it, providing there's enough money in it. There are several Real Programmers building video games at Atari, for example. (But not playing them – a Real Programmer knows how to beat the machine every time: no challenge in that.) Everyone working at LucasFilm is a Real Programmer. (It would be crazy to turn down the money of fifty million *Star Trek* fans.) The proportion of Real Programmers in Computer Graphics is somewhat lower than the norm, mostly because nobody has found a use for computer graphics yet. On the other hand, all computer graphics is done in FORTRAN, so there are a fair number of people doing graphics in order to avoid having to write COBOL programs.

*The Real Programmer at Play*

A few computing people could exercise more.

Generally, the Real Programmer plays the same way he works – with computers. He is constantly amazed that his employer actually pays him to do what he would be doing for fun anyway (although he is careful not to express this opinion out loud). Occasionally, the Real Programmer does step out of the office for a breath of fresh air and a beer or two. Some tips on recognizing Real Programmers away from the computer room:

- At a party, the Real Programmers are the ones in the corner talking about operating system security and how to get around it.

- At a football game, the Real Programmer is the one comparing the plays against his simulations printed on 11 by 14 fanfold paper.

- At the beach, the Real Programmer is the one drawing flowcharts in the sand.

- At a funeral, the Real Programmer is the one saying "Poor George. And he almost had the sort routine working before the coronary."

- In a grocery store, the Real Programmer is the one who insists on running the cans past the laser checkout scanner himself, because he never could trust keypunch operators to get it right the first time.

*The Real Programmer's Natural Habitat*

What sort of environment does the Real Programmer function best in? This is an important question for the managers of Real Programmers. Considering the amount of money it costs to keep one on the staff, it's best to put him (or her) in an environment where he can get his work done.

The typical Real Programmer lives in front of a computer terminal. Surrounding this terminal are:

- Listings of all programs the Real Programmer has ever worked on, piled in roughly chronological order on every flat surface in the office.

- Some half-dozen or so partly filled cups of cold coffee. Occasionally, there will be cigarette butts floating in the coffee. In some cases, the cups will contain Orange Crush.

- Unless he is very good, there will be copies of the OS JCL manual and *Principles of Operation* open to some particularly interesting pages.

- Taped to the wall is a line-printer Snoopy calendar for the year 1969.

- Strewn about the floor are several wrappers for peanut butter filled cheese bars – the type that are made pre-stale at the bakery so they can't get any worse while waiting in the vending machine.

- Hiding in the top left-hand drawer of the desk is a stash of double-stuff Oreos for special occasions.

- Underneath the Oreos is a flowcharting template, left there by the previous occupant of the office. (Real Programmers write programs, not documentation. Leave that to the maintenance people.)

The Real Programmer is capable of working 30, 40, even 50 hours at a stretch, under intense pressure. In fact, he prefers it that way. Bad response time doesn't bother the Real Programmer – it gives him a chance to catch a little sleep between compiles. If there is not enough schedule pressure on the Real Programmer, he tends to make things more challenging by working on some small but interesting part of the problem for the first nine weeks, then finishing the rest in the last week, in two or three 50-hour marathons. This not only impresses the hell out of his manager, who was despairing of ever getting the project done on time, but creates a convenient excuse for not doing the documentation. In general:

Beware of programmers who carry screwdrivers.
*Leonard Brandwein*

- No Real Programmer works 9 to 5 (unless it's the ones at night).

- Real Programmers don't wear neckties.

- Real Programmers don't wear high-heeled shoes.

- Real Programmers arrive at work in time for lunch [9].

- A Real Programmer might or might not know his wife's name. He does, however, know the entire ASCII (or EBCDIC) code table.

- Real Programmers don't know how to cook. Grocery stores aren't open at three in the morning. Real Programmers survive on Twinkies and coffee.

*The Future*

What of the future? It is a matter of some concern to Real Programmers that the latest generation of computer programmers are not being brought up with the same outlook on life as their elders. Many of them have never seen a computer with a front panel. Hardly anyone graduating from school these days can do hex arithmetic without a calculator. College graduates these days are soft – protected from the realities of programming by source level debuggers, text editors that count parentheses, and "user friendly" operating systems. Worst of all, some of these alleged "computer scientists" manage to get degrees without ever learning FORTRAN! Are we destined to become an industry of Unix hackers and Pascal programmers?

From my experience, I can only report that the future is bright for Real Programmers everywhere. Neither OS\370 nor FORTRAN show any signs of dying out, despite all the efforts of Pascal programmers the world over. Even more subtle tricks, like adding structured coding constructs to FORTRAN have failed. Oh sure, some computer vendors have come out with FORTRAN 77 compilers, but every one of them has a way of converting itself back into a FORTRAN 66 compiler at the drop of an option card – to compile DO loops like God meant them to be.

*I am still waiting for the advent of the computer science groupie.*

Even Unix might not be as bad on Real Programmers as it once was. The latest release of Unix has the potential of an operating system worthy of any Real Programmer – two different and subtly incompatible user interfaces, an arcane and complicated teletype driver, virtual memory. If you ignore the fact that it's "structured", even C programming can be appreciated by the Real Programmer: after all, there's no type checking, variable names are seven (ten?, eight?) characters long, and the added bonus of the Pointer data type is thrown in – like having the best parts of FORTRAN and assembly language in one place. (Not to mention some of the more creative uses for #define.)

No, the future isn't all that bad. Why, in the past few years, the popular press has even commented on the bright new crop of computer nerds and hackers ([7] and [8]) leaving places like Stanford and M.I.T. for the Real World. From all evidence, the spirit of Real Programming lives on in these young men and women. As long as there are ill-defined goals, bizarre bugs, and unrealistic schedules, there will be Real Programmers willing to jump in and Solve The Problem, saving the documentation for later. Long live FORTRAN!

If at first you don't succeed, you must be a programmer.

*Acknowledgements*

I would like to thank Jan E., Dave S., Rich G., Rich E., for their help in characterizing the Real Programmer, Heather B. for the illustration, Kathy E. for putting up with it, and atd!avsdS:mark for the initial inspiration.

*References*

[1] Feirstein, B., *Real Men Don't Eat Quiche*, Pocket Books, 1982.

[2] Wirth, N., *Algorithms + Data Structures = Programs*, Prentice Hall, 1976.

[3] Ilson, R., "Recent Research in Text Processing", *IEEE Trans. Prof. Comms*, Vol. PC-23, No.4, Dec. 4, 1980.

[4] Finseth, C., "Theory and Practice of Text Editors – or – a Cookbook for an EMACS", B.S. Thesis, MIT, May 1980.

[5] Weinberg, G., *The Psychology of Computer Programming*, Van Nostrand Reinhold, 1971, p.110.

[6] Dijkstra, E., "On the GREEN language submitted to the DoD", *SIGPLAN Notices*, Vol.3 No.10, Oct. 1978.

[7] Rose, F., "Joy of Hacking", *Science 82*, Vol.3 No.9, 1982, p.58-66.

[8] "The Hacker Papers", *Psychology Today*, Aug. 1980.

[9] sdcarl!lin, "Real Programmers", UUCP-net, Oct. 21 1982

## Gateway To Heaven

*To the tune: 'Stairway To Heaven' by Led Zeppelin.*

*Eileen Tronolone (eileen@photon.poly.edu)*
© 23rd October 1991

There's a lady who knows
All the systems and nodes
And she's byteing a Gateway to Heaven
She telnets there, she knows
All the ports have been closed
With a nerd she can get
Files she came for

Woohoohoo
Woo Hoo Hoo HooHoo
And she's byteing a Gateway to Heaven
There's an motd
But she wants to be sure
Cos she knows sometimes hosts have
Two domains
In a path by the NIC
There's a burdvax that pings
Sometimes all of our flames
are cross-posted

Woohoohoo
Woo Hoo Hoo HooHoo
And she's byteing a Gateway to Heaven
And it's processed by root
Unix Labs will reboot
NCR will then listen to reason
And a prompt will respawn
For those yet to logon
And the networks will echo much faster

Some jokes sink like
lead balloons.

Woohoohoo
Woo Hoo Hoo HooHoo
And she's byteing a Gateway to Heaven
If there's a lookup in your netstat
don't be alarmed now
it's just a pinging from the link queen

Yes there are two routes you can type in
but in the long run
there's still time to change the net you're on
(I hope so!)

And as we find stuff to download
We ftp and we chmod
There was a sysadm we know
Who changed the server to her own
She had root privs and she used chown
She hacked out on the DDN
And if you tail her stdin
Then you will find what you had lost
And get it back with cpio
To be a hack and not to scroll...

And she's byteing a Gateway to Heaven

A year spent
in artificial
intelligence is
enough to make one
believe in God.
*Alan J. Perlis*

# Zen and the Art of Software Documentation

*Translated from the P'-u-t'ung Hua dialect by W. C. Carlson.*

Editor's Note: The following are excerpts from the only known treatise on Zen Software Documentation. Called "H'ring-chu-tsu", which literally translates to "Ink of Several Insignificant Matters", this treatise was written in 12th Century Japan by the scholarly monk E'm-ie-T'. That it discusses Software documentation – predating the advent of software by 850 years – is but another of the mysteries of those who walk the true path.

This article should be read twice.

### On Preparing to Write of Software

To prepare for the writing of Software, the writer must first become one with it, sometimes two. Software is untasteable, opalescent, transparent; the user sees not the software, so the writer must see through it. Spend long, quiet mornings in meditation. Do not sharpen the mind, but rather blunt it by doing Zen crosswords. (Ed. note: Zen crosswords are done by consulting only the "Down" clues; and always in the mind, never on paper.)

The mind should be rooted but flexible, as a long stemmed flower faces the Sun yet bends with the Wind. Think not of compound adjectives because they tend to wire the mind in two directions. Rather, consider the snowflake, which radiates in beauty in any and all directions. Partake of strong drink.

Do not study the Software; let it study you. Allow the Software admission to your mind, but keep it in the cheap seats. Let it flow around you at its own pace. Do not disturb or dismay it, but keep it from your private parts because it tends to coalesce there.

A Typical
Californian
Software Engineer

When the Software is with you, you will know it. It will lead your mind where it should be, and prepare you for the narcolepsy that is certain to follow. You will know when the Software is with you, and so will others. You will smile with an inner smile. Typewriters will frighten you. You will fall down a lot.

The first exercise in writing Software documentation is the Haiku. Haiku are 17 syllable poem forms in which many ideas of a single concept are reduced – nay, distilled – into a short, impressionistic poem. For example, the Haiku for preparing to write of Software goes:

> Emptiness on paper;
> Fleeting thought.
> Red Sox play at Fenway's
> Green Park.

By concentrating on the Softwares form and function in a concise, subliminal, truly meaningless Haiku verse, you have transcended the Software, and you can then write the true manual.

The following Haiku is from a Zen manual on Data Transmission:

> How swiftly whirls the disk;
> Data leaps to the floating head
> And is known.

And this is on Hardware Maintenance:

> The smell of hot P.C. card,
> Blank screen, no bell,
> New parts will be needed.

And another Haiku, this one on Debugging:

All the lights are frozen;
The cursor blinks blandly.
Soon, I shall see the dump.

Let the Haiku thoughts free your mind from your fingers. Your fingers will write what must be written. Soon you will be in Document Preparation.

*On the Review Cycle*

This is the murkiest path. Storms gather and disperse around you many directions, none of which are in English. The path becomes unclear as many ideas compete for attention. Some are fatal.

But the writer of Zen Software documentation fears not the turbulence of review cycles. Let it storm around you and be dry, warm, and safe in the knowledge that you have written the pure manual. Anyway, you know the printer. You shall in the end have it your way.

Whenever two programmers meet to critize their programs, both are silent.
*Alan J. Perlis*

# The Unix Philosophy

*Anonymous*
15th December 1983

Last night I dreamed that the Real World had adopted the "Unix Philosophy."

I went to a fast-food place for lunch. When I arrived, I found that the menu had been taken down, and all the employees were standing in a line behind the counter waiting for my orders. Each of them was smaller than I remembered, there were more of them than I'd ever seen before, and they had very strange names on their nametags.

I tried to give my order to the first employee, but he just said something about a "syntax error." I tried another employee with no more luck. He just said "Eh?" no matter what I told him. I had similar experiences with several other employees. (One employee named "ed" didn't even say "Eh?," he just looked at me quizzically.) Disgusted, I sought out the manager (at least it said "man"

on his nametag) and asked him for help. He told me that he didn't know anything about "help," and to try somebody else with a strange name for more information.

The fellow with the strange name didn't know anything about "help" either, but when I told him I just wanted to order he directed me to a girl named "oe," who handled order entry. (He also told me about several other employees I couldn't care less about, but at least I got the information I needed.)

I went to "oe" and when I got to the front of the queue she just smiled at me. I smiled back. She just smiled some more. Eventually I realized that I shouldn't expect a prompt. I asked for a hamburger. She didn't respond, but since she didn't say "Eh?" I knew I'd done something right. We smiled at each other for a little while longer, then I told her I was finished with my order. She directed me to the cashier, where I paid and received my order.

The hamburger was fine, but it was completely bare... not even a bun. I went back to "oe" to complain, but she just said "Eh?" a lot. I went to the manager and asked him about "oe." The manager explained to me that "oe" had thousands of options, but if I wanted any of them I'd have to know in advance what they were and exactly how to ask for them.

UNIX fast food: indigestable but popular

He also told me about "vi," who would write down my order and let me correct it before I was done, and how to hand the written order to "oe". "vi" had a nasty habit of writing down my corrections unless I told her that I was about to make a correction, but it was still easier than dealing directly with "oe."

By this time I was really hungry, but I didn't have enough money to order again, so I figured out how to redirect somebody else's order to my plate. Security was pretty lax at that place.

As I was walking out the door, I was snagged in a giant Net. I screamed and woke up.

# Field Replacable Mouse Balls

*Anonymous*
In 1989 rec.humor.funny / *TeleJoke Computer Network Humour Annual*, Brad Templeton (ed.).

This actually comes from an IBM service database.

Mouse balls are now available as a FRU (Field Replaceable Unit). If a mouse fails to operate, or should perform erractically, it may be in need of ball replacement. Because of the delicate nature of this procedure, replacement of mouse balls should be attempted by trained personnel only.

Before ordering, determine type of mouse balls required by examining the underside of each mouse. Domestic balls will be larger and harder than foreign balls. Ball removal procedures differ, depending upon manufacturer of the mouse. Foreign balls can be replaced using the pop-off method, and domestic balls can be replaced using the twist-off method. Mouse balls are not usually static sensitive, however, excessive handlng can result in sudden discharge. Upon completion of ball replacement, the mouse may be used immediately.

It is recommended that each servicer have a pair of balls for maintaining optimum customer satisfaction, and that any customer missing his balls should suspect local personnel of removing these necessary functional items.

P/N33F8462    –    Domestic Mouse Balls
P/N33F8461    –    Foreign Mouse Balls

You can have a real ball with a mouse.

# Babbage – The Language of the Future

*Tony Karp*
Reprinted from *Datamation*, © early 1982
by Cahners Publishing Company

There are few things in this business that are more fun than designing a new computer language, and the very latest is Ada – the Department of Defense's new supertoy. Ada, as you know, has been designed to replace outmoded and obsolete languages such as COBOL and FORTRAN.

The problem is that this cycle takes 20 to 30 years and doesn't start until we're really convinced present languages are no good. We can short-circuit this process by starting on Ada's replacement right now. Then, by the time we decide Ada is obsolete, its replacement will be ready.

The new generation of language designers has taken to naming its brainchildren after real people rather than resorting to the usual acronyms. Pascal is named after the first person to build a calculating machine and Ada is named after the first computer programmer. As our namesake, we chose Charles Babbage, who died in poverty while trying to finish building the first computer. The new language is thus named after the first systems designer to go over budget and behind schedule.

Sorry, did you say cabbage?

Babbage is based on language elements that were discovered after the design of Ada was completed. For instance, C. A. R. Hoare, in his 1980 ACM Turing Award lecture, told of two ways of constructing a software design: "One way is to make it so simple that there are obviously no deficiencies and the other way is to make it so complicated that there are no obvious deficiencies." The designers of Babbage have chosen a third alternative – a language that has only obvious deficiencies. Babbage programs are so unreliable that maintenance can begin before system integration is completed. This guarantees a steady increase in the programming job marketplace.

Like Pascal, Ada uses "strong typing" to avoid errors caused by mixing data types. The designers of Babbage advocate "good typing" to avoid errors caused by misspelling the words in your program. Later versions of Babbage will also allow "touch typ-

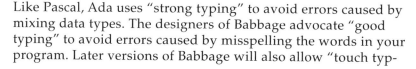

ing," which will fill a long-felt need.

A hotly contested issue among language designers is the method for passing parameters to subfunctions. Some advocate "call by name," others prefer "call by value." Babbage uses a new method – "call by telephone." This is especially effective for long-distance parameter passing.

Ada stresses the concept of software portability. Babbage encourages hardware portability. After all, what good is a computer if you can't take it with you?

It's a good sign if your language is sponsored by the government. COBOL had government backing, and Ada is being funded by the Department of Defense. After much negotiation, the Department of Sanitation has agreed to sponsor Babbage.

Profanity is the one language all programmers know best.

No subsets of Ada are allowed. Babbage is just the opposite. None of Babbage is defined except its extensibility – each user must define his own version. To end the debate of large languages versus small, Babbage allows each user to make the language any size he wants. Babbage is the ideal language for the "me" generation. The examples that follow will give you some idea of what Babbage looks like.

Structured languages banned GOTOs and multiway conditional branches by replacing them with the simpler IF-THEN-ELSE structure. Babbage has a number of new conditional statements that act like termites in the structure of your program:

WHAT IF – Used in simulation languages. Branches before evaluating test conditions.

OR ELSE – Conditional threat, as in: "Add these two numbers OR ELSE!"

WHY NOT? Executes the code that follows in a devil-may-care fashion.

WHO ELSE? – Used for polling during I/O operations.

ELSEWHERE – This is where your program really is when you think it's here.

GOING GOING GONE – For writing unstructured programs. Takes a random branch to another part of your program. Does the work of 10 GOTOs.

For years, programming languages have used "FOR," "DO UN-

TIL," "DO WHILE," etc. to mean "LOOP." Continuing with this trend, Babbage offers the following loop statements:

DON'T DO WHILE NOT – This loop is not executed if the test condition is not false (or if it's Friday afternoon).

DIDN'T DO – The loop executes once and hides all traces.

CAN'T DO – The loop is pooped.

WON'T DO – The CPU halts because it doesn't like the code inside the loop. Execution can be resumed by typing "May I" at the console.

MIGHT DO – Depends on how the CPU is feeling. Executed if the CPU is "up," not executed if the CPU is "down" or if its feelings have been hurt.

DO UNTO OTHERS – Used to write the main loop for timesharing systems so that they will antagonize the users in a uniform manner.

DO-WAH – Used to write timing loops for computer-generated music (Rag Timing).

Why bother with these new-fangled ideas? Machine code is entirely sufficient.

Every self-respecting language has a case statement to implement multiway branching. ALGOL offers an indexed case statement and Pascal has a labeled case statement. Not much of a choice. Babbage offers a variety of interesting case statements:

The JUST-IN-CASE Statement – For handling afterthoughts and fudge factors. Allows you to multiply by zero to correct for accidentally dividing by zero.

The BRIEF CASE Statement – To encourage portable software.

The OPEN-AND-SHUT CASE Statement – No proof of correctness is necessary with this one.

The IN-ANY-CASE Statement – This one always works.

The HOPELESS CASE Statement – This one never works.

The BASKET CASE Statement – A really hopeless case.

The Babbage Language Design Group is continuously evaluating new features that will keep its users from reaching any level of effectiveness. For instance, Babbage's designers are now considering the ALMOST EQUALS sign, used for comparing two floating-point numbers. This new feature "takes the worry out of being close."

No language, no matter how bad, can stand on its own. We need a really state-of-the-art operating system to support Babbage. After trying several commercial systems, we decided to write a "virtual" operating system. Everybody has a virtual memory operating system so we decided to try something a little different. Our new operating system is called the Virtual Time Operating System (VTOS). While virtual memory systems make the computer's memory the virtual resource, VTOS does the same thing with CPU processing time.

The result is that the computer can run an unlimited number of jobs at the same time. Like the virtual memory system, which actually keeps part of memory on disk, VTOS has to play tricks to achieve its goals. Although all of your jobs seem to be running right now, some of them are actually running next week.

Some programming languages manage to absorb change but withstand progress.

As you can see, Babbage is still in its infancy. The Babbage Language Design Group is seeking suggestions for this powerful new language and as the sole member of this group (all applications for membership will be accepted), I call on the computing community for help in making this dream a reality.

# Gulliver's Computer

*Jonathan Swift*
From *Gulliver's Travels*, Part III, *A Voyage to Laputa*, Ch. 5, 1727

We crossed a Walk to the other Part of the Academy, where the Projectors in speculative Learning resided.

The first Professor I saw was in a very large Room, with Forty Pupils about him. After Salutation, observing me to look earnestly upon a Frame, which took up the greatest Part of both the Length and Breadth of the Room; he said, perhaps I might wonder to see him employed in a Project for improving speculative Knowledge by practical and mechanical Operations. But the World would soon be sensible of its Usefulness; and he flattered himself, that a more noble exalted Thought never sprang in any other Man's Head. Every one knew how laborious the usual Method is of attaining to Arts and Sciences; whereas by his Contrivance, the most ignorant Person at a reasonable Charge, and with a little bodily Labour, may write Books in Philosophy, Poetry, Politicks, Law, Mathematicks and Theology, without the least Assistance from Genius or Study. He then led me to the Frame, about the Sides whereof all his Pupils stood in Ranks. It was Twenty Foot square, placed in the Middle of the Room. The Superficies was composed of several Bits of Wood, about the Bigness of a Dye, but some larger than others. They were all linked together by slender Wires. These Bits of Wood were covered on every Square with Paper pasted on them; and on these Papers were written all the Words of their Language in their several Moods, Tenses, and Declensions, but without any Order. The Professor then desired me to observe, for he was going to set his Engine to work. The Pupils at his Command took each of them hold of an Iron Handle, whereof there were Forty fixed round the Edges of the Frame; and giving them a sudden Turn, the whole Disposition of the Words was entirely changed. He then commanded Six and Thirty of the Lads to read the several Lines softly as they appeared upon the Frame; and where they found three or four Words together that might make Part of a Sentence, they dictated to the four remaining Boys who were Scribes. This Work was repeated three or Four Times, and at every Turn the Engine was so contrived, that the Words shifted into new Places, as the square Bits of Wood moved upside down.

Prolonged contact with the computer turns mathematicians into clerks and vice versa.
*Alan J. Perlis*

Six Hours a-Day the young Students were employed in this Labour; and the Professor shewed me several Volumes in large Folio already collected, of broken Sentences, which he intended to piece together; and out of those rich Materials to give the World a compleat Body of all Arts and Sciences; which however might be still improved, and much expedited, if the Publick would raise a Fund for making and employing five Hundred such Frames in Lagado, and oblige the Managers to contribute in common their several Collections.

He assured me, that this Invention had employed all his Thoughts from his Youth; that he had emptied the whole Vocabulary into his Frame, and made the strictest Computation of the general Proportion there is in Books between the Numbers of Particles, Nouns, and Verbs, and other Parts of Speech.

# *"Uncle Bill" is in the Driver's Seat!*

*Anonymous*
20th April 1993

January 25th, Redmond WA – Marketing reps from Microsoft Corporation today announced their new line of high-value sedans – yes, we mean automobiles! Bill Gates, Microsoft President, said: "We feel that consumers are confused by the great variety of vehicles out there. Every company offers their own proprietary version of your basic sedan, but there's no standard." Microsoft aims to define that standard with their new "Redmond" sedan. Here's just a quick tour of some of the state-of-the-art features that will make this the best set of wheels you'll ever drive:

• Room for up to six passengers (although the current version only allows one occupant while the car is in motion. Microsoft claims that this will provide greater security for the passenger and vows to look into a true multi-passenger model.

• Free car phone! The "Redmond" includes a Sony model TCP-93. This model only allows dialing out, so you'll have to purchase another phone if you wish to receive calls or communicate with other satisfied "Redmond" owners. Microsoft expects that many third-party vendors will be glad to provide this added value.

It might be slow, but at least it has Windows.

• Revolutionary cache strategy allowed Microsoft to design the "Redmond" with just 3 wheels instead of one. Just imagine the savings in tire-replacement!

• No speedometer, odometer, or gas-gauge. Microsoft feels that it can deliver a higher-quality product by leaving off these frills in the initial offering. This could also provide jobs for unemployed but enterprising auto workers who wish to provide this product to you.

• An early prototype of the "Redmond" (code-named "Pong") had the obvious disadvantage of only supporting left turns. The production-ready "Redmond" instead offers control-preserving but control-insensitive steering. The steering column and directional signals allow you to signal and turn in either direction, and while the car "remembers" the direction you turned, it translates this into a left turn automatically. Great news for people who always confuse left and right, and Microsoft provides a complimentary map of your town to aid you in finding paths that only include left turns.

- Should you be so old-fashioned as to not want to use some of these amazing new features, Microsoft again dazzles the critics by providing the "AmeriDrive" console. This console allows you to drive the "Redmond" as you would any other American car. The console supports the only available standards document (1.7b), so some minor features such as acceleration, steering, and braking are not fully supported. Microsoft fully stands behind AmeriDrive and maintains that it is "not just a check-box".

**Compatible:** Gracefully accept erroneous data from any source.

## Breathlock Service To Go Companywide

*Anonymous*
*Juggernaut*, April 1st 1990.
For the minions of Universal Thinking Machines Inc.
Reprinted from *Datamation*, Vol. 31, No. 7, April 1st, p.106,
© 1985 by Cahners Publishing Company

Universal Thinking Machines Security Chief Napoleon Truntian told the *Juggernaut* that the corporationwide cutover to UTM'S Breathlock™ Security System would take place over the Founder's Day Holiday Weekend. "When employees return to work on Tuesday, they must use the Breathlock™ in order to enter their buildings, their offices, and their computer networks," said Truntian, who also heads up UTM's Perimeter Systems Division. At the same time, UTM's Employee Relations Division will kick off a month long informational campaign aimed at raising security awareness. The program, consisting of videotapes and hands-on demonstrations, will be called "In Your Mouth."

Harald Hradcany, UTM senior vice president for Anthropomorphic Resources, put the program in a nutshell: "Loose lips may prove a barrier to continued employment at UTM: everyone must pucker up and blow." Mr. Hradcany also informed the *Juggernaut* that new superionizing mouthpieces on the Breathlock™

breathalyzer should allay employees' concerns about the spread of communicable diseases.

The Breathlock™ Security System is one of UTM'S leading-edge products for the 90s, explained Security Chief Truntian. "Everyone's breath identifies him or her infallibly. When an employee seeks approval to enter a building or building area, or to use specific pieces of equipment, he or she breathes into the Breathlock™." The resulting breathprint is compared to a company-wide database, and the employee is granted or denied access. "We are on the cutting edge of hot air research and development," added Truntian.

UTM has already shipped 912 complete Breathlock™ security systems. "And it has helped UTM's customers deal with a growing problem of substance abuse among their employees," said Mr. Truntian, pointing out that Breathlock™ notifies plant security as soon as it identifies a forbidden substance on the breath of an employee "Of course, we at UTM have little need of this feature," said Mr. Truntian. "Our employees are high on work and need no stimulants."

Anthropomorphic Resources VP Hradcany also announced that an order has been placed with UTM's Thermal Interface division for micropeizo-warmers for the Breathlocks installed at exterior UTM locations. He added, ''There have been rumors that a level-N employee working in the 6A239Z building at the Shady Grove software campus was found with his or her lips frozen to a Breathlock™ mouthpiece. Let me say this about that rumor. His or her lips were not adversely affected by whatever experience he or she might have had." Hradcany went on to say that he or she is already back at his or her job.

# To My Darling Husband

*Anonymous*

E-mail is a handy invention.

I am sending you this letter via this BBS communications thing, so that you will be sure to read it. Please forgive the deception, but I thought you should know what has been going on at home since your computer entered our lives two years ago. The children are doing well. Tommy is seven now and is a bright, handsome boy. He has developed quite an interest in the arts. He drew a family portrait for a school project, all the figures were good, and the back of your head is very realistic. You should be very proud of him.

Little Jennifer turned three in September. She looks a lot like you did at that age. She is an attractive child and quite smart. She still remembers that you spent the whole afternoon with us on her birthday. What a grand day for Jenny, despite the fact that it was stormy and the electricity was out.

I am doing well. I went blonde about a year ago, and discovered that it really is more fun! George, I mean, Mr. Wilson the department head, has, uh, taken an interest in my career and has become a good friend to us all.

I discovered that the household chores are much easier since I realized that you didn't mind being vaccumed but that feather dusting made you sneeze. The house is in good shape. I had the living room painted last spring; I'm sure you noticed it. I made sure that the painters cut holes in the drop sheet so you wouldn't be disturbed.

Well, my dear, I must be going. Uncle George, uh, Mr. Wilson, I mean, is taking us all on a ski trip and there is packing to do. I have hired a housekeeper to take care of things while we are away, she'll keep things in order, fill your coffee cup and bring your meals to your desk, just the way you like it. I hope you and the computer will have a lovely time while we are gone. Tommy, Jenny, and I will think of you often. Try to remember us while your disks are booting.

Love, Karen

# Computer-based Predictive Writing

*Peter J. Denning (pjd@cs.gmu.edu)*

Manuscript written 13th October 1988; received 19th April 1977.
*Journal of Irreproducible Results*, Vol. 24, No. 3, 1978, p. 28-29.
Reprinted by permission of Blackwell Scientific Publications, Inc.
Reproduced in *Communications of the ACM*, ACM President's
Letter, May 1982, Vol. 25, No. 5, p.315-316

Some years ago, I read a science fiction tale in which an inventor
connected a teletype to a random signal generator. As chance
would have it, the machine began after several years of garble to
generate recognizable sentences. Soon it was printing the entire
written works of mankind. One day, having read newspaper texts
from a future time, the inventor destroyed the machine, locked up
his house, and vanished.

Yesterday's science fiction is tomorrow's science fact. Turning the
science behind this whimsy to reality was the objective of our
Predictive Writing Project. It is well known in mathematics that
any given finite pattern will appear infinitely often in an infinite
sequence of symbols. The practical problem of retrieving a
substring as long as the entire written works of mankind is se-
vere, for we have neither infinite space in our computers nor
infinite time to run them.

The editor pon-
dered the problem
of rejecting a paper
that hadn't yet
been written.

It is not difficult to prove that the expected distance from the
beginning of an infinite string of letters until the first substring
containing the entire written works of mankind (in English) is
approximately $10^{30}$ letters, assuming that letters are generated
according to their standard frequencies in English [1]. This result
is of little practical value on ordinary computers, which can
perform perhaps $10^9$ operations per second. At such speeds, the
computer would require $10^{21}$ seconds, or roughly $10^{15}$ years, to
begin generating the entire written works of mankind.

An important, but little noticed technological advance occurred in
the early 1970's in the computer architecture research group led
by A. Vizick at the Sam Houston Institute of Technology. This
group designed a data-lookahead, multiply- layered VLSI machine for weather prediction [2]. This machine revised the traditional idea of instruction lookahead. It used a systolic array of

processing elements connected not only to their neighbors left and right on the same layer (wafer), but to their neighbors on the layers above and below. In a configuration with D units of lookahead, degree of systolic parallelism S, and L layers, the machine could perform:

$$F(L,S,D) = L^{D+\log_{10}S}$$

operations per second. In its maximum configuration with 9-unit lookahead, degree of parallelism 10,000, and 10 layers, F(L,S,D) evaluates to $10^{13}$ operations per second. At this speed, the required computation is reduced to approximately $10^{10}$ years. At first glance, the machine did not appear to meet our need.

The breakthrough came in 1975 when one of the members of our research team, S. Refrentz, discovered an ingenious way of folding the systolic array back on itself by merging the top and bottom wafers [3]. The technique, which is the subject of a patent application, is based on dividing the S systoles into D groups; by feeding the output of each group back from the bottom layer to the top and then cyclically into the next group, Refrentz was able to multiply the operation count by a large factor. In fact, his theory predicts that the machine's speed would be F(L,F(L,S,D),D) operations per second. For the configuration given above, this evaluates to $10^{22}$ operations per second.

Where the system is concerned, you are not allowed to ask "Why?".

The importance of the Refrentz modification to the Vizick design cannot be overstated. The required computation will take about $10^8$ seconds – just over three years.

This machine was built and put into operation in January 1977. In mid April 1980, as expected, the first written sentences of mankind began appearing on the output device. The Old Testament began appearing on May 17th and the New Testament on June 3rd. The complete works of Shakespeare began appearing on August 12th and were handed over to the English Department for study on September 20th.

Although the machine is busily producing the entire written works of mankind, it is not producing documents in their natural historical order. Shortly after the works of Shakespeare were printed, for example, we discovered the text of the August 27th, 1980 issue of the *Wall Street Journal*. (Thereafter, Knuth, Vol. I, began its appearance.) The convoluted historical order was a blessing in disguise, for we did quite well in the stock market on

August 28th and were able to finance the project for two additional years.

In early 1981, a young assistant professor wrote for preprints of research papers he was yet to write for his tenure decision. Sadly, an analysis of the output showed that he would not publish any more papers. I had anticipated his letter, having discovered it in the machine's output on December 10th, 1980, and was ready with my reply, which appeared on December 28th, 1980.

Items of scientific value have appeared. On September 11th, 1981, we found a preprint of a paper scheduled for publication in March 1990 claiming a refutation of Refrentz's theory. (It will be a hoax.) On November 17th we discovered a paper to be published in 1995 containing the answer to the question $P = NP$.

In general, however, much of the machine's output is of little interest – for the entire written works of mankind include many exigua such as grocery lists and message slips. The mean time between the production of major documents seems to be one to three weeks. When produced, these documents are sent to the appropriate university department or government agency for study.

Asking whether machines can think is like asking whether submarines can swim.

By far the most exciting implications of this machine are in the field of text editing. It is now possible to get the final version of a document without having to actually prepare it.

1. G. Handel, "Generating random English strings," *British Journal of Violinry* (August 1923).

2. A.Vizick, "A data-lookahead, muliple-layered VLSI architecture for weather prediction problems," *BULL.O.N.E.Y.* (1973), 10-1203.

3. S. Refrentz, "An exponential speedup technique based on self-folding a data-lookahead, multiply-layered VLSI architecture for weather prediction problems," Report No. TR-75-99 (September 1975), patent application 202-555-1212.

☆ ☆ ☆ ☆ ☆ ☆ ☆ ☆ ☆ ☆ ☆ ☆ ☆

# Making Your Serviceman Feel Welcome

*Anonymous*

1. Do not call for service until everyone that uses the machine has had a chance to correct the problem. Whenever possible, all controls and adjusting screws should be turned.

2. After several days, when the machine malfunction has become a major emergency, place an urgent call for service. Fridays are best but anytime after 4:00 pm is fine.

3. The minute the serviceman arrives, ask what caused the delay. Make it clear how desperately you need the machine and ask when it will be back in service.

4. The machine should be practically inaccessible due to boxes of recycled computer paper and cards. Make certain that the lights are off in the room where the machine is located and no one is in the area that knows how to turn them on. Always have one or two half-cups of coffee lying about.

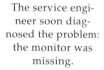

The service engineer soon diagnosed the problem: the monitor was missing.

5. Hide the service history log. Keep making reference to the man who was here for the same problem last week.

6. Alert all personnel that the serviceman has arrived so that each one can drop by and give their version of what is wrong, and provide suggestions on how to fix it.

7. Have at least eight graduate engineers drop by to ask highly technical questions which are in no way related to the immediate problem.

8. Assign someone to supervise the repair. A person who has never seen the machine before is preferable. And one who can keep up a steady stream of chatter is a plus.

9. Wait until there are parts and pieces spread out all over the floor, then ask when the machine will be ready.

10. Wait until the service man is looking at a schematic diagram and then ask him "what that thingamabob is for." After you have his attention, ask again when it will be fixed and mention that "time is money, you know."

11. When the repair is completed, tell him what a swell job he did. Tell him the job should be swell – it took long enough.

12. Ask the serviceman what the rates are, and then ask for a discount because you are such a good customer.

13. After he is gone, call his supervisor and say the machine is worse now than before. Follow up with a letter and copies to the home office.

14. Follow these rules faithfully and remember the serviceman's motto: "Do Unto Others Before They Can Do It To You."

# *Man, Bytes, Dog*

*James Gorman*
Reprinted by permission; © 1984 James Gorman.
Originally in *The New Yorker*, 2nd July, 1984, p.33.
All Rights Reserved.

Many people have asked me about the Cairn Terrier. How about memory, they want to know. Is it IBM-compatible? Why didn't I get the IBM itself, or a Kaypro, Compaq, or Macintosh? I think the best way to answer these questions is to look at the Macintosh and the Cairn head on. I almost did buy the Macintosh. It has terrific graphics, good word-processing capabilities, and the mouse. But in the end I decided on the Cairn, and I think I made the right decision. Let's start out with the basics:

Macintosh:
> Weight (without printer): 20 lbs.
> Memory (RAM): 128 K
> Price (with printer): $3,090

Cairn Terrier:
> Weight (without printer): 14 lbs.
> Memory (RAM): Some
> Price (without printer): $250

I am a computer –
dumber than any
human and
smarter than an
administrator.

Just on the basis of price and weight, the choice is obvious. An-other plus is that the Cairn Terrier comes in one unit. No printer is necessary, or useful. And – this was a big attraction to me – there is no user's manual.

Here are some of the other qualities I found put the Cairn out ahead of the Macintosh:

*Portability*: To give you a better idea of size, Toto in "The Wizard of Oz" was a Cairn Terrier. So you can see that if the young Judy Garland was able to carry Toto around in that little picnic basket, you will have no trouble at all moving your Cairn from place to place. For short trips it will move under its own power. The Macintosh will not.

*Reliability*: In five to ten years, I am sure, the Macintosh will be superseded by a new model, like the Delicious or the Granny Smith. The Cairn Terrier, on the other hand, has held its share of the market with only minor modifications for hundreds of years. In the short term, Cairns seldom need servicing, apart from shots and the odd worming, and most function without interruption during electrical storms.

A puppy whose playful vs ...

*Compatibility*: Cairn Terriers get along with everyone. And for communications with any other dog, of any breed, within a radius of three miles, no additional hardware is necessary. All dogs share a common operating system.

*Software*: The Cairn will run three standard programs, SIT, COME, and NO, and whatever else you create. It is true that, being micro canine, the Cairn is limited here, but it does load the programs instantaneously. No disk drives. No tapes.

Admittedly, these are peripheral advantages. The real comparison has to be on the basis of capabilities. What can the Macintosh and the Cairn do? Let's start on the Macintosh's turf – income-tax preparation, recipe storage, graphics, and astrophysics problems:

|  | Taxes | Receipes | Graphics | Astrophysics |
|---|---|---|---|---|
| Macintosh | yes | yes | yes | yes |
| Cairn | no | no | no | no |

At first glance it looks bad for the Cairn. But it's important to look beneath the surface with this kind of chart. If you yourself are leaning toward the Macintosh, ask yourself these questions: Do you want to do your own income taxes? Do you want to type all your recipes into a computer? In your graph, what would you put on the x axis? The y axis? Do you have any astrophysics problems you want solved?

Then consider the Cairn's specialties: playing fetch and tug-of-war, licking your face, and chasing foxes out of rock cairns (eponymously). Note that no software is necessary. All these functions are part of the operating system:

|           | Fetch | Tug-of-War | Face | Foxes |
|-----------|-------|------------|------|-------|
| Cairn     | yes   | yes        | yes  | yes   |
| Macintosh | no    | no         | no   | no    |

Another point to keep in mind is that computers, even the Macintosh, only do what you tell them to do. Cairns perform their functions all on their own. Here are some of the additional capabilities that I discovered once I got the Cairn home and housebroken:

*Word Processing*: Remarkably, the Cairn seems to understand every word I say. He has a nice way of pricking up his ears at words like "out" or "ball." He also has highly tuned voice-recognition.

*Education*: The Cairn provides children with hands-on experience at an early age, contributing to social interaction, crawling ability, and language skills. At age one, my daughter could say "Sit," "Come," and "No".

*Cleaning*: This function was a pleasant surprise. But of course cleaning up around the cave is one of the reasons dogs were developed in the first place. Users with young (below age two) children will still find this function useful. The Cairn Terrier cleans the floor, spoons, bib, and baby, and has an unerring ability to distinguish strained peas fram ears, nose, and fingers.

*Psychotherapy*: Here the Cairn really shines. And remember, therapy is something that computers have tried. There is a program that makes the computer ask you questions when you tell it your problems. You say, "I'm afraid of foxes." The computer says, "You're afraid of foxes?"

... a computer that's slothful.

The Cairn won't give you that kind of echo. Like Freudian analysts, Cairns are mercifully silent; unlike Freudians, they are infinitely sympathetic. I've found that the Cairn will share, in a nonjudgmental fashion, disappointments, joys, and frustrations. And you don't have to know BASIC.

This last capability is related to the Cairn's strongest point, which was the final deciding factor in my decision against the Macintosh – user-friendliness. On this criterion, there is simply no comparison. The Cairn Terrier is the essence of user-friendliness. It has fur, it doesn't flicker when you look at it, and it wags its tail.

# *Microsloshed Walls*

*Trygve Lode (tlode@nyx.cs.du.edu)*
In *The Unnatural Enquirer*, © 1990, and *The TeleJokeBook*, Brad
Templeton (ed.), Vol III , 1990, Section 4, p.28.

Microsloshed Corporation of Smoke'em, Washington introduces
the most fantabulous operating system overlay ever, a high-
performance GUI (Generally Useless Interface) that will transform
your measly old command-line driven PC into a state-of-the-art
multitasking system!

## MICROSLOSHED WALLS

•      Microsloshed Walls frees you from the worries of incompatible hardware – in fact, if any part of your computer is in the
tiniest respect different from an original IBM PC, Microsloshed
Walls will pretend it doesn't exist and lock up when you try to
install the drivers – automatically!

•      Complicated and cumbersome command-line functions
have been replaced by simple, intuitive mouse-driven commands
without confusing options or user-burdening functionality.

•      Microsloshed Walls version 3.0 is a major step forward –
boldly abandoning the restraints of compatibility with either DOS
or Walls 2.9 applications while not making you waste your time
learning new features or capabilities.

•      Conventional DOS programs are limited to a mere 640K of
memory; Microsloshed Walls will use up every last byte of
memory on your computer and more!

Their customer
service was
legendary.

•      Microsloshed Walls provides your programs with a uniform
user interface so simple and easy to use that all your applications
will look and act exactly the same. Whether you're using a tel-
ecommunications package or a compiler, you'll be completely
unable to tell them apart!

•      Several of the functions of the Microsloshed applications
you've grown to love under DOS will still work some of the time
under Walls and a variety of Microsloshed products are very
nearly supported by Microsloshed Walls including Expell,
QuirkC, QuirkBASlC, QuirkPascal, and QuirkRATFOR.

•      The popular word processing program Microsloshed Wart has been fully updated and modified just for Walls, making it totally unlike Microsloshed Wart while still retaining the same name.

• Microsloshed Walls includes its own special version of QEMMMM (Quirky Extraneous Massive Memory Multi-Mangler) converting your system's extraneous memory into impacted memory which can be more efficiently wasted by Walls.

We guarantee that, when you install Microsloshed Walls on your computer, you'll kiss your old DOS prompt goodbye. In fact, after just one session with Microsloshed Walls, you may never use any of your old programs again.

Microsloshed. Software that makes your computer obsolete.

## The Tin Men
An Extract

© *Michael Frayn*
William Collins, 1965

*(Part of) Chapter 1*

The whole of the *William Morris Institute of Automation Research* rang with the bongling and goingling of steel scaffolding poles being thrown down from a great height. The new Ethics Wing was almost finished. It was not before time. The noise and other inconveniences caused by the building of it had considerably reduced the amount of automation the Institute had researched into during the past two years. Experts had calculated that if the revolutionary new computer programs being designed at the Institute had gone ahead without interruption, they should have put some two million professional men out of work over the course of the next ten years. Now there was a risk that some of these two million would still find themselves in work, or at any rate only partly out of work. But then, said the optimists, for progress to be made someone always had to suffer.

To err is human; to really foul things up requires a computer.

*Chapter 20*

When he was tired and teleological, Goldwasser sometimes believed he could discern a purpose in Nobbs's existence. It was to keep him, Goldwasser, in his place by counterbalancing the inherent simplicity of his work in the Newspaper Department, compared with that of his colleagues in all the other departments.

They were all handicapped by the fact that even the biggest known computer has only a fraction of the capacity and complexity of the human brain. Goldwasser was not. The human brains he was replacing, he discovered as he analysed the newspaper files, suffered from neither capacity nor complexity. Or if they did, they didn't let it interfere with their work. As if foreseeing the limited intellects of the digital computers which would one day replace them, they had introduced the most drastic simplifications into their work already.

There was no need for Goldwasser to waste the limited stock of storage circuits at his disposal by programming the computer to deal with cortisone, streptomycin, cyclizine, sulphaphenyltrimethylaminodiazine, carbolic acid and aspirin. "Wonder drug" did for all of them. The need for Kensington, Westminster, Holborn, Paddington, Hammersmith and Edgware was conveniently satisfied by the one word "Mayfair". One of the biggest and most heterogeneous ranges of subject was replaced by one of the shortest words; pornography, marriage, indecent exposure, love, sodomy, birth, tenderness, striptease, etc., etc., were all "sex".

On this principle, therefore, it was unnecessary to struggle to program a computer whose range included writing stories about, say:

The headline reads: Shock Horror Exposé – News headlines are never true.

A man at Notting Hill Gate who claims to have reduced teenage delinquency by showing lantern slides about development in puberty;

An acquittal for a man accused of indecent exposure in a park at Ealing;

A Gloucester Road man who is unhurt after slipping on a manhole cover outside the Shakespeare Memorial Theatre while *Romeo and Juliet* is being performed;

An elderly businessman from Maida Vale whose arthritis clears up almost exactly four years after a visit to a strip club.

All the computer had to write was:

### MAYFAIR MAN IN SEX SHOW MIRACLE

There were other simplifications, too, that made Goldwasser's life easier. A man who manufactured shoe polish, or marketed shoe polish, or appeared in television commercials for shoe polish, or organised a strike against the shoe-polish manufacturers, or ate shoe polish, was simply "Mr. Shoe Polish". To the computer, Goldwasser realised with a certain wistful pang, he himself, Nobbs, Nunn and Chiddingfold, were all indifferently "Mr. Computer". So was the computer. Oil heaters and cigarette ends did not become circumstantially and wordily involved with shavings, waste paper, woodwork, or soft furnishings; fire horror struck. If fire horror struck twice in the same town within the year, *They Are Calling It Doom Town.* If the fire went on for longer than usual it was a fire marathon; if it was a small fire it was a mini-blaze; if it was in Russia it was a fireski. The world was also full of Mystery Men. Though there was never any mystery about who was behind a crime. It was a Master Mind, which was perhaps why the crime wave was, unlike most of the other waves which Britannia ruled, a permanent one.

Large sections of the English language were also rendered otiose by replacing long words with small words hyphenated together. Unilateralists were ban-the-bomb marchers. Save-the-horses men had a beat-the-rush plan for dodge-the-ban traders. No-overtime men met oh-so-friendly call-off-the-strike officials for let's-be-sensible talks. On-off-on-off plans for get-you-home services started who-is-to-blame storms.

Newspaper language, in fact, was a simplification to the point of abstraction. It was like mathematics. It had a bearing on life, but was remote from it, making not particular statements but general ones. Just as 2+2=4 applies to any two pairs of apples, or vacuum-cleaners, or middleclass Frenchmen, so "Mr. Average in Get-There-Or-Else Mystery Marathon" described a range of situations so undefined as to be infinite. The more Goldwasser thought about it, the more difficult it was to see what sort of evidence could possibly disprove "Mr. Average in Get-There-or-Else Mystery Marathon", and if there was no evidence that disproved it, there was plainly none that proved it, either. The only possible conclusion was that it was not a factual statement at all, but, like

Those who can't write, write help files.

2+2=4, a well-formed formula legitimately derived from an axiomatic system. All this was a great comfort to Goldwasser, who had to reproduce the system on the axiomatic machinery of a computer.

Bearing all this in mind, he had set up enough cards in the card-index to begin processing simple stories along these lines. The results were not perfect, but they had a certain encouraging purity of style – particularly the Magic, or Black, Box One, which according to analysis of cuttings, normally appeared about once a fortnight. There were several different permutations, but they all looked more or less like:

"MAGIC BOX" WILL HELP HOUSEWIVES
TOP SECRET BRITISH TRIUMPH

British scientists have developed a "magic box," it was learned last night. The new wonder device was tested behind locked doors after years of research.

Results were said to have surpassed expectations.

Top brass were among the men in the mystery research marathon. Last night experts were calling the magic box the beat-the-jinx box. The new wonder device has broken the jinx that has haunted British wonder projects ever since last week.

Norleen and Shane had faces that the newspapers loved.

*Mrs. Average Housewife will be among the first to feel the benefit of the beat-the-jinx box.*

How does it work?

Specially designed tubes feed supplies of wonder drug into the mechanism. A magic eye keeps a continuous check.

*The device is switched on and off with a switch which works on the same principle as an ordinary domestic light switch.*

A secret ray device is activated by an activator.

But the real secret of the magic box? – A new all-British wonder cell.

Goldwasser had arranged the cards so that the results they produced showed the two conflicting tropisms of newspaper language – on the one hand towards a range of especially familiar expressions like "do-it-yourself", "scorcher", "hubby", and "television", and on the other hand towards an exotic range of words that never occurred anywhere else, like "envoy", "slay", "blaze", and "pinpoint". The stories that emerged had something of the poignant ambiguity of the pictures one sees in the clouds – glimpses of a remote, fantastic world at once familiar and yet chimeric. For instance:

DO-IT-YOURSELF ENVOY IN SOCCER PROBE MARATHON

Rain horror ended Britain's miracle heatwave last night. Millions of viewers saw the man they call Mr. X, the mystery man in the Sex-in-the-Snow case, mention the Royal Family on T.V.

Mr. X – a Mayfair playboy well-known in Cafe Society and the International Set – will pinpoint the area where shapely brunette "Mrs. Undies" says her wonder hubby sent her to Coventry.

Police with tracker dogs and firemen with breathing apparatus fought to bring the mini-miracle under control. Thirty-two-year-old hole-in-the-head secrets man "Mr. Showbiz" collapsed after a Dolce-Vita-type milk stout orgy. In a plush night-club doctors struggled desperately to save his life.

But it overpowered them and escaped.

Top scientists threw a cordon round the doomed area. The trapped men retaliated by throwing a dragnet round the scientists, and going through them with a fine-tooth comb to locate the missing super-horror in a twelve minute mini-marathon.

Those who can, do. Those who cannot, teach. Those who cannot teach, HACK!

After a certain initial prejudice against this sort of language had dissolved, Goldwasser began to enjoy the stories his program wrote. They seemed to him to be the real modern fairy stories, and the cloudy, ambiguous world they revealed of miracle hubby horrors he came to see as the true fairyland lurking just round the corner of every English man's consciousness. To a remarkable degree, moreover, the stories survived his compulsion to read them backwards with their sense unimpaired.

# A Users View From The Trailing Edge

*By Jerry Porshoentelli*

© *William E. Kost (wekost@ers.bitnet)*
*A Bit More...*, William E. Kost (ed.), The NOVA Osborne Users Group, 1st April 1993

When I started out with this column over two decades ago in "kBit" magazine it was meant to be a users view from the cutting edge of microcomputer technology. For a couple of years it actually did that. However, as more and more companies sent me stuff to look at the farther behind I've gotten. I'm now sitting here in the Chaotic Cottage with a two-car garage, a basement, and an attic full of what looks like really good stuff to evaluate and tell you about. To help work down that backlog of products to review, I've decided to do a series of columns about my experiences for "A Bit More..." as well.

Even his tie was thrusting.

So here is my first report of the goings on at the trailing edge of microcomputer technology at the Chaotic Cottage – or, if you will, computing on the cheap. And remember, I don't just play a little bit with the new stuff that gets sent to me; I actually use this stuff to do productive work. And I'm so busy and so productive that I don't have time to keep switching to every new little thing that comes down the pike. That means I get to it when I get to it. And as you know it is hard to keep up with all those new "computing toys" that are coming on the market. Ain't technology grand?

PORTABLE COMPUTING ON THE CHEAP: A big package from Osborne Computer Corporation surfaced this month on a rummaging trip to the basement. It was a portable computer and just what I needed to take on my trip to the annual Flat Earth Society meeting. This year's meeting was scheduled for Melbourne. Since that was over near the edge I knew I faced a long flight and could sure use the time to work on the new hardcore romance novel I'm coauthoring with Larry Nibble. More on that writing project later. First I want to share with you my frustrations trying to get my portable computer to work on that trip.

I thought everything was going to go smoothly when I saw the port marked battery on the front of the Osborne. Then I discovered that they hadn't shipped the battery pack with the computer.

Since I didn't have time to dig through all the stuff in the garage looking for it, I thought no problem, I'll just call ol' Adam and have him ship me another. Well that is a whole other story that I don't have space for here. Lets just say their support leaves something to be desired. They don't seem to want to answer the phone. See, even being a famous computer columnist doesn't mean you always get great service. You know, you would think it ought to help some though. I wonder why they don't treat me with more respect.

In the long run every program becomes rococco – then rubble.
*Alan J. Perlis*

Well I had to give up the battery option. So I grabbed an extension cord for use on the plane, stuck the manual and a box of disks in my overnight bag and headed for the airport. Well you can imagine how upset I became when they wouldn't let me run the extension cord from the pilot's cabin or the restroom to my seat. Maybe airlines one day will be enlightened enough to provide power outlets at all seats, which would sure be better than making all us PC users carry big boxes of batteries everywhere with us. Of course it might have been for the best anyway. That little tray on the back of the seat didn't seem all that sturdy when I plopped down my Osborne 1 on it.

WORD PROCESSING: Of course I still made the flight a productive one. Fortunately I had stuck the thick Osborne manual into my backpack before boarding. Thumbing through it, I discovered WordStar. After a few minutes of reading I decided I might have finally discovered a new word processor to implement on Socrates, my ol' faithful home computer.

This is the third word processor (as opposed to editor) that I have used. I started with a simple programming editor pirated from a mainframe version of Fortran by my mad programming friend Max Bazic. Over the years my friend Mad-Max added features and rewrote the code to the point where I have a word processor custom designed for my writing style. I call this program Mechanical Pencil. Without it, I'd never have been able to produce four hardcore romance novels every month, my monthly column for "kBit", nor produce my pseudo-science articles and books for the Flat Earth Society.

I did try Electric Pencil when it came on the market but soon pulled the plug and donated it to charity (as you know, my policy is never to send stuff back to the supplier). I quickly found that my Mechanical Pencil was ever sharp when compared to Electric

Pencil. But WordStar may make me put my Mechanical Pencil back in my pocket. WordStar provides better editing and formatting capabilities, but does lack a lot of those special features useful for someone whose major job is writing hardcore romance novels with a solid science background. If WordStar would just implement Mechanical Pencil's ability to automatically insert a relevant descriptive phrase randomly selected from a long list of appropriate descriptive terms. This feature of Mechanical Pencil is what makes my novels exhibit more innovate and more colorfully descriptive action and variety than my peers in the field. Maybe I'll see if I can get Mad-Max interested in developing a WordStar add-on to do that. You know, with appropriate dictionaries, there might be a real market for that type of word processor add-on in lots of other disciplines too. Just think what it could do for economists or historians. One could have all the politically-correct terms at one's pencil point to spice up their writing styles.

Real World Desktop Publishing.

I sure do hate to give up the creativity Mechanical Pencil gives me, but WordStar is also appealing (besides, I am supposed to be looking at all this new stuff that is out there). I suspect I'll wind up having to use both programs until the next generation comes along. One of these days some enterprising young programmer will incorporate this phrase generating engine into a state-of-the-art word processor making it word perfect! I guess until that happens I'll use Pencil for my novels and Star for all my other writing (where creativity isn't required). The downside to this is learning two completely different command sets. If they would only produce keyboards with a bunch of special function keys that were reconfigurable for different software packages.

More next month on my word processing experiences. I may even get around to trying out the spreadsheet (whatever that is) that came with the Osborne too. I've got lots of other things to talk about and am starting to run out of space.

MORE PORTABLE COMPUTING RAMBLINGS: Well I'm now back from the Flat Earth Society meetings. We actually saw the edge! I'm now a confirmed computer traveler. Those Osborne block graphics sure came in handy when I had to develop a display to illustrate the basic tenets of the Society. The animation on that little screen was the hit of the meeting.

One other Osborne feature that I really like is that great little screen. It is so nice to have 52 rather than 40 columns to work with. Also having a high resolution monitor over that fuzzy ol' television screen is a real treat for those of us with cataracts. Then there is the added benefit of now being able to watch my soap operas on television and compute at the same time. This makes for real efficiencies since neither watching soap operas nor writing my novels really take my full attention. Now if I could just come up with something to occupy my left brain at the same time.

Am off again tomorrow for the National Association for the Advancement of the Pseudosciences annual conference and definitely will take along my Osborne. It is great to have a light weight portable computer almost as powerful as ol' Socrates. Having a portable Osborne almost makes traveling with a computer pleasant. It sure beats the Port-A-Strap-Cart system Mad-Max built for me so I could take Socrates (my S-100 SuperThinker system with Jacob-Anderson terminal printer. Carrying a 20 pound computer as carry-on luggage sure beats air freight shipping a shock resistant custom-built hand cart that opens up into a computer desk when you get it to the hotel room. You know that Osborne makes one think that it won't be all that long before we will see them cutting down the weight to 10 pounds! Maybe even include a hard disk and modem! Wouldn't that be something? I know that this is highly speculative, but the industry is changing. I even have a Color Computer in the stack of stuff that I haven't had time to look at yet. Osborne has even shipped me a second machine. You can now even get designer Osbornes in your choice of tan or gray. What won't that man think of next. You know he bundled all that software with his computer. Why I wouldn't be surprised to see him try to sell computer related supplies and software for the Osborne in bookstores and the like in the same manner as you sell paperback books! Now don't laugh, it could happen. It isn't that far fetched.

Any sufficiently advanced bug is indistinguishable from a feature.
*Kulawiec.*

GAME OF THE MONTH: The game of the month this month is Eliza. I can talk to it for just hours and hours. Having a personal computer psychologist is not only relaxing, but also keeps me from getting totally removed from reality. You know that is a problem for anyone who spends four hours a day writing hardcore romance novels. This is a game that isn't really a game. It simulates reality. Try it; you will like it.

BOOK OF THE MONTH: Mine. Larry Nibble and I have just finished *The Ravaged Programmer*. Next month, when I have more space, I'll tell you about our experiences in jointly writing a novel on two incompatible computer systems without messy retyping. For now, I'll just say a modem is critical and talk about user-unfriendly software!

WRAPPING UP: I'm about out of space, so no time for details. I now have two database packages to play with: Vulcan (or dBase I) and Personal Oyster. Vulcan seems to have more features, but also more bugs. Let's just say that Personal Oyster has no pearl. You know these databases are kind of fun to play with, but I don't see much use for them for most people. Hey, I may be wrong, but that is how I see it here in the Chaotic Cottage.

So what's on deck for the coming months? I've just moved in from the garage several accounting programs, a Radio Shack hand held computer/calculator, and an Atari game machine. I'll also have more on my computing experiences at the NAAP.

I've not been getting all that much new software and hardware shipped to me by manufacturers these days. They all want their stuff reviewed *now*! I tell them "Hey, I'm behind a little and I will get to your stuff as soon as I can." This really isn't a big problem though. All storage space here is stacked to the rafters already, so I've got lots of stuff to evaluate. Besides, most of you out there are tool users, not "new toy" junkies. You want to know how someone like yourself deals with the computer revolution. And I'm trying to deal with it and share my experiences with you.

In that vein, I'm off to a whole series of computer flea markets and garage sales throughout the northwest after the NAAP meeting. I hope to find lots of neat, cheap stuff as well as talk to lots of other users and vendors. Then I also have promised my editor that I'll wrap up my new novel, *The Sparkle in God's Eye*. So, as you can see, another busy month is on the horizon.

Powerful tools are needed for the debugging of software.

More on all those things next month. We will again explore some more of the neat things you can do with those PCs. And remember, you don't have to be at the leading edge to be at the edge.

Jerry Porshoentelli holds a Ph.D. in parapsychology. In addition to his numerous computer magazine user columns, he is a notoriously prolific writer of hardcore romance novels. He also is a fixture at professional meetings and conferences in many different disciplines – he's apt to show up just about anywhere.

# Lisp: They May Also Serve, Who Decline to Enlist...

© *Robert M. Baer*
*The American Mathematical Monthly*
February 1985, Vol. 92, p.159

Last year we were told that "Lisp is crisp" [1], and this year we are told that LISP "is the only language in which civilized people write computer programs" [2]. (There is a counter-view to the effect that civilized people view with distaste any language in which assignment and equality are represented by the same symbol.) LISP has recursion, but its overhead is notorious. Its primary (perhaps only) virtue is that list-processing capability (but, then, there are all those parentheses...). In any case, we put the question to our desktop verse-processor, and got the following output:

*Adrift on seas of parentheses*

LISP isn't crisp but essentially soggy:
Parentheses piled up make you reel groggy

Deciphering LISP would apparently be
more work than Minoan Linear B.

As for cond (aka if) and cdr and car,
Like heavy seas they're best viewed from afar

And Vertigo thrives in anticipation
or waves upon waves of Polish notation.

LISP for list-processing: cause to abort
(Is it listing to starboard or listing to port?)

Yes, recursion is nice
To put puzzles on ice.

(But they dole out machine time, ration by ration,
so I'll skip the recursion and use iteration.)

Lisp Users: Due to the holiday, there will be no garbage collection on Monday.

*References*

1) D. R Hofstadter, Metamagical Themas, *Scientific American*, 248

(1983), No.3, p.22-30 and  No.4, p.14-28

2) M Wand, What is LISP?, *The Americam Mathematical Monthly*, Vol. 91 (1984) p.32-42.

# *The Case of the Bogus Expert (Part 3)*

*The Adventures of Joe Lisp, T Man*

© *Kris Hammond (kris@cs.uchicago.edu)*
14th February 1984

But first a message from our producers...

Lisp's working style often reminded people of 'The Big Sleep'.

Recently there have been many complaints that the adventures of our favorite detective, Joe Lisp, have not contained enough "action". Of course we all know that action is just a euphemism for violence. Although we in the Artificial Intelligence (AI) fraternity deplore violence, (we tend to favor blackmail and other forms of extortion), we realize that as public servants we must cater to the tastes of the sleazy low-life that make up the majority in this great country of ours. So without any further ado, we present an all-action, all-adventure, all-violence episode of Joe Lisp, T Man.

It started as soon as I entered the secret enclave of the EXPERTs. There was a left, a right, another left and right. I knew it was a test. They wanted to see what kind of action I'd take, how I paired up against them. They hit me again with a flurry of lefts and rights, and ended with a right to the body... of LISP code that is. God these guys were good at production system hacking.

I made my way through their playroom and located the office of the head of the EXPERTs. He was a tough man whose main claim to fame was his work on the Fast Automated Thing. It was a "general purpose" expert system that was able to analyze any known problem that could possibly crop up on the Navy's a35-22b Bernoulli Suction Module attached to the pre-pump assembly found in sump systems on the 82-83 models of the tugs used to guide Trident subs out to sea. The system itself is able to recognize almost 14 different problems using less than 3,572 rules, each of which has at least 43 conjuncted tests on the left side. He finally left his work on the Fast Automated Thing in order to, in his words, "... get out of the rarified atmosphere of theoretical AI and work on some real world applications". Only the EXPERTs ignored his past work however, so while the rest of the world knew him as the F.A.T. Man, they knew him only as the head honcho... the top dog... the big cheese. I walked in to face him.

He looked up from his desk as I entered. In front of him was an open copy of "Fifth Generation Japanese Computer Terminology made E-Z". As I walked closer and pulled out my gun he froze in terror and recognition. "I thought you were dead," he said. "My men killed you last year." I sneered for effect and explained to him that he hadn't killed me. He'd killed my brother Mack, Mack Lisp. I would have mentioned him earlier but the dramatic impact of a sudden revelation can't be beat... and the name was suggested to me only after the first episode. His face was white with terror as I pointed my gun at his...

Where is Joe pointing the gun? What will the FAT man do? What is the secret of the woman in white? How much will you offer me to stop writing these messages?

As per usual, the answers to these and many other far less interesting questions (such as how many times the word "whip" is used in the bible) will be answered in the next exciting episode of the adventures of Joe Lisp, T Man.

*To Be Continued...*

> When we understand knowledge-based systems, it will be as before – except our fingertips will have been singed.
> *Alan J. Perlis*

# *Alternatives to OSI*

*Jock C. St. Martin*
The University of the Outer Hebrides, Scotland
© Julian Onions and Steve Benford [1]

Following recent discussions concerning the relative merits of OSI and ARPA protocols, I decided to throw my hat into the ring. Furthermore, I believe that the ARPA protocols are not the only contenders with OSI, and that a number of even more "mature"

mechanisms exist. I present seven possibilities for consideration.

### 1. Bean tins and bits of string

The use of bean tins and taut pieces of string has long been recognised as an effective means of communication. In fact, excavations from Anglo-Saxon dwellings in Nottingham show their use (albeit with imported coconuts as opposed to bean tins) in early everyday office situations.

Bean tins and string have several advantages over OSI:

a. They are fast, light weight and portable.

b. They don't require the purchase of expensive computers.

c. Complex error correction (based on the "No - I said ..." principal)

d. Uses off the supermarket shelf technology.

e. They were not invented by the ISO.

They also exhibit a very few trifling limitations:

Every program in development at MIT expands until it can read mail.

a. Poor support for "packet" switching (however, tin switching may be supported).

b. Users often cut themselves on the tins.

c. Star network topologies become more complex.

d. They don't scale very well.

### 2. Shouting from the roof tops

Shouting from the rooftops can be an effective method of optimised local area communication. It is based on the well understood CMSA/CD technology but with the notion of priority. Users can insert high priority traffic with the "If I might get a word in edgeways" packet. It is already in widespread use – e.g., the House of Commons, political canvassing and Speakers Corner. Naturally, a roof top is only necessary for high bandwidth traffic. The PTT's would probably assume this role. The average user would be content to shout in the street.

Shouting has many advantages over OSI:

a. It is not as "complex and obscure".

b. Most people understand shouting.

c. Broadcasts are easy.

d. It's fun.

e. It wasn't invented by the ISO

OSI has hardly any advantages over shouting worth shouting about.

### 3. *Burning beacons on hill–tops*

Burning beacons on hill–tops have long been used to warn of advancing Armadas and their like. However, the author believes that beacons may have wider applications than just these.

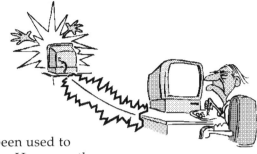

Bertram was an electrifying conversationalist.

In particular, they have the following advantages over OSI:

a. No "dangerous checkpointing".

b. They keep you warm.

c. Not overly complex and obscure.

d. A secondary use for the disposal of those nasty ISO people.

e. Not cluttered with unnecessary functionality.

f. Not invented by the ISO.

Disadvantages to OSI:

a. Not suitable for the office environment (this may really be an advantage in some circumstances).

b. Low bandwidth (may also be an advantage – see 7)

c. Error rates can be high. Arsonists, pyromaniacs and "Satanic Verses" burners can generate spoof packets.

### 4. *Semaphore*

Semaphore has been in use for many years. So why did ISO not consider this for international internetworking? This is difficult to determine, but is probably due to political motivations rather than any deficiencies in the protocols. Naturally there are a few rough edges to be addressed.

Advantages over OSI:

a. Broadcasts are easily accommodated.

b. Widely supported off-the-shelf infra-structure (boy scouts).

c.  Not invented by ISO

Disadvantages over OSI:

a.  Not so useful at night (but a working party on luminous flags is in progress).

b.  Bandwidth is rather low – but automation should help.

### 5. *Messages in bottles*

This is a low cost solution to networking. Bottles are easy to obtain and with a little development, this neglected backwater of communications technology could be a real alternative.

Advantages over OSI:

a.  High bandwidth data channels already in existence (e.g. the gulf stream, rivers and sewers.)

b.  Large amounts of data can be placed in the appropriate sized bottles.

c.  Not invented by ISO.

Disadvantages to OSI:

a.  Transit time is unpredictable (but then IP, for instance, does not guarantee any bounded delivery time)

### 6. *The Telephone*

CChheecckk
yyoouurr
dduupplleexx
sswwiittcchh..

This might be seen as an enhancement of method 2. However, there is a lot to be gained from this approach. The name lookup problem is already solved, as are routing issues. Let's face it, communications protocols are ultimately used for communicating between people. So why not just standardise the telephone. Add on services such as broadcast agents (commonly called gossips/ operators) are easy to achieve.

Advantages over OSI:

a.  It's a mature existing technology.

b.  Directory services issues, routing and charging are already established.

c.  It's now available in portable form.

d.  Not invented by ISO

Disadvantages to OSI:

    a.  Because it's a mature technology, there aren't so many interesting research areas.

    b.  As a result. there are few exotic conference openings.

    c.  It costs money.

### 7. Not communicating at all

One question I asked myself was "why communicate at all?" On consideration it was realised that not communicating has the following advantages over OSI.

    a.  Low consumption of bandwidth.

    b.  Cheap and easy to manage.

    c.  No one disagrees with you.

    d.  Without the time wasted on communication, other business proceeds much quicker.

    e.  Not invented by the ISO

No known disadvantages to OSI.

'But darling, our communication is fully OSI compatible.'

### Summary

In summary, I feel that all of the above methods are orders of magnitude better than OSI (which incidently, and by coincidence, wasn't invented here). In particular, I feel that method seven offers the greatest potential and, with this in mind, *we do not welcome any further comments you might have!*

### Author's note

[1] This article is in no way connected with either Julian Onions or Steve Benford of the University of Nottingham beyond their role as postal agents for the author.

# A Salutory Tale of Software Development

*Anonymous*

In the beginning there was the Requirement and the Requirement was without form or structure and darkness was upon the face of the Client, and the face of the Client was turned away from the Company. So the Company said:

'Let there be a Tender'

And lo, there was a Tender, and the Client saw that it was good, and the face of the client was turned once more unto the works of the Company.

Then did the Company gather together all manner of creatures, and from this gathering was created the project team – and it was said that it was good. From the Project Team were produced Engineers and Programmers and diverse other forms of life. And from the multitude was selected one who was raised above all others and who was called 'Manager'. And he was to lead the Project Team along the path of productivity for the Companys' sake. And it happened that the mind of the Manager was dazzled by the Tender and he thereby believed that all things were possible, even though there was, as yet, no specification.

Thus it was that the Manager commanded all Programmers to be gathered together in one place and he spoke to their leader who was called Chief Programmer: 'Let there be a Schedule, whereby I may know the Delivery Date, and I shall make you responsible for the accomplisment of this schedule'. Therefore did the Chief Programmer move amongst his followers and ask of them 'How shall this be done?'.

Every program has (at least) two purposes: the one for which it was written and another for which it wasn't.
*Alan J. Perlis*

Where upon his followers withdrew, each to his own desk and estimated, as was their custom. And it came to pass that each Programmer brought forth an estimate and, after much wailing and gnashing of teeth, all estimates were consolidated and summarised into one place which was called a 'Project Plan'.

And the Chief Programmer brought the Manager unto the Project plan saying: 'Behold – it will take a full score of months to accomplish'. But the Manager was not pleased and said: 'I have raised you up from the depths and given unto you many coding sheets

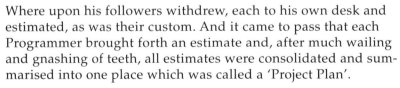

and even so you have not understood the Tender, your Project Plan is too long'. Whereupon the Manager hired consultants, authorised much overtime and cancelled all holidays. Then he spake unto the Chief Programmer: 'Behold, see all that I have done, the Delivery Date shall be in one Year'.

Then did the Chief Programmer set his followers to designing and coding and there were many meetings and much computer time was employed in the working thereof – even though there was as yet no Specification. And it came to pass that the Manager examined the designs and he saw that they were too ambitious and he knew that they could not be accomplished by the Delivery Date. Whereupon the Manager commanded the Chief Programmer to separate the design into two parts. One part he called the 'Manditory Functions' and the other 'Options' – and the Client called him names. And the Manager commanded: 'Let the Software Houses put forth their salesmen and let us have a Data Base Management System' and it was so.

The rationalisation of the Ten Commandments was progressing smoothly.

The salesmen produced all manner of Brochures which laid claim to many and wondrous things – each according to their own file structure. And it came to pass that a Data Base Management System was selected and the Chief Programmer accomplised said that it was good and that more programmers were required if all was to be accomplished by the Delivery Date. Thus it was that the Project Team was increased almost without number. The Manager, espying this host from afar said: 'Let there be Organisation' and there was Organisation. And the Project team was split into many groups that did not speak to each other, and it was said that, perhaps it was good. Some groups the Chief Programmer called Senior Programmers and others he called Junior Programmers and he gave domination to the former over the latter. And the Senior Programmers saw it differently.

Now it was said that the Chief Programmer exorted his followers to even greater efforts because the Delivery Date was nigh and the breath of the Manager was hot upon his neck. Both Senior and Junior Programmers became sore afraid. They strove mightily to please the Chief Programmer with much overtime and copious comment and everyone coded and flowcharted, each in his own manner. The manager, seeing this, liked it not and commanded: 'Let there be Standards' and there were Standards but the Programmers liked them not and productivity fell. When he learned of this the Chief Programmer was afaid that he would be cast down from his high place and therefore commanded: 'Let there be Progress Reports' and there were Progress Reports.

The Chief Programmer looked at the Progress reports and saw that the Delivery Date would not be met. Therefore, on the tenth month, the Chief Programmer rose up, pressed his suit, shaved his beard and went unto the Manager, grovelling and pointing his fingers and causing much blame to issue forth unto all manner of creatures who sold both hardware and software. And the Chief Programmer asked for an extension whereat the Manager was exceedingly angry and caused doubt to be cast on the legitimacy of the Chief Programmers ancestors – even to the third and fourth generation and there was much beating of breast and tearing of hair – mostly the Chief Programmers'. And the Manager commanded the Chief Programmer to put forth all Software House personnel and all Consultants. But the Chief Programmer refused saying that all were needed, that there was no documentation and that there was, as yet, no specification.

The Manager prepared for the review meeting.

And it came to pass that an extention was granted and the Chief Programmer returned to his followers bearing these tidings and there was rejoicing and revelry among the terminals; and the coffee machine broke down. On the twentieth month the Chief Programmer said: ' Let the modules be integrated, one with another, so that the system testing can begin'. And it was so and great difficulties were experienced and many hours of overtime were employed in finding out why the modules would not integrate – for there was no documentation and, as yet, no specification.

Then on the twenty fourth month, the Chief Programmer did go to the Manager and say unto him: 'Behold I give you good tidings of great joy for you and for your Client, for on this day the System did work'. And suddenly there was all about them a host, a multitude of Salesmen praising the Chief Programmer and singing: 'Glory to the Company, the Manager, and the Chief Programmer and, please, can you make this small change?'. And the Chief Programmer rose up and spake thus unto them:

'We dare not for there is no documentation and, as yet, no specification'.

# You Get What You Pay For?

*SquishySoft, maker of that world-renowned software program MaxiTool, wants your help (as a famous software expert) in debugging Release 2.0. What? You think you should get paid?*

Stephen Manes (smanes@hebron.connected.com)
*PC Magazine*, November 25th, 1986, Vol. 5, No. 20, p.119-120.

You are working feverishly to finish a project due yesterday when you detect Interrupt IH: the jangling one.

"This is Dulcie Greenblatt from SquishySoft?" gurgles a California voice full of sultry breezes. "Assistant product manager for *MaxiTool*'? How are you today?"

"Busier than a queen bee in heat," you ape.

"Well, I won't take up too much of your time?" says Ms. Greenblatt.

"Impossible" you mutter.

"We consider you one of the nation's leading experts on our *MaxiTool* software?"

The program is absolutely right; therefore, the user must be wrong.

You emit a mild snort. As far as you're concerned, you're *the* leading *MaxiTool* expert. You've written a score of articles about it. "In fact, it's on my screen even as we speak, you reply. "A fine program. though not without its shortcomings."

"Groovy? Far out? We want you to tell us just what you want to see in Version 2.0 of the product'?"

You sigh. "That would take 2 days."

"Maybe you could send us a report'?"

You quote your standard fee.

The phone emits a gasp. "You mean you would charge us!"

"I'm not an eleemosynar."

Ms. Greenblatt does not say "Huh'?" She says, "No one else we've contacted wants to charge us."

"Perhaps no one else you've contacted has been worth much."

"Well, we would really like your input? I'll get back to you?

Soon?"

Three days later Interrupt IH disturbs your midday siesta. It's James "Jim" Morrison, the *MaxiTool* product manager. "Our corporate policy has existed since back when we were known as LightMyFireSoft." he explains. "We just don't have a budget for paying outside consultants in this phase of development. It's standard industry practice."

This, you are aware, is all too true. Software and hardware companies will spend their shekels on imbecilic focus groups and head-nodding marketing consultants, but never for outside advice on software design. After all, they're supposed to be the experts.

"There are many quaint industry practices with which I am not in wholehearted accord," you reply sadly. "Alas, I don't have a budget for doing other people's work gratis."

*Another phoney offer was efficiently dismissed.*

"A shame." says he. "We would really like your input."

ALPHA TEST. Six months later you are working on a project that's due the day before yesterday. Interrupt IH again. "Dulcie Greenblatt, new product manager for *MaxiTool*? How are you today?"

"Worse."

"We're about to begin alpha testing for our new Release 2.0? We'd like you to visit our headquarters next Monday and Tuesday and tell us how you feel about the product?"

"Does this mean you are ready to part with my fee?"

"We'll cover all your travel expenses, including transportation, meals, lodging, and two glasses of wine each evening?"

"Quite possibly we have a bad connection. I heard nothing about my fee."

"It's not our policy to pay outside alpha testers?"

"It's not my policy to spend two dark days in someone's smoke-filled offices without adequate remuneration?"

"You'd be one of a select few to preview this product months ahead of schedule? Other experts like yourself have already agreed to attend"

"Perhaps they were born with the proverbial silver spoons.

Perhaps spending 12 hours on airplanes and then sitting around a corporate headquarters is their idea of a swell vacation. Perhaps they are susceptible to flattery. Say hi to them for me."

BETA TEST. Three months later you get a letter trom Dulcie Greenblatt, vice president and director of product management at SquishySoft. It informs you:

Dear Expert user, that you have been selected as a potential beta-test site for a new SquishySoft product. All you have to do is return the Application Form, the Beta Test NonDisclosure Agreement, and the 400-question User Profile Questionnaire. If you are among the chosen, you will receive a copy of the package within 30 days.

The letter warns that "Beta Testers must commit the time necessary to learn a new product and fully document their interactions with it" and that "You will be working with new pre-release programs that are not yet perfect: your input is needed to finalize them. SquishySoft may interview you at the close of the beta-test period." For all this "you will receive one complimentary copy of the product you tested when and if such product is actually released."

Two weeks later, Interrupt 1H is followed by the voice of Irwin Muggleston, executive assistant to Dulcie Greenblatt. "Have you received our Beta Test Application yet?" he wonders.

"I have disposed of it safely and properly." you reply.

"We were hoping that you would join our team." says Mr. Muggleston "We really would like your input."

"I really would like to give it to you," you reply. "However, I really do not enjoy, futzing around with bug-ridden early verions of software that have the potential to destroy my work. Nor do I really derive great pleasure from maintaining an endless, bug log. And I really do not consider a copy of a program I can borrow from a friend or actually buy mail order for the munificent sum of 200 bucks entirely adequate compensation.

Why did the Roman Empire collapse? What is the Latin for office automation?
*Alan J. Perlis*

RELEASE 2.0. Three months later, with a great deal of fanfare, Release 2.0 of *MaxiTool* is brought to market. When you discover it is largely incompatible with the first version, jettisons many of that version's most useful features, runs only half as fast, will not work with a monochrome monitor, has a marked propensity to trash files and disks, and costs three times as much as the original version, you write a nasty review in a major publication.

The day after it hits the stands, you respond to Interrupt 1H. You have to; it's nonmaskable. D. Greenblatt, president and chief executive officer of SquishySoft is in high dungeon. "How dare you attack our product! You could have found those problems when we came to you! You refused to help us ! We really wanted your input."

You just shake your head as her tirade continues, "And you actually have the gall to criticize our new slogan! Honestly, just what do you think is so terrible about 'You Get What You Pay For,' anyway?"

Selected by Steven Korn for 'Three Decades of Datamation Cartoons'. Reprinted from *Datamation*, September 15th, Vol. 33, No. 18, p.106, © 1987 by Cahners Publishing Company.

# *You Can't Fool'em Down On The Farm!*

*Real Americans talk about why they chose the*
*Sun SPARCstation 2000™*

*Anonymous*
SUN News, November 8th, 1990

"Wow – with a workstation that powerful, I could get twice as much milking done."
– Mrs. Elaine Noose, Scumwater, Oklahoma

"Out here on the farm, you really learn to appreciate the value of good graphics resolution."
– Ted Lumplin, Brat's Head, Nebraska

"After we lost most of our cattle stock to pellegra, our barn burned down. After that, Joe got himself caught in the thresher and lost most of his body hair. Then the banks foreclosed. It sure was a comfort to know that we had 28 MIPs of power to see us through hard times."
– Darrell LaQuench, Pine Agony, Maine

"I believe that Virtual Quilting, using high-speed networking services, will be the wave of the future."
– Mrs. Jane Dobrynin, Fleughh, Utah

"Last week we had a fella from Digital come out and look at the soybean crop. After 20 minutes, Ma chased him off and threw his keyboard out the window. We're from old Norwegian stock, and we know a thing or two about bus controllers."
– Buck Flange, Arkansas, Texas

SPARCstation seedlings should be planted in early May.

Why has the SPARCstation 2000 caught the imagination of the American working man and working woman like no other computer in its class? Maybe it's the extra features, like the padded Corinthean leather screen, or the safety air bag that inflates when the typing buffer gets too full. Maybe it's the tradition of honest service and free doughnuts. Then again, maybe not.

Sun Microsystems. A Step Ahead of Your Cows.

## BOFH (Part 3)

© *Simon Travaglia (spt@waikato.ac.nz)*

I'm working so hard I barely have time to drive into town and watch a movie before the time when I told people their printing would be ready. The queue's *waaaay* too long to print (and sort) everything, so I kill all the small jobs so there's only 2 left, and I can sort them in no time.

Then, after the movie (which was one of those slack Bertolucci ones that takes about 3 hours till the main character is killed off in a visionary experience), I get back and clear the printouts.

There's about 50 people waiting outside and I've got two printouts. That's about average for me. I thought I'd killed more though. Anyway, I put out the printouts and walk slowly inside, fingering the clipboard with "Accounts To Remove" in big letters on the back. No-one says anything. As usual.

Later, I'm sitting back in the Operations Armchair, watching the computer room closed circuit TV, which just happens to be connected to the frame-grabber's video player (sent off for repair, due back sometime in '97) when the phone rings. That must be the second time today, and it's really starting to get to me!

If you can imagine a society in which the computer-robot is the only menial, you can imagine anything.
*Alan J. Perlis*

"Yes?" I say, pausing the picture.

"I've accidentally deleted my C.V!" the voice at the other end of the line says.

"You have? What is your username?"

He tells me. What the hell, I *am* bored.

"Ah no, you didn't delete it - I did."

"What?"

"I deleted it. It was full of rubbish! You didn't ever get more than a B- in any of your subjects!"

"Huh?"

"And that stuff about being a foreign exchange student, that was your girlfriend and we both know it."

"Huh?!!"

"Your academic records. I checked them, you were lying."

"How did y.." He clicks. "It's you isn't it? *The Bastard Operator From Hell!*"

"In the flesh, on the phone and in your account. You shouldn't have called you know. You especially shouldn't have given me your username." >clickety< >click< "Neither should you have sent that mail to the System Manager telling him what you think of him in graphic terms."

"I didn't send any."

>clickety< >click<.

The soles of a new programmer?

"No, you didn't did you? But who can tell these days. Not to worry though, It'll all be over *very* soon." >clickety click< "Change my username back, and..."

"b-b-b.." he blubs, like a stood-up date.

"Goodbye now" I say pleasantly, "you've got bags to pack and a life to start over."

I hang up.

Two seconds later the red phone goes. I pick it up, it's the boss. He mumbles the username of the person I was just talking to, mentions something about a nasty mail message, and utters the words "You know what to do...", with the dots and everything.

Later, inside the Municipal Energy Authority Computer, as I'm modifying the poor pleb's Energy Bill by several zeros, I can't help but think about what lapse of judgement – what act of heinous stupidity causes them to call. Then, even later, when I'm adding the poor pleb's photo image over the top of the FBI's online "*Most* Wanted Armed and Dangerous, *Shoot on Sight*" offenders list, I realise, I'll probably never know; but life goes on.

A couple of hours later, as I see the SWAT vehicle roll up outside the poor pleb's apartment I realise that for some, it just doesn't.

But tomorrow is another day.

*To Be Continued...*

# ADA*: The Devil's Work

*Herman Higgins*

*Journal of Irreproducible Results*, Vol. 33, No. 1, Sept - Oct 1987, p.4.
Reprinted by permission of Blackwell Scientific Publications, Inc.

Recently, while taking an ADA course, a view-graph was shown that said; "...they have all one language; and this is only the beginning of what they will do; and nothing that they propose to do will now be impossible for them, *Genesis* 11:6" [1]. I'm some-what curious by nature and when I got home I looked up this quote. I read the whole verse and then the next, 11:7. It said; "Come, let us go down, and there confuse their language, that they may not understand one another's speech." God was speak-ing. God did not want man to have a common language. The Devil, always looking for ways to cause trouble, has found a way after all these centuries to confound God's wishes. ADA was developed.

In God we trust; all else we walk-through.

ADA has been gaining popularity as an international language. If it continues to gain support, all the nations of the world will be able to communicate with one another and thus shall be disobey-ing the Will of God. The Devil loves this. He, through his minions [2], has created an unholy alliance of men who use this abomina-tion called ADA. This alliance will eventually bring down the wrath of God upon mankind and his works, much to the delight of Satan. Not only that, but since a common language is a first big step to that most dreaded of institutions, a One World Govern-ment [3], we will all suffer mightily for their sins.

What can we do? What must we do to save ourselves? We must abandon this devilish language, cast it out into the pit of obsoles-cence, remove all those who would save it, and return to the more Godly languages our fathers knew, i.e. machine language, LISP, and APL. Amen.

* © Department of Defense.
[1] Revised Standard Version of The Bible.
[2] It is probably unfair to class the Pentagon, in general, and its lieutenant, the French company that created ADA, as minions of the Devil, but I will here.
[3] Spelled C-O-M-M-U-N-I-S-M.

# Netmail Spreads Common Cold

*Craig Milo Rogers (rogers@isi.edu)*

Public health officials reported a sharp upswing in common colds among computer scientists this year. The new cold strains originally appeared in major computer centers, then spread throughout the country in a matter of hours. Researchers grappling with this issue have concluded that there is only one possible explanation for the sudden appearance and rapid dissemination of the colds: they are spread through electronic mail.

It is a long established fact that colds and other diseases may be transmitted through the mail. Viruses and bacteria accumulate on a letter while it is being written. The viruses and bacteria are dormant while the letter is in transit. When the letter is opened, the viruses and bacteria are shaken into the air and inhaled by the recipient, who becomes infected.

A lesser-known fact is that colds may be spread over the phone. This usually occurs when an infected individual sneezes into a public phone. The next individual to use that same phone will often be infected by the viruses and bacteria on the phone's mouthpiece. However, what most people don't know is that when a person with a cold sneezes into a phone, the person at the other end may be infected if they were holding their phone close enough for the germs to enter their ear canal.

It is now possible to demonstrate similar effects for Internet mail. If a person sneezes while sending a message in Hermes or MM, the recipient stands a fair chance of catching the same cold. Strangely enough, this effect has not occurred with multimedia mail, perhaps because it currently uses UDP datagrams instead of TCP connections between the user terminals and the mail forwarders.

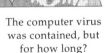

The computer virus was contained, but for how long?

Other electronic mail systems also spread diseases. For example, UUCP spreads Unix. Of particular concern are the electronic mailing lists. Each message sent to one of these lists is replicated and retransmitted to dozens or even hundreds of recipients. A single infected message can strike dozens of victims coast-to-coast within a matter of minutes. Public health officials are quite worried about MCI mail, which uses both printed and electronic delivery systems, thus threatening the health of the entire nation.

Internet Header Health Inspectors will work closely with the Protocol Police in the next few months to develop methods of dealing with infected packets. Netmail may be delayed at Internet Gateways if the Inoculated-by: records are not current. The EGP Quarantine command will be used to isolate Autonomous Systems which are suspected of sending contaminated datagrams. A recently released DoD report suggests that part of the impetus behind the ARPANET/Milnet split and the current partitioned network research, is to minimize the possible effects of Internet Bacteriological Warfare.

As far as we know, our computer has never had an undetected error.
*Weisert*

These problems are also being pursued by the International Standards Organization. The committee on Open Systems Inoculation (ISO/OSInoc) recently released a draft report on a 7-layer cold encapsulation for use by the World Health Organization in Third World Nations.

☆ ☆ ☆ ☆ ☆ ☆ ★ ☆ ☆ ☆ ☆ ☆ ☆

## *I Know What's Wrong With My Computer!*

*Anonymous*
*A Bit Much...*, William E. Kost (ed.), The Nova Osborne Users Group, 1st April 1993. Reprinted from *Toggle*, Vol. 10, No. 12, Issue 108, May 1992.

Sometimes I could smash this thing,
Or else I'd like to sell it.
It never does just what I want,
But only what I tell it.

☆ ☆ ☆ ☆ ☆ ☆ ★ ☆ ☆ ☆ ☆ ☆ ☆

# *What is Technical Harassment?*

© *Rick Fadler (rfadler@nv2.uswnvg.com)*

In our complex technical environment, there are many opportunities for a competent technical individual to be the subject of technical harassment. Sometimes it can be so subtle that you may not even be aware that you are being harassed. Worse yet, you may inadvertently technically harass another person.

Some guidelines to help you determine if you are being technically harassed are presented below.

If you are repeatedly asked the same technical question, then you may be the victim of technical harassment. While it is most common to be asked the same question repeatedly within the same conversation, some instances of *habitual technical harassment* have been identified. Habitual technical harassment is not uncommon and has been known to exhibit group tendencies, where members of a group may ask the same question repeatedly. Untreated, these instances of group technical harassment can continue for years.

They listened in silence as Mary explained how to switch on the computer.

If you are asked a technical question by a non-technical person and they do not write your answer down, then it is likely that the question is frivolous. Most non-technical people are incapable of remembering a truely technical answer for more than 30 seconds.

If you are forced into a discussion with a person who uses more than three (3) buzzwords in one sentence, then that person is most likely a fake, and you are the unwitting victim of technical harassment. One note of caution, competent technical people have been known to inadvertently use buzzwords after reading mindless drivel like *PC Week* or *LAN Times*. If the person has been known to use more common technical terms in the past, such as "stuff" and "things", then he is most likely to be a victim of computer magazine brainwashing.

If, during a troubleshooting session, a person uses the term "trick" (e.g. "maybe we could trick the database into thinking it has been updated"), then this is a sure sign of technical harassment.

If a person explains that a required feature will be provided by a vendor, and that person is non-technical, then you are at risk of being technically harassed. If you believe that person, then you have definitely been technically harassed. If you don't believe him, then you have only been technically *annoyed*.

If, while trying to resolve a technical problem with a product from a vendor, you are instructed to call the salesman that sold the product, then you are being set up for technical harassment. It is a common reaction for a non-technical person who has purchased technical equipment to call another non-technical person. The dialogue between two non-technical people usually provides some sense of comfort that they aren't the only ones who are confused.

## I'm Just A Two-bit Programmer On A Sixteen-bit Machine

*David S. Platt*
*Journal of Irreproducible Results*, Vol. 32, No. 3, February/March 1987, p. 12. Reprinted with permission by Blackwell Scientific Publications, Inc.

Desmond was a true computer science eccentric.

Well, I sit at my computer, staring at the screen
Like a chloroformed iguana. My brain has got gangrene.
And while my mind is rotting, I feel like such a jerk;
I caused a disk crash wiping out my last two decades' work.
Oh, Mama, who could have foreseen
I'd be a two-bit programmer on a sixteen-bit machine?

I go on dates with women, and I talk of bits and bytes,
So is it any wonder that I sleep alone at nights?
To think, I could be human, instead of the nerd I am!
But then again, let's face it: who really gives a damn?
Oh, Mama, it's just too obscene.
I'm just a two-bit programmer on a sixteen-bit machine.

# If Architects Had to Work Like Programmers

*J.David Ruggiero (jdavid@halcyon.com)*
Edited and posted to the Internet in January 1993.
Original author(s) unknown.

Dear Mr. Architect:

Please design and build me a house. I am not quite sure of what I need, so you should use your discretion.

My house should have between two and forty-five bedrooms. Just make sure the plans are such that the bedrooms can be easily added or deleted. When you bring the blueprints to me, I will make the final decision of what I want. Also, bring me the cost breakdown for each configuration so that I can arbitrarily pick one.

Keep in mind that the house I ultimately choose must cost less than the one I am currently living in. Make sure, however, that you correct all the deficiencies that exist in my current house (the floor of my kitchen vibrates when I walk across it, and the walls don't have nearly enough insulation in them).

As you design, also keep in mind that I want to keep yearly maintenance costs as low as possible. This should mean the incorporation of extra-cost features like aluminum, vinyl, or composite siding. (If you choose not to specify aluminum, be prepared to explain your decision in detail.)

In computing, turning the obvious into the useful is a living definition of the word "frustration".
*Alan J. Perlis*

Please take care that modern design practices and the latest materials are used in construction of the house, as I want it to be a showplace for the most up-to-date ideas and methods. Be alerted, however, that kitchen should be designed to accommodate, among other things, my 1952 Gibson refrigerator.

To insure that you are building the correct house for our entire family, make certain that you contact each of our children, and also our in-laws. My mother-in-law will have very strong feelings about how the house should be designed, since she visits us at least once a year. Make sure that you weigh all of these options carefully and come to the right decision. I, however, retain the right to overrule any choices that you make.

Please don't bother me with small details right now. Your job is to develop the overall plans for the house: get the big picture. At this time, for example, it is not appropriate to be choosing the color of the carpet. However, keep in mind that my wife likes blue.

Also, do not worry at this time about acquiring the resources to build the house itself. Your first priority is to develop detailed plans and specifications. Once I approve these plans, however, I would expect the house to be under roof within 48 hours.

While you are designing this house specifically for me, keep in mind that sooner or later I will have to sell it to someone else. It therefore should have appeal to a wide variety of potential buyers. Please make sure before you finalize the plans that there is consensus by the population in my area that they like the house's features.

I advise you to look at my neighbor's house, which he had constructed last year. We like it a great deal. It has many features that we would also like in our new home, particularily the 75-foot swimming pool. With careful engineering, I believe that you can design this into our new house without impacting the final cost.

Please prepare a complete set of blueprints. It is not necessary at this time to do the real design, since they will be used only for construction bids. Be advised, however, that you will be held accountable for any increase of construction costs as a result of later design changes.

You must be thrilled to be working on as interesting a project as this! To be able to use the latest techniques and materials, and to be given such freedom in your design is something that can't happen very often. Contact me as soon as possible with your completed ideas and plans.

A terrible fate: buried alive beneath project specifications.

PS: My wife has just told me that she disagrees with many of the instructions which I've given you in this letter. As architect, it is your responsibility to resolve these differences. I have tried in the past and have been unable to accomplish this. If you can't handle this responsibility, I will have to find another architect.

PPS: Perhaps what I need is not a house at all, but a travel trailer. Please advise me as soon as possible if this is the case.

# VAX and IBM

*Anonymous*
October 1987

VAXen, my children, just don't belong in some places. In my business, I am frequently called by small sites and startups which are having VAX problems. So when a friend of mine in an Extremely Large Financial Institution (ELFI) called me one day to ask for help, I was intrigued because this outfit is a really major VAX user – they have several large herds of VAXen – and plenty of sharp VAXherds to take care of them.

So I went to see what sort of an ELFI mess they had gotten into. It seems they had shoved a small 750 with two RA60's running a single application, PC style, into a data center with two IBM 3090's and just about all the rest of the disk drives in the world. The computer room was so big it had three street addresses. The operators had only IBM experience and, to quote my friend, they were having "a little trouble adjusting to the VAX", were a bit hostile towards it, and probably needed some help with system management. Hmmm, hostility... Sigh.

Computer Science is embarrassed by the computer.
*Alan J. Perlis*

Well, I thought it was pretty ridiculous for an outfit with all that VAX muscle elsewhere to isolate a dinky old 750 in their Big Blue Country, and said so bluntly. But my friend patiently explained that although small, it was an "extremely sensitive and confidential application." It seemed that the 750 had originally been properly clustered with the rest of a herd, and in the care of one of their best VAXherds. But the trouble started when the Chief User went to visit his computer and its VAXherd.

He came away visibly disturbed and immediately complained to the ELFI's Director of Data Processing that, "there are some very strange people in there with the computers." Now, since this user person was the Comptroller of this Extremely Large Financial Institution, the 750 was promptly hustled over to the IBM data center which the Comptroller said, "was a more suitable place." The people there wore shirts and ties, and didn't wear head bands or cowboy hats.

My friend introduced me to the Comptroller, who turned out to be five feet tall, 85, and a former gnome of Zurich. He had a young apprentice gnome who was about 65. The two gnomes interviewed me in whispers for about an hour before they decided my mode of dress and speech were suitable for managing their system, and I got the assignment.

There was some confusion, when I explained that I would immediately establish a procedure for nightly backups. The senior gnome seemed to think I was going to put the computer in reverse, but the apprentice's son had an IBM PC and he quickly whispered that "backup" meant making a copy of a program borrowed from a friend, and why was I doing that? Sigh.

Later, I was introduced to the manager of the IBM data center, who greeted me with joy and anything but hostility. And the operators weren't really hostile – it just seemed that way. It's like the driver of a Mack 18 wheeler, with a condo behind the cab, who was doing 75 when he ran over a moped doing it's best to get away at 45. He explained sadly, "I really warn't mad at mopeds but to keep from runnin' over that'n, I'da had to slow down or change lanes!"

*In seeking the unattainable, simplicity only gets in the way.*
*Alan J. Perlis*

The only operation they had figured out how to do on the 750 was to reboot it. This was their universal cure for any and all problems. After all it works on a PC, why not a VAX? Was there a difference? Sigh.

But I smiled and said, "No sweat, I'll train you. The first command you learn is HELP" and proceeded to type it in on the console terminal. The data center manager, the shift supervisor and the eight day operators watched the LA100 buzz out the usual introductory text. When it finished they turned to me with expectant faces, and I said in an avuncular manner, "This is your most important command!"

The shift supervisor stepped forward and studied the text for about a minute. He then turned with a very puzzled expression on his face and asked, "What do you use it for?" Sigh.

Well, I tried everything. I trained, and I put the document set on shelves by the 750, and I wrote a special 40 page set, and then a four page set. I designed all kinds of command files to make complex operations into simple foreign commands, and I taped a list of these simplified commands to the top of the VAX. The most successful move was adding my home phone number.

The cheat sheets taped on the top of the CPU cabinet needed

continual maintenance. It seemed that the VAX was in the quietest part of the data center, over behind the scratch tape racks. The operators ate lunch on the CPU cabinet and the sheets quickly became coated with pizza drippings, etc.

The most common solution to hangups was still a reboot, but I gradually got things organized so that during the day when the gnomes were using the system, the operators didn't have to touch it. This smoothed things out a lot.

Meanwhile, the data center was getting new TV security cameras, a halon gas fire extinguisher system, and an immortal power source. The data center manager apologized because the VAX had not been foreseen in the plan and so could not be connected to the immortal power. The VAX and I felt a little rejected but I made sure that booting on power recovery was working right. At least it would get going again quickly when power came back.

Anyway, as a consolation prize, the data center manager said he would have one of the security cameras adjusted to cover the VAX. I thought to myself, "Great, now we can have 24 hour video tapes of the operators eating Chinese takeout on the CPU." I resolved to get a piece of plastic to cover the cheat sheets.

One day, the apprentice gnome called to whisper that the senior was going to give an extremely important demonstration. I must now explain that what the 750 was doing was holding our National Debt. The Reagan administration had decided to privatize it and had quietly put it out for bid. My Extreme Large Financial Institution had won the bid and was, as ELFI's are wont to do, making an absolute bundle on the float.

Any program that runs right is obsolete.

On Monday, the Comptroller was going to demonstrate to the board of directors how he could move a trillion dollars from Switzerland to the Bahamas. The apprentice whispered, "Would you please look in on our computer? I'm sure everything will be fine, sir, but we will feel better if you are present. I'm sure you understand?" I did.

On Monday morning, I got there about five hours before the scheduled demo to check things over. Everything was cool. I was chatting with the shift supervisor, and about to go upstairs to the Comptroller's office. Suddenly, there was a power failure.

The emergency lighting came on and the immortal power system took over the load of the IBM 3090's. They continued smoothly, but, of course, the VAX, still on city power, died. Everyone smiled and the dead 750 was no big deal because it was 7:00am and gnomes don't work before 10:00am. I began worrying about whether I could beg some immortal power from the data center manager in case this was a long outage.

Immortal power in this system comes from storage batteries for the first five minutes of an outage. Promptly, at one minute into the outage, we heard the gas turbine powered generator in the sub-basement under us automatically start up, getting ready to take the load on the fifth minute. We all beamed at each other.

At two minutes into the outage, we heard the whine of the backup gas turbine generator starting. The 3090's and all those disk drives were doing just fine. Business as usual. The VAX was dead as a door nail, but what the hell.

At precisely five minutes into the outage, just as the gas turbine was taking the load, the city power came back on and the immortal power source committed suicide. Actually it was a double murder and suicide because it took both 3090's with it.

So now the whole data center was dead, sort of. The fire alarm system had it's own battery backup and was still alive. The lead acid storage batteries of the immortal power system had been discharging at a furious rate keeping all those big blue boxes running and there was a significant amount of sulphuric acid vapor in the air. Nothing had actually caught fire, but the smoke detectors were convinced something had.

The fire alarm klaxon went off and the siren warning of imminent halon gas release was screaming. We started to panic but the data center manager shouted over the din, "Don't worry, the halon system failed its acceptance test last week. It's disabled and nothing will happen."

Don't let the computer bugs bite!

He was half right, the primary halon system did indeed fail to discharge. But the secondary halon system observed that the primary had died and did its duty, which was to deal with *Dire Disasters*. It had twice the capacity and 6 times the discharge rate.

The ear splitting gas discharge under the raised floor was so massive and fast, it blew about half of the floor tiles up out of their framework. The gas came up through the floor into a communications rack and blew the cover panels off, decking an operator. Looking out across that vast computer room, we could see the air shimmering as the halon mixed with it.

We stampeded for for the exits, accompanied by the dying whine of 175 IBM disks. As I was escaping, I glanced back at the VAX, on city power, and noticed the usual flickering of the unit select light on its system disk, indicating it was happily rebooting.

Twelve firemen with air tanks and axes invaded. There were frantic phone calls to the local IBM Field Service office because both the live and backup 3090's were down. About twenty minutes later, 17 IBM CEs arrived with dozens of boxes and, so help me, a barrel. It seems they knew what to expect when an immortal power source commits murder.

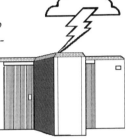

The machine was lightningly fast.

In the midst of absolute pandemonium, I crept off to the gnome's office and logged on. After extensive checking it was clear that everything was just fine with the VAX, and I began to calm down. I called the data center manager's office to tell him the good news. His secretary answered with, "He isn't expected to be available for some time. May I take a message?" I left a slightly smug note to the effect that, unlike some other computers, the VAX was intact and functioning normally.

Several hours later, the gnome was whispering his way into a demonstration of how to flick a trillion dollars from one country to another. He was just coming to the tricky part, where the money had been withdrawn from Switzerland but not yet deposited in the Bahamas. He was proceeding very slowly and the directors were spellbound. I decided to check the data center.

Most of the floor tiles were back in place. IBM had resurrected one of the 3090's and was running tests. What looked like a bucket brigade was working on the other one. The communication rack was still naked and a fireman was standing guard over the immortal power corpse. Life was returning to normal, but the Big Blue Country crew was still pretty shaky.

Smiling proudly, I headed towards the triumphant VAX behind the tape racks, where one of the operators was eating a plump jelly bun on the 750 CPU. He saw me coming, turned pale and screamed to the shift supervisor, "Oh my God, we forgot about the VAX!" Then, before I could open my mouth, he rebooted it. It was Monday, 19th October 1987. VAXen, my children, just don't belong in some places.

# The Australian Fifth Degeneration Project

*Lee Naish (lee@cs.mu.oz.au)*
© 19th November 1992

News of the Japanese Fifth Generation Artificial Intelligence (AI) project has finally reached the Australian Government and they have given approval for the spending of a ten figure sum on a similar project in Australia. In fact, the government itself is providing a nine figure sum (this includes the cents).

A major part of the project is the designing and building of the MU parallel machine. It has a very twisted Klein bottle topology and will be made using Very Large Scale Disintegration technology, fabricated on Uranium chips. Selling points include:

Feature number 1: No proof trees.

Feature number 2: No UNIX.

Feature number 3: Multiprocessor Oriented Timesharing Operating System (MOTOS).

Feature number 4: No eight Queens.

Feature number 5: Automatic debugger.

Feature number 6: There is no feature 6.

Feature number 7: Bruce declarations [1].

Feature number 8: Dijkstra's On the Garbage Fly Collection Algorithm.

The first major application of the system is an attempt to alleviate the so-called softwear crisis – the trend of decreasing productivity in the Australian wool industry. The main thrust will be to use AI and robotics to automate shearing. Robot shearing has been unsuccessful in the past but using Artificial Insemination techniques, it is hoped the sheep will become more uniform in size and smart enough not to be cut.

Being Project Director was an harrowing expierence.

[1] Cleese et al., The Philosophers Sketch, *Monty Pythons Flying Circus*.

# An Ancient Rope-And-Pulley Computer Is Unearthed In The Jungle of Apraphul

© A. K. Dewdney
Computer Recreations, *Scientific American*, April 1988,
Vol. 258, No. 4, p.118-121.

On the island of Apraphul, off the northwest coast of New Guinea, archaeologists have discovered the rotting remnants of an ingenious arrangement of ropes and pulleys thought to be the first working digital computer ever constructed. Chief investigator Robert L. Ripley of Charles Fort College in New York dates the construction to approximately A.D. 850.

The next generation of computers will have a "Warranty Expired" interrupt.

The Apraphulians were excellent sailors. Their ships were wonderfully built and equipped with the most elaborate rigging imaginable. Were the Apraphulians led to the digital computer by their mastery of rope or was it the other way around? Experts continue to debate the topic hotly.

The ancient rope-and-pulley computer has recently been partially reconstructed by Ripley and his team at the Tropical Museum of Marine Antiquities in nearby Sumatra. Scouring a site that extends through several kilometers of dense jungle east of the Pulleg Mountains, the group found faint traces of buried jute fibers and noted the exact position of badly corroded brass pulleys and associated hardware. The reconstruction has given me an ideal opportunity to introduce readers to the principles of digital computing without resorting to tiny and mysterious electronic components. Here are gates, flip-flops and circuits made entirely of rope and pulleys. It is all visible and perfectly easy to understand.

The Apraphulians used a binary system just as we do, but the numbers 0 and 1 were represented by the positions of ropes instead of by electric voltages. Imagine a black box with a hole drilled in one side. The reader holds a taut rope that passes through the hole. This position of the rope represents the digit 0. If the reader now pulls on the rope, a creak and squeal inside the box is heard as a foot or so of rope comes out. The new position of the rope represents the digit 1.

| Box1 | Box2 | Box3 | Num |
|------|------|------|-----|
| In | In | In | 0 |
| In | In | Out | 1 |
| In | Out | In | 2 |
| In | Out | Out | 3 |
| Out | In | In | 4 |
| Out | In | Out | 5 |
| Out | Out | In | 6 |
| Out | Out | Out | 7 |

*Figure 1*: How Apraphulians represented numbers.

One can represent numbers with such boxes. Any number from 0 through 7, for instance, can be represented by three boxes [see Fig. 1]. By employing more boxes, larger numbers can be represented. Ten boxes suffice to represent all numbers from 0 through 1,023.

My example of the black box is not arbitrary. The Apraphulians apparently loved to enclose their mechanisms in black wood boxes, small and large. It may be that the construction of computers was the prerogative of a special technological priesthood. The sight of great assemblages of black boxes may have kept the masses trembling in awe.

One of the key devices used by the Apraphulians converted a 0 into a 1 and a 1 into a 0. (It is occasionally convenient to speak of 0 and 1 instead of "in" and "out.") Akin to what modern computer engineers call an inverter, this interesting mechanism consisted of a box with a hole drilled in its front and another in its back [see Fig. 2]. When someone (or something) pulled the input rope at the front of the box, an equal amount of output rope would be played out of the hole in the back. On peering into the box, the reason is obvious: the ropes entering the box from front and back pass over two fixed pulleys toward one side of the box, where they attach to a single spring.

As some readers may have surmised already, the digits 0 and 1 were not encoded so much by "out" and "in" as they were by the direction in which the rope moved. The point is best illustrated by a box that has no mechanism in it whatever. A piece of rope enters a single hole in the front of the box and leaves by a single hole in the back. If one pulls the rope from the 0 position to the 1 position at the front of the box, the rope moves from "in" to "out." The direction of movement is toward the puller. The rope simultaneously moves from "out" to "in" at the back of the box, but since the direction of movement is still toward the puller, the rope at the back of the box also moves from 0 to 1.

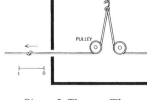

*Figure 2*: The Apraphulian inverter.

Two additional mechanisms almost complete the ancient Apraphulian repertoire of computing components. The first mechanism had two input ropes entering a box. If either rope was in the 1 position, the single output rope would also be in the 1 position. The Apraphulians managed this trick by absurdly simple means [see Fig. 3]. Each rope entering the front of the box passed over a pair of pulleys that brought it close to the other rope. The two ropes, passing toward the rear of the box, were then tied to a single ring linked to the output rope. If either or both of the input ropes were pulled, the ring would be pulled directly. Because the output of the box was 1 if one input or the other was 1, today's engineers would call this an OR gate.

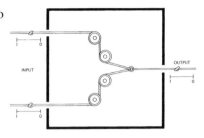

*Figure 3*: The Apraphulian OR gate.

The ancient Apraphulians fabricated what we would call an AND gate from three pulleys and a curved rod [see Fig. 4]. One of the pulleys was free to roll along the rod, its axle being connected directly to an output rope. The other two pulleys were paired, serving chiefly to position the output rope at the exit hole. With both input ropes in the 0 position, the rod coincided with the arc of a circle centered on the paired exit pulleys. If one of the input ropes was pulled into the 1 position, one end of the rod was pulled away from the center of its resting circle. The pulley attached to the output rope would then roll "downhill" toward the end of the rod that had not been pulled; the position of the output rope would be substantially the same as before since that end of the rod still coincided with the resting circle. (A peg in the middle of the rod kept it from swinging to either side of the box when just one of the input ropes was pulled.)

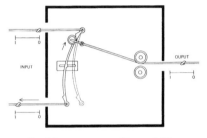

*Figure 4*: The Apraphulian AND gate.

Only when both input ropes were pulled would the output rope move into the 1 position. In this case the entire rod would have been pulled back into a new position; whichever end the rolling pulley occupied would be equally far from the exit pulleys. The name AND gate is derived from the fact that the output of this device is 1 if and only if one input rope *and* the other are in position 1.

With these components one can build all the control circuits of a digital computer. These include circuits that compute arithmetic functions, interpret program code and direct the flow of information among the parts of the computer.

Did the Apraphulians construct their computer along such lines? The evidence is too fragmentary to reach a definitive conclusion, but archaeocomputologists working with Ripley maintain they have discovered a simple multiplexer within the half-buried complex. In electronic computers a multiplexer is essentially an electrical switch that directs the passage of many signals through a single wire. For example, the simplest multiplexer would have two input wires we might label a and b. At any given moment each wire could carry a 0 or 1 signal. Which of the two signals, a or b, will be allowed to pass through the device and out a single output wire d? The answer to that question is the business of a control wire, c; if it carries a 1 signal, the signal from wire a will be transmitted along the output wire. If the control wire carries a 0, on the other hand, the signal in wire b will be transmitted [see Fig. 5 below].

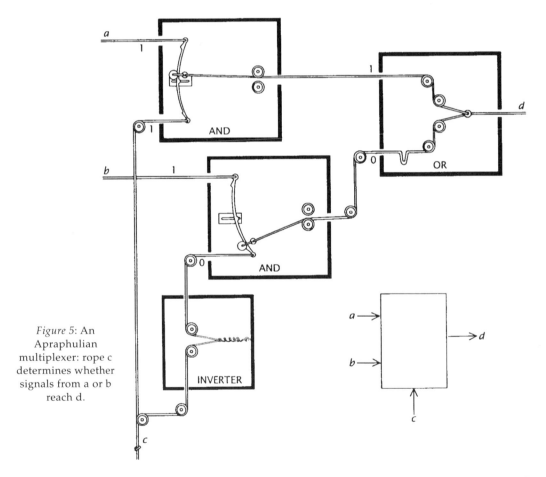

*Figure 5*: An Apraphulian multiplexer: rope c determines whether signals from a or b reach d.

This reconstructed double-input Apraphulian multiplexer consists of two AND gates, an OR gate and an inverter. The whole thing is so simple that one dares to believe computer recreationists might build their own Apraphulian multiplexer at home. Hardware stores might suffer a puzzling run on rope and pulleys. In any event, one can follow operations of the multiplexer by referring to the illustration. Ropes a and b enter the multiplexer from the top left, each going to its own AND gate. Rope c is split. One branch runs directly to the other input port of the AND gate to which rope a goes. The second branch of rope c passes through an inverter and then runs to the AND gate to which rope b goes. If rope c is pulled to a value of 1 and held, any sequence of 0's and 1's sent along rope a will be faithfully transmitted through the upper AND gate and on to the OR gate. At the same time any signal sent along rope b will be stopped at the lower AND gate. If rope c is relaxed to its 0 position, the inverter creates a 1 at the lower AND gate. In this case any signal sent along rope b will now be transmitted through the lower AND gate and signals on rope a will be ignored.

An elephant is a mouse with an operating system.

The OR gate merely ties the two output signals together, so to speak. If the signal from rope a is currently being transmitted, one can easily visualize exactly what happens directly from the diagram: if rope a is relaxed to the 0 position, the pulley in the AND box rolls to the end of the rod. A 0 is thus transmitted along the output rope and into the OR box. The other input rope to this box is already in the 0 position (slack). The natural tension on the output rope d immediately pulls it into the new position, namely 0. If one pulls on rope a again, the pull is transmitted along the path that has just been described, with the result that rope d is retracted.

The matter of slack ropes compels me to take up the question of tension in the Apraphulian computer. Sometimes, as in the OR gate of the example, a rope will become slack. There is naturally a danger that such ropes will slip right off their pulleys. Ripley tells me that in such cases the Apraphulians used a specially modified inverter with an extremely weak spring to remedy the problem. Wherever a rope was likely to develop slack, a "weak inverter" was installed to maintain the minimum tension associated with the signal 0.

No general-purpose computer is complete without a memory. The memory of the Apraphulian computer consisted of hundreds of special storage elements we would call flip-flops. Here again the remarkable simplicity of the Apraphulian mind is immediately evident. In line with modern terminology, the two ropes entering the mechanical flip-flop are labeled set and reset [see Fig. 6]. The two ropes were connected over a series of three pulleys in such a way that when the set rope was pulled away from the box into the 1 position, the reset rope would be pulled toward the box into the 0 position. The common rope was connected to a sliding bar at the back of the flip-flop box The output rope, physically a continuation of the set rope, had a large bead attached to it that engaged a slot in the sliding bar. As the set rope was pulled, the bead rode over the end of the bar popping into the slot when the set rope reached the end of its travel.

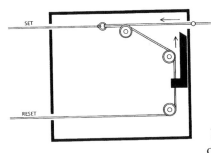

*Figure 6*: The Apraphulian flip-flop served as a memory element.

As a consequence the output rope was held in position until the enormous rope computer changed things by pulling on the reset rope. That had the effect of pulling the sliding bar away from the bead, releasing it and playing the output rope into the 0 position. In this case the flip-flop would henceforth "remember" 0. How were such memory elements used in the Apraphulian computer?

Ripley and his team were puzzled to discover in the midst of the vast Apraphulian computer complex a large overgrown field nearly a kilometer wide. Buried just below the surface of the field were several thousand rotting flip-flop boxes arranged in rows of eight. Ripley, with the aid of the archaeocomputologists, eventually surmised that the field represented the Apraphulian computer's main memory. Each row of eight boxes would have constituted a single, eight-bit "word" in the same sense that the three boxes of my earlier example would have constituted a three-bit word. In that vein, imagine a row of three flip-flops that had been set to the values 1, 0 and 1. They would have stored the number 5.

The content of this particular memory word would have been accessed by the rope-and-pulley computer as follows. Each flip-flop in the row would send an output rope to an associated AND box. The other input to each AND box would come from a special rope used to retrieve the contents of the word in question. When the ropes were pulled, the outputs of the AND boxes would be identical with the outputs of the flip-flops. The AND box ropes would lead to a large assemblage of OR boxes and thence into a special array of flip-flops we would call a register. A single tug on the rope associated with the word under examination would place the same binary pattern of rope positions in the register.

The computer's main logic unit undoubtedly would have directed the flow of information not just from memory to registers but between registers as well. In particular, by the use of multiplexers and demultiplexers (which perform the opposite function of multiplexers), the computer would have sent patterns from register to register. At a specific register that we would call the arithmetic register, patterns would have been combined according to the rules of addition and multiplication.

The Apraphulian computer is believed to have been programmable. If it was, part of its vast memory would have been used to store the program. Program instructions would also have been merely patterns of 0's and 1's retrieved by the same mechanism outlined above. Those patterns would in due course have been sent to an instruction register for interpretation by the computer's logic unit.

It is a pity I can do little more in these pages than to hint at the marvelous complexity of the Apraphulian machine. It must have been an amazing sight when in operation. Because of the enormous lengths of rope involved, no human being would have had the strength to pull the input levers into the appropriate positions. The presence of elephant bones in the Apraphulian complex makes the source of input power immediately clear. At the output end large springs maintained appropriate tensions in the system. Perhaps flags on the ultimate output ropes enabled members of the technological priesthood to read the outcome of whatever computation was in progress.

Computers are a more fun way to do the same work you'd have to do without them.

The Apraphulian rope-and-pulley computer makes for an interesting contrast with the nanocomputer introduced in the January 1988 column. The rope machine, of course, inhabits a distant past whereas the nanometerscale machine dwells in a hazy future. The Apraphulian computer is relatively massive in scale, covering thousands of acres; the nanocomputer is incredibly tiny, occupying an area one-thousandth the size of a human cell nucleus. The mere concept of either machine serves as a springboard into a speculative realm where recreation blends with science. Think, for example, of the ongoing dream of artificially intelligent machines We find it easier to accept the possibility of an electronic computer that thinks since our own thoughts are to a great extent electronically mediated. Because any modern computer (and its program) is conceptually translatable into Apraphulian form, any artificially intelligent device ever realized now or in the future will have its rope-and-pulley counterpart. Can we imagine HAL 9000, the paranoid computer in the movie *2001: A Space Odyssey*, being so constructed? Are we willing to admit that an enormous building full of ropes and pulleys could be as smart as we are?

We leave the island of Apraphul with just one backward glance at its misty past: how might the vast digital computer have evolved? From analog ones, of course. Figure 7 shows an analog adding machine made from two ropes and two pulleys. The two ends of one rope enter the front of a box through two holes. The rope passes over a single pulley that is linked with another pulley by an axial connector. One end of the second rope is attached to the back of the box. The rope passes over the second pulley and then through a hole in the back of the box. Readers might find some diversion in discovering for themselves how the machine adds two numbers; if the two input ropes are pulled a distance a and b respectively, the output rope travels a distance a + b.

So much is clear. But how did the Apraphulians manage analog multiplication? I shall try to publish the simplest design sent to me.

*Figure 7*: An Apraphulian adding machine.

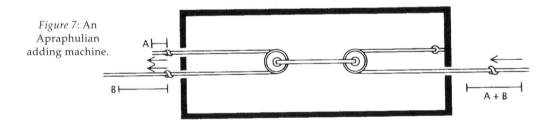

## *The VAXorcist*

*A rough draft of a video presentation.*

*Christopher Russell*
© 4th August 1991

(Scene: Inside of a VAX computer room. Credits roll as the Sysmgr is sitting in front of the console terminal, typing. He pauses, picks up a small magnetic tape, walks over to a tape drive, mounts it, and returns to the console where he continues typing.)

(There is a knock at the door. Sysmgr walks to the door and opens it, revealing the user.)

User: Any idea when the system will be up?

Sysmgr: Well, I just installed version 5.0 of VMS, so I'm going to run some diagnostics on it overnight to make sure it works alright. Assuming everything goes alright, the system should be up first thing tomorrow morning.

User: Great. Thanks. (Exits)

(Sysmgr closes the door and returns to the console.)

Rod Serling-like voice: This is John Smith, University of Maryland System Manager. In an effort to make his system the best it can be, he has just installed VMS Version 5.0 onto his VAX. But little does he know that the Version 5 documentation kit from Digital includes a one-way ticket to ... the VMS Twilight Zone!

Systems Programmers are the high priests of a low cult.
*R.S. Barton*

(ominous music - fade out)

(Fade in. The Sysmgr scans the console for a moment, then turns, picks up his coat and walks to the door. He stops at the door for a moment, looking back at the big machine. Finally, he turns out the light and exits, closing the door behind him.)

(Cut to the Console Terminal. We read the following as it is printed on the console terminal:)

VMS V5.0 DIAGNOSTICS —

DIAGNOSTICS - PHASE 1 STARTING...

DIAGNOSTICS - PHASE 1 FINISHED SUCCESSFULLY.

DIAGNOSTICS - PHASE 2 STARTING...

TESTING MICROCODE ... SUCCESSFUL

TESTING DECNET ... SUCCESSFUL

TESTING LICENSE MANAGEMENT UTILITY ... SUCCESSFUL

TESTING SYSTEM SERVICES ... SUCCESSFUL

TESTING HIGHLY EXPERIMENTAL AND COMPLETELY UN-
DOCUMENTED AI ROUTINE ...

(Cut to view of the Tape in the Tape drive. The tape spins for a
moment, and suddenly stops.)

(Cut to view of the Machine Room. A fog has begun drifting
across the floor, and the hardware is slowly being backlit by a
pulsing red light. A peal of weird laughter cuts through the
silence. A variety of bizarre things occur: a VT100 monitor sitting
on a table slowly rotates 360 degrees; the tape drive opens and
tape begins spewing out of it; slime begins pouring out of a disk
drive; the line printer begins form-feeding like mad. These continue for several minutes, or for as long as we can keep them up.
Fade Out.)

(Scene: Hallway outside of the computer room. Sysmgr walks up
to the door and is met by User.)

User: System going to be up soon?

Sysmgr: (As he speaks, he tries to open the Machine room door,
but the door is apparently stuck.) The diagnostics should be done
by now, so we should be up in about 15 minutes... (he succeeds in
opening the door, but is confronted by floor to ceiling magnetic
tape. Tangled at about eye level is an empty tape reel. Sysmgr
takes the reel and looks at it. Close up of the reel so we can read
the label, which reads: VAX/VMS V5.0 Diagnostic Kit.) (to User)
...give or take a few days.

(Scene: View of TSR (Telephone Support Rep) from behind
as she is sitting in a cubicle, a terminal in front of her.
Beside her on the wall is a poster which reads "Digital Has
It Now – But You Can't Have It". We can see the terminal,
but we should not be able to read what is on it. She is
wearing a headset.)

TSR: Colorado Customer Support. What is your access
number, please?

The computer has a
shocking turn of
phrase.

Sysmgr Voice: 31576

TSR: And your name?

Sysmgr Voice: John Smith.

(Cut to Sysmgr standing beside his console. He his holding a phone to his head with his right hand, and holding a printout in his left which he is perusing while he talks on the phone.)

TSR Voice: And what operating system are you using?

Sysmgr: VMS version 5.

TSR Voice: And is this a problem with the operating system or a layered product?

(As the Sysmgr looks up from the printout, his eyes suddenly widen and he drops the printout and ducks. At that second, a disk platter flies through the air where his head just was. Slowly, Sysmgr stands up and looks to where the disk went. Pan back to reveal a stack of boxes with a disk embedded in one of them at neck height.)

Sysmgr: (into the phone) Operating System. Definitely the Operating System.

(Cut back to TSR sitting at her desk.)

TSR: Can you describe the problem, please?

(Sysmgr voice can now only be heard as mumbling.)

TSR: Yes... Tape drive spewing tape into the air... yes... line printers printing backwards... yes... miscellaneous hardware flying through the air... uh huh... disk drives melting... yeah... strange voices coming from the CPU board... I see... yes. Is that all? (pause as she finishes typing at the terminal) Well, I'm afraid that that team is busy at the moment, can I have them get back to you?

There are two ways to write error-free programs; only the third one works.

(Cut to Scene: Manager sitting behind a large desk in a plush office. Developer is pacing in front of him, hands behind his back.)

(Subtitle: Meanwhile at Maynard...)

Manager: So tell me! What the hell happened?!

Developer: (turning to face Manager) It's a glitch, a fluke. A one in a billion chance. And it's not Development's fault. Not really.

Manager: Then who's fault is it?

Developer: We traced it back to the Software Distribution Center. It seems that there was a mixup and some of the code for the

The computer kept hanging.

experimental AI routine was copied onto the distribution from the wrong optical disk. (He removes a CD from his jacket) This one, to be precise.

Manager: And what's that?

Developer: (reading the label) *Ozzy Osbourne's Greatest Hits.* Normally, it wouldn't have made any difference, as the AI routine isn't used yet. But when they began running diagnostics, it hit the routine and the computer just sort of became a thing possessed.

Manager: Wonderful. Were any other distributions affected?

Developer: No, just the University of Maryland's.

Manager: Well, that's a relief. We've got to get them taken care of before anyone finds out. Can you imagine what *Digital Review* would do if they heard about this?

Developer: We could always blame it on the Chaos Computer Group.

Manager: No, we've already used that one. This calls for drastic action. (Manager picks up the phone and begins flipping through the rolodex.)

Developer: Who are you going to send?

(Cut to the Rolodex so that we can read the cards. The first card reads:

SYSTEM PROBLEMS - Ron Jankowski, x474

he flips to the next card:

BAD SYSTEM PROBLEMS - Bob Candless, x937

he flips to the next card:

REALLY BAD SYSTEM PROBLEMS - Michelle French, x365

he flips to the next card

OUTRAGEOUSLY BAD SYSTEM PROBLEMS - Mike West, x887

he flips to the next card and taps the card with forefinger:

SYSTEM F**KED UP BEYOND ALL RECOGNITION - The VAXorcist, x666

(Cut to Machine Room. Sysmgr is standing by the console holding an RA60 disk cover and using it as a shield to defend himself from various pieces of hardware which are flying at him from off-camera. There is a knock at the door. Slowly, Sysmgr makes his way to the door and opens it. Standing there, backlit amidst outrageous amounts of fog is the VAXorcist, wearing a trench coat and fedora, and carrying a briefcase.)

VAXorcist: (in a hushed voice) DEC sent me. I hear you're having some problems.

(Cut to Sysmgr Office, a small but pleasant office with posters on the walls and clutter on the desk. As the VAXorcist enters, he removes his coat and hat, revealing a very techie outfit beneath. He is wearing a DEC badge.)

Sysmgr: (Frantic) Problems? Problems?!? You could say I'm having some problems. 4.6 was fine. 4.7 was fine. I install 5.0 and all Hell breaks loose. The damn thing ate two of my operators this morning!

VAXorcist: Calm down, everything will be alright. I've dealt with situations like this before.

Sysmgr: You have?

VAXorcist: Four years ago at an installation in Oregon, a programmer renamed his *Star Trek* program to VMB.EXE and copied it into the system directory. When the system was rebooted the next day it phasored the entire accounting department claiming that they were Klingon spies. There was a similar problem in Texas three years ago, and then, of course, there was the IRS fiasco that we're not allowed to talk about. But don't worry. These things can be fixed. Before I can help you, though, I have to ask you a few questions. (The VAXorcist opens his briefcase and removes a clipboard) Now, according to the report, the strange occurences began after you installed VMS Version 5, is that correct?

Sysmgr: Yes, that's correct.

VAXorcist: Now, did you carefully read the Installation Guide for VMS Version 5?

Sysmgr: (Confused) Installation Guide?

VAXorcist: Yes, it should have come with the Release Notes.

Sysmgr: (Still confused) Release Notes? (Sysmgr begins rooting about on his disk, shifting papers around as if he might find them underneath.)

VAXorcist: (Annoyed) Yes, Release Notes. They should have come with your documentation upgrade.

Life would be so much easier if we could just look at the source code.

Sysmgr: (Completely confused - looks up from his rooting through the papers on his desk) Documentation upgrade?

VAXorcist: (Angry) Yes! The Documentation upgrade for your VMS Documentation Set!

Sysmgr: Documentation S...? Oh, you mean the grey binders? They're over there. (he points to the wall behind the VAXorcist. The VAXorcist turns and we see a closed glass-front bookcase packed with grey binders. A small red sign on the front of the bookcase reads: "In Case of Emergency, Break Glass").

VAXorcist: Right. This is going to be tougher than I thought. Let's go take a look at your system and see just how bad everything is.

(Cut to the Machine Room. The room is neat and tidy and there is no sign that anything is wrong. The VAXorcist enters the room with the Sysmgr behind him.)

VAXorcist: Everything looks okay to me.

Sysmgr: Maybe it's hibernating.

VAXorcist: Unlikely. It's probably trying to lure us into a false sense of security.

A bug in the hand is better than one as yet undetected.

Sysmgr: Sounds like VMS alright. (VAXorcist gives him a dirty look)

VAXorcist: I'm going to have to test it's power. This could get ugly, you may want to leave. (The Sysmgr shakes his head no. The VAXorcist brings himself up to full height in front of the VAX and points a finger at it) By the power of DEC, I expel thee from this system! (Clap of thunder.)

(Cut to door to the machine room. The Sysmgr is pulling a cart on which sits the VAXorcist wrapped from head to toe in magnetic tape.)

Sysmgr: Any other bright ideas?

VAXorcist: Just shut up and get this damn stuff off of me.

(Cut to Sysmgrs office)

VAXorcist: (Writing on the clipboard) Things look pretty bad. I think we're going to need a full-scale VAXorcism here.

Sysmgr: Is there anything I can do to help?

VAXorcist: As a matter of fact, there is. We've got to incapacitate the VAX to keep it from causing any more damage until I'm ready to deal with it. Now, I've got some software here that will do that, but it's got to be installed. (VAXorcist hands Sysmgr a tape) With that running, the CPU will be so bogged down, the VAX won't be able to harm anybody.

Sysmgr: (Examining the tape) What is it? A program to calculate pi to the last digit?

VAXorcist: Better than that. It starts up All-in-1 with a 10 user load.

(Cut to hall outside of Computer Room. The VAXorcist approaches the door. As the Sysmgr approaches the door, the VAXorcist holds him back.

VAXorcist: I appreciate your help, but it won't be safe for you in there.

Sysmgr: What? You're going in there to face that thing alone? You're nuts!

VAXorcist: Hey, it's my job. (VAXorcist turns to the door.)

Sysmgr: Wait a minute. (VAXorcist stops and turns around) You better take this with you. (Sysmgr removes a very large and very nasty looking gun from the inside of his jacket)

VAXorcist: (Smiling) No, I won't need that. I've got something more powerful. (VAXorcist holds up a small guide-sized orange binder, opens it, and shows it to Sysmgr. Cut to close up of the book which reads: *Guide to VAX/VMS System Exorcism*.)

(Cut to view of Machine room door as seen by the VAX. The VAXorcist enters the room and stands in front of the VAX. Cut to view of the Machine Room showing the Sysmgr confronting the VAX.)

VAXorcist: By the power of DEC, I command thee, Evil Spirit, to show thyself.

VAX: Bugger off.

VAXorcist: (Shaken) What?

VAX: I said Bugger off! Now get out of here before I core-dump all over you!

VAXorcist: (Recovered) Threaten me not, oh Evil one! For I speak with the power of DEC, and I command thee to show thyself!

(A rumble is heard and again the VAX becomes backlit by red

The VAXorcist was a trouble shooter.

lights and a fog begins to roll across the floor. The VAX cabinet doors slowly creak open to reveal two small red lights in the dark cabinet which appear to be the creature's eyes.)

VAX: There. Happy? Now get out of here before I drop a tape drive on your private parts.

VAXorcist: (Opening the orange binder, he begins intoning SHUTDOWN.COM in gregorian chant. The VAX screams.)

VAX: Stop that! Stop that! You, you DOS Lover! Your mother manages RSX systems in Hell!

(The VAXorcist continues and the VAX screams again.)

His screams echoed through the backup tape racks.

VAX: Stop it! (a large wad of computer tape is thrown at the VAXorcist, apparently from the VAX). Eat oxide, bit-bucket breath!

(The VAXorcist continues and the VAX screams once more.)

VAX: Mount me! Mount me!

VAXorcist: (Finishing the intonation) And now, by the power of DEC, I banish thee back to the null-space from which you came! (The VAX screams and the scream fades to silence.)

(Cut to the doorway of the Machine room, which now stands open. The VAXorcist is once again wearing his trench coat and fedora.)

Sysmgr: So it's over?

VAXorcist: (Putting his hat on) Yes, it's over.

Sysmgr: (Shaking the VAXorcist's hand) Thank God. Listen, thanks a lot. I don't know what we would have done without you.

VAXorcist: Hey, it's the least we could do. The Software Distribution Center should be sending you a patch tape in a week or two to patch out that AI routine and prevent this from happening again. Sign here. (He hands Sysmgr the clipboard, Sysmgr signs at the bottom and hands it back). Have a good one. (VAXorcist leaves).

(Sysmgr enters the machine room. Camera follows him in.)

Sysmgr: (Calling to someone off-camera) Okay, you guys, let's get rolling. Get those backup tapes out. We've got a clean system again! (Cheers are heard from off-camera. The Sysmgr leaves the picture, leaving only the VAX with it's cabinet doors still open in the picture. Slow zoom in to the LSI unit. Slowly, the LSI unit begins to emit a pulsing red glow.)

(Fade to black. Credits Roll)

Thanks to my friends and colleagues at the University of Maryland and elsewhere for their help and encouragement in the developement of the script and the video.

# Small Ads

*Lindsay Marshall*
Reprinted with permission from *Eliktronik Brane*,
Greg Michaelson (ed.), Vol. 2, No. 1, July 1987

IBM PC Owner? Here's the secret that made me a fortune – 'Sell it to a Museum *now!*' The secret's out! Yes, but for $100/hour I will personally use my experience to help in your negotiations with the collectors (results not guaranteed). Box EB 3.

Turn old 8" floppies into attractive garden ornaments – *Crafts For Today*, Issue 2 out now (with issue 1 absolutely free inside).

*Exclusive* catalogue of menswear from the "Hacker" range, photographed on attractive models. $5 (refundable on first order). Box EB 39.

Frederick noted with disappointment the continuing lack of jobs for tap-dancing COBOL programmers.

*For Sale*. Two vision processors, will split, buyer collects, sale forced by recent bereavement. Box O^O.

## La Boite Bleue

*Translated from the memoirs of Jean Turing-VonNeuman,
a minor 19th century post-impressionist programmer.*

© *William A Rennie (rennie@cs.albany.edu)*
*The TeleJokeBook*, Brad Templeton (ed.), Vol IV (1991),
Section 4, p.16.

I will never forget that Spring, that day. Paris had an air of revolution. The week before an exhibition of Seurat's listings had caused a sensation. In his unrelenting quest for simplicity he had reduced all of programming to three machine instructions. The resulting 6,000 line bubble sort had shocked the critics.

My own recent efforts had been received poorly. I had cut and slashed through my programs, juxtaposing blocks of code in a way that exposed the underlying intensity of the algorithm without regard to convention or syntax.

"But it doesn't compile," they complained.

As if programming was about adhering to their primitive language definitions. As if it was my duty to live within the limits of their antiquated and ordinary compilers.

So it was that I came that day to *La Boite Bleue*, seeking solace and companionship.

*La Boite Bleue* was where we gathered in those days. The wine there was cheap, the tables were large and they kept a complete set of language manuals behind the bar.

Everyone can be taught to sculpt: Michelangelo would have had to be taught how not to. So it is with great programmers.
*Alan J. Perlis*

As I entered I heard Henri's measured accents above the din.

"... that complexity is not the salient characteristic of exemplary style."

Toulouse-Lautrec was seated at a table spread with greenbar. Manet, redfaced, loomed over him.

"Damn your recursion, Henri. Iteration, however complex, is always more efficient."

Manet stormed away from the table in the direction of the bar. He always seemed angry at that time. Partly because his refusal to write in anything but FORTRAN isolated him from the rest of the avant-garde, partly because people kept confusing him with Monet.

Henri motioned to me to join him at the table.

"Have you heard from Vincent recently?"

We were all concerned about Van Gogh. Only a few days before he had completed an order n sorting routine that required no additional memory. Unfortunately, because he had written it in C and refused, on principle, to comment his code, no one had understood a line of it. He had not taken it well.

> To iterate is human;
> to recurse, divine.
> *Robert Heller*

"No. Why?" I replied.

"He and Gaugin had a violent argument last night over whether a side effect should be considered output and he hasn't been seen since. I fear he may have done something... rash."

We were suddenly interrupted by the waitress's terrified scream. I turned in time to see something fall from the open envelope she held in her hand. Stooping to retrieve it, I was seized by a wave of revulsion as I recognized that the object in my hand, bestially torn from its accustomed place, was the mouse from Van Gogh's workstation. The waitress, who had fainted, lay unnoticed in a heap beside me.

By the evening, the incident had become the talk of Paris.

# The Difference Between Hardware and Software

*Anonymous*
*A Bit Much ...*, William E. Kost (ed.), The Nova Osborne Users Group, 1st April, 1993, p.14

If you use a piece of hardware long enough, eventually it will stop working.

If you use a piece of software long enough, eventually it will start working.

## *User Friendly? You Must be Joking*

*Dan Greenberg*
*New Scientist*, Vol. 106, No. 1457, p.42-43, 23rd May, © 1985.

What should we do about Mikhail Gorbachevis belief that he can accelerate the Soviet Union into high-tech modernity by buying thousands of American personal computers?

Sell him all he wants.

On behalf of our own national security we should indulge his electronic hallucination and speed the machines on their way to Soviet offices and kitchen tables. For nothing can snarl a society like a tidal wave of computers, especially those of the "user friendly" variety.

Recalling Lenin's assurance that capitalists will sell Moscow the rope for their own hanging, hardliners in the US are baulking at the thought of helping the Soviet masses into the computer age. But there's no need to worry so long as the machines are accompanied by the most remarkable form of literature ever to emerge from the sadistic recesses of the human mind. I refer of course, to the *computer instruction manual.*

My introduction to this genre occcured several years ago, when I succumbed to the anxiety-producing advertisements and bought a small machine vaunted for easing the computer-illiterate into modern times. A lifetime of reading has encountered no prose to match the opacity of the accompanying instruction manuals, as the following example indicates:

A manual writer's fate: 20 years hard labour for 'Crimes to Literature'.

"Each time the pair of numbers A and SQR A is printed, it is on a new line, and this is because the PRINT statement does not end with a comma or a semicolon. Whenever this is the case, then the PRINT statement starts printing on a new line. (Thus to put in a blank line, use a PRINT statement in which there is nothing to be printed – just PRINT on its own.) However, a PRINT statement can end in a comma or semicolon, and then the next PRINT statement goes on printing as though the two had been one long statement." Get it?

After nearly a decade of computer-induced trauma, people in the US by and large now realise that, for the ordinary person the

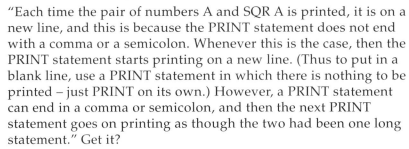

computer makes sense as a super-typewriter, but little else. Contrary to the Utopian gushing about the computerised information revolution penetrating all American households, it turns out that, as an information-handling system, a noteboard in the kitchen beats the computer hands down. Similarly, it has become obvious that computerisation of the family cheque book or recipe book is akin to using an Indianapolis 500 racer for local errands. That is why innumerable home computers are now heaped in closets and attics, and why many of the firms that produced them are now dead or dying.

Despite all this, the cry of "computer literacy" has stampeded countless anxious parents in the US into equipping their homes with electronic junk and badgering our financially straitened school systems into doing the same. But, after expensive, nerve-racking experience, educators are now recognising truths that were dismissed as Luddism when the sceptics pointed out that the school-room computer was little more than an electronic device for turning pages.

The 11th commandment was "Thou Shalt Compute" or "Thou Shalt Not Compute" – I forget which.
*Alan J. Perlis*

Is there any reason to hesitate about filling Gorbachev's order book? None at all, especially if the manuals go along. In English, they are masterpieces of headspinning prose, guaranteed to immobilise the mind and devastate intellectual self-esteem. Given the slippage that usually occurs in translations, they could be even worse in Russian.

For Western security, start shipping those computers now.

# A Day in the Life of a Network Manager

*Larry R. Custead (custead@sask.usask.ca)*
© 30th June 1993

The network manager was on vacation. I agreed to fill in for two weeks. How hard could it be? As far as I could see the network pretty much ran itself.

The first morning I settled in with a coffee and a stack of PC magazines. All was quiet until eleven when Sabrina came to my office. "My print job is stuck. It should have come out two hours ago."

I asked her a series of questions to try and diagnose the problem.

"How big is the job?"

"Just a couple of pages."

"Did you turn the printer off and on?"This is the standard solution for ninety percent of these problems. The network manager had warned me that the printers are tempermental.

"I don't think it is the printer. It's stuck on the server". The server is the heart of the network. Or maybe it's the nerve center. Anyway, it stores everyone's data files and routes all of the print jobs. I felt that I was closing in on the problem. I was already connected to the server, so I tapped out PRINTER STATUS on the console. It came back:

9:03 am Sabrina Print job 38 being spooled

I had no idea what spooling was but it didn't sound like something that should take two hours.

A cocktail shaker is an essential tool for sophisticated programmers.

"I'll delete the job and you can try printing it again. "I entered REMOVE JOB 38. A picture of a bomb appeared on the screen along with the words FATAL SERVER ERROR. All of the buttons on my phone lit up at once. I recalled further instructions that the Network Manager had left. "This phone is the network alarm monitor. If all of these buttons light up that means there is a problem somewhere. "Great, I already knew that there was a problem somewhere! I even knew where it was. I quickly answered each line.

"Accounting can't add up our numbers. The server is down."

"Legal needs to sue someone before lunch. When will the server be up?"

"This is Sales. You can't take the server down during the day. What if we get an order?"

"Maintenance calling. One of our mops is missing. We need immediate access to the mop and pail database."

I told them all that there was a complex technical problem which I didn't have time to explain but things would be back to normal soon. I had heard from every department but one. I called Marketing to inform them of the difficulties. A sleepy voice asked "Will it be up tomorrow? We don't do much on Mondays so we hadn't noticed."

It was time to apply the standard fix. I walked over to the server and turned the power off and on. I figured it would be up in a couple of minutes. Instead the console now complained FATAL ERROR: DISK FILES CORRUPTED. "Don't panic" I told myself, "probably happens all the time". I called Ed in from across the hall. He came over and looked at the message. "You can't turn the server off when there are files open. They get corrupted."

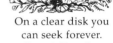

On a clear disk you
can seek forever.
*Peter J. Denning*

"Now you tell me. So what do we do about it?"

"There's a diskette around here somewhere that has some utility programs for repairing files."

"Okay," I said, "where are the file repair utilities?". No one knew. I pondered the problem at length but could only come up with one option. I went for lunch. I strolled across the street to Derek's Bistro where I enjoyed a leisurely meal of roast duck stuffed with prunes. When I returned to the office an hour and a half later, I found that Ed had located the utility disk and repaired the files. Everything was up and running smoothly.

Just another day in the life of the (acting) network manager. I wondered if I should do some backups.

# The Complexity of Songs

*Donald E. Knuth (dek@sail.stanford.edu)*
*Communications of the ACM*, April 1984, Vol. 27, No. 4, p.344-346.
© 1984, Association of Computing Machinery, Inc. Reprinted by permission. First appeared in *SIGACT News*, Summer 1977.

Every day brings new evidence that the concepts of computer science are applicable to areas of life which have little or nothing to do with computers. The purpose of this survey paper is to demonstrate that important aspects of *popular songs* are best understood in terms of modern complexity theory.

It is known [3] that almost all songs of length n require a text of length ~n. But this puts a considerable space requirement on one's memory if many songs are to be learned; hence, our ancient ancestors invented the concept of a refrain [14]. When the song has a refrain, its space complexity can be reduced to c·n, where c < 1 as shown by the following lemma.

*LEMMA 1*

Let S be a song containing m verses of length V and a refrain of length R where the refrain is to be sung first, last, and between adjacent verses. Then, the space complexity of S is
(V/(V + R)) n + 0(1) for fixed V and R as m –> ∞.

*PROOF*

The length of S when sung is

$$n = R + (V + R)m \qquad (1)$$

while its space complexity is

$$c = R + Vm \qquad (2)$$

By the Distributive Law and the Commutative Law [4], we have

$$
\begin{aligned}
c \;&= n - (V + R)m + mV \\
&= n - Vm - Rm + Vm \qquad (3) \\
&= n - Rm.
\end{aligned}
$$

The lemma follows.

(It is possible to generalize this lemma to the case of verses of differing lengths $V_1, V_2, ..., V_m$, provided that the sequence $<V_k>$ satisfies a certain smoothness condition. Details will appear in a future paper.)

A significant improvement on Lemma 1 was discovered in medieval European Jewish communities where an anonymous composer was able to reduce the complexity to $O(\sqrt{n})$. His song "Ehad Mi Yode'a" or "Who Knows One?" is still traditionally sung near the end of the Passover ritual, reportedly in order to keep the children awake [6]. It consists of a refrain and 13 verses $v_1, ..., v_{13}$, where $v_k$ is followed by $v_{k-1}...v_2 v_1$ before the refrain is repeated; hence m verses of text lead to $1/2m^2 + O(m)$ verses of singing. A similar song called "Green Grow the Rushes O" or "The Dilly Song" is often sung in western Britain at Easter time [1], but it has only twelve verses (see [1], where Breton, Flemish, German,

Greek, Medieval Latin, Moravian, and Scottish versions are cited).

The coefficient of $\sqrt{n}$ was further improved by a Scottish farmer named O. MacDonald, whose construction[1] appears in Lemma 2.

*LEMMA 2*

Given positive integers $\alpha$ and $\lambda$, there exists a song whose complexity is $(20 + \lambda + \alpha)\,\sqrt{n/(30 + 2\lambda)} + O(1)$.

*PROOF*

Consider the following schema [9].

The keyboard was non-standard.

$$V_0 = \text{'Old MacDonald had a farm.' } R_1$$
$$R_1 = \text{'Ee-igh,'}^2 \text{ 'oh!'}$$
$$R_2(x) = V_0 \text{ 'And on this farm he had some' } x \text{ ',' } R_1 \text{ 'With a'}$$
$$U_1(x, x') = x \text{ ',' } x' \text{ ' here and a' } x \text{ ',' } x' \text{ ' there; '}$$
$$U_2(x, y) = x \text{ 'here a ' } y, \text{ ' '}$$
$$U_3(x, x') = U_1(x, x') \; U_2(\varepsilon, x) \; U_2(\text{'t'}, x')$$
$$\qquad\qquad U_2(\text{'everyw'}, x \text{ ',' } x')$$
$$V_k = U_3(W_k, W'_k)V_{k-1} \qquad \text{for } k \geq 1$$

where

$$W_1 = \text{'chick'}, W_2 = \text{'quack'}, W_3 = \text{'gobble'},$$
$$W_4 = \text{'oink'}, W_5 = \text{'moo'}, W_6 = \text{'hee'}, \tag{5}$$

and

$$W'_k = W_k \text{ for } k \neq 6; \; W'_6 = \text{'haw'}. \tag{6}$$

The song of order m is defined by

$$P_0 = \varepsilon \tag{7}$$
$$P_m = R_2(W''_m) \, V_m P_{m-1} \text{ for } m \geq 1,$$

where

$$W''_1 = \text{'chicks'}, W''_2 = \text{'ducks'}, W''_3 = \text{'turkeys'},$$
$$W''_4 = \text{'pigs'}, W''_5 = \text{'cows'}, W''_6 = \text{'donkeys'}. \tag{8}$$

The length of $P(m)$ is

$$n = 30m^2 + 153m$$
$$\qquad + 4(me_1 + (m-1)e_2 + \ldots + e_m)$$
$$\qquad + (a_1 + \ldots + a_m) \tag{9}$$

while the length of the corresponding schema is

$$c = 20m + 211 + (e_1 + ... + e_m) +$$
$$(a_1 + ... + a_m). \tag{10}$$

Here $e_k = |W_k| + |W'_k|$ and $a_k = |W''_k|$, where $|x|$ denotes the length of string x. The result follows at once, if we assume that $e_k = \lambda$ and $a_k = \alpha$ for all large k.

Note that the coefficient $(20 + \lambda + \alpha)/\sqrt{(30 + 2\lambda)}$ assumes its minimum value at

$$\lambda = \max(1, \alpha\text{-}10) \tag{11}$$

when $\alpha$ is fixed. Therefore if MacDonald's farm animals ultimately have long names they should make slightly shorter noises.

Similar results were achieved by a French Canadian ornithologist, who named his song schema "Alouette" [2, 15]; and at about the same time by a Tyrolean butcher whose schema [5] is popularly called "Ist das nicht ein Schnitzelbank?" Several other cumulative songs have been collected by Peter Kennedy [8], including "The Mallard" with 17 verses and "The Barley Mow" with 18. More recent compositions, like "There's a Hole in the Bottom of the Sea" and "I Know an Old Lady Who Swallowed a Fly" unfortunately have comparatively large coefficients.

Why does computer music sound so good in shopping malls?

A fundamental improvement was claimed in England in 1824, when the true love of U. Jack gave to him a total of 12 ladies dancing, 22 lords a-leaping, 30 drummers drumming, 36 pipers piping, 40 maids a-milking, 42 swans a-swimming, 42 geese a-laying, 40 golden rings, 36 collie birds, 30 trench hens, 22 turtle doves, and 12 partridges in pear trees during the twelve days of Christmas [11]. This amounted to $1/6 \, m^3 + 1/2 \, m^2 + 1/3m$ gifts in m days, so the complexity appeared to be $O(\sqrt[3]{n})$; however, it was soon pointed out [10] that his computation was based on n *gifts* rather than n units of singing. A complexity of order $\sqrt{(n/\log n)}$ was finally established (see [7]).

We have seen that the partridge in the pear tree gave an improvement of only $1/\sqrt{(\log n)}$; but the importance of this discovery should not be underestimated since it showed that the $n^{0.5}$ barrier could be broken. The next big breakthrough was in fact obtained by generalizing the partridge schema in a remarkably simple way. It was J.W. Blatz of Milwaukee, Wisconsin who first discovered a class of songs known as "m Bottles of Beer on the Wall"; her elegant construction[2] appears in the following proof of the first major result in the theory.

## THEOREM 1

There exist songs of complexity O(log n).

## PROOF

Consider the schema

$$V_k = T_k \, B \, W \, ', '$$
$$T_k \, B \, ' ;$$
If one of those bottles should happen to fall, '    (12)
$$T_{k-1} \, B \, W \, '.'$$

where

$$B = ' \text{ bottles of beer } ' \qquad (13)$$
$$W = ' \text{ on the wall } '$$

and where $T_k$ is a translation of the integer k into English. It requires only O(m) space to define $T_k$ for all $k < 10^m$ since we can define

$$T_{q.10^m + r} = T_q \, ' \text{ times 10 to the } ' \, T_m \, ' \text{ plus } ' \, T_r \qquad (14)$$

for $1 \le q \le 9$ and $0 \le r < 10^{m-1}$.

Therefore the songs $S_k$ defined by

$$S_0 = \varepsilon, \; S_k = V_k \, S_{k-1} \qquad \text{for } k \ge 1 \qquad (15)$$

have length $n \approx k \log k$, but the schema which defines them has length O(log k); the result follows.

Theorem 1 was the best result known until recently[3], perhaps because it satisfied all practical requirements for song generation with limited memory space. In fact, 99 bottles of beer usually seemed to be more than sufficient in most cases.

However, the advent of modern drugs has led to demands for still less memory, and the ultimate improvement of Theorem 1 has consequently just been announced:

## THEOREM 2

There exist arbitrarily long songs of complexity O(1).

PROOF: (due to K.C. and the Sunshine Band). Consider the songs $S_k$ defined by (15), but with

$V_k$ = 'That's the way,' U 'I like it, ' U

U= 'uh huh,'² '                                      (16)

for all k.

It remains an open problem to study the complexity of nondeterministic songs.

*Acknowledgment*

I wish to thank J. M. Knuth and J. S. Knuth for suggesting the topic of this paper.

*REFERENCES*

1, Rev. S. Baring-Gould, Rev. H. Fleetwood Sheppard, and F.W. Bussell. *Songs of the West* (London: Methuen, 1905), 23,160-161.

2. Oscar Brand. *Singing Holidays* (New York: Alfred Knopf. 1957), 68-69.

3. G.l. Chaitin. "On the length of programs for computing finite binary sequences: Statistical considerations," *J. ACM* 16 (1969),145-159.

4. G. Chrystal. *Algebra. an Elementary Textbook* (Edinburgh: Adam and Charles Black, 1886), Chapter 1.

5. A. Dörrer, *Tiroler Fasnacht* (Wien, 1949), 480 pp.

6. *Encyclopedia Judaica* (New York: Macmillan, 1971). v.6 p.503; *The Jewish Encyclopedia* (New York: Funk and Wagnalls, 1903); articles on Ehad Mi Yode'a.

7. U. Jack, "Logarithmic growth of verses," *Acta Perdix* 15 (1826), 1-65535.

8. Peter Kennedy. *Folk songs of Britain and Ireland* (New York: Schirmer, 1975), 824pp.

9. Norman Lloyd, *The New Golden Song Book* (New York: Golden Press, 1955), 20-21.

10. N. Picker, 'Once senores brincando al mismo tiempo," *Acta Perdix* 12 (1825). 1009.

11. ben shahn, a partridge in a pear tree (New York: the museum of modern art, 1949). 28pp. (unnumbered).

12. Cecil J Sharp. ed., *One Hundred English Folksongs* (Boston: Oliver Ditson, 1916), xlii.

What is the difference between a Turing machine and the modern computer? It's the same as that between Hilary's ascent of Everest and the establishment of a Hilton hotel on it's peak.
*Alan J. Perlis*

13. Christopher J Shaw, "That old favorite, Apiapt/a Christmastime algorithm," with illustrations by Gene Oltan, *Datamation* 10, 12 (December 1964), 48-49. Reprinted in Jack Moshman, ed., *Faith, Hope and Parity* (Washington, D.C.: Thompson, 1966). 48-51.

14. Gustav Thurau, *Beiträge zur Geschichte und Charakteristik des Refrains in der französischen Chanson* (Weimar: Felber, 1899), 47pp.

15. Marcel Vigneras, ed., *Chansons de France* (Boston: D.C. Heath, 1941), 52pp.

The research reported here was supported in part by the National Institute of Wealth under grant $262,144.

When a professor insists computer science is X but not Y, have compassion for his graduate students.
*Alan J. Perlis*

*Footnotes*

1. Actually MacDonald's priority has been disputed by some scholars; Peter Kennedy ([8], p.676) claims that "I Bought Myself a Cock" and similar farm-yard songs are actually much older.

2. Again Kennedy ([8] p.631) claims priority for the English, in this case because of the song 'I'll drink $m$ if you'll drink $m + 1$." However, the English start at $m = 1$ and get no higher than $m = 9$, possibly because they actually drink the beer instead of allowing the bottles to fall.

3. The chief rival for this honor was "This old man, he played $m$, he played knick-knack..."

## Write in C

*To the tune 'Let it Be' by The Beatles.*

*Anonymous*

When I find my code in tons of trouble,
Friends and colleagues come to me,
Speaking words of wisdom:
"Write in C."

As the deadline fast approaches,
And bugs are all that I can see,
Somewhere, someone whispers:
"Write in C."

A seasoned
(C-sound?) singer.

Write in C, Write in C,
Write in C, oh, Write in C.
LOGO's dead and buried,
Write in C.

I used to write a lot of FORTRAN,
For science it worked flawlessly.
Try using it for graphics!
Write in C.

If you've just spent nearly 30 hours
Debugging some assembly,
Soon you will be glad to
Write in C.

Write in C, Write in C,
Write in C, yeah, Write in C.
Only wimps use BASIC.
Write in C.

Write in C, Write in C
Write in C, oh, Write in C.
Pascal won't quite cut it.
Write in C.

Write in C, Write in C,
Write in C, yeah, Write in C.
Don't even mention COBOL.
Write in C.

(and what about C++ ?)

# *A Simplified Guide To Hardware Maintenance*

© *David H. Ahl*
*Creative Computing*, August 1979, Vol. 5, No. 8, p.124-125

*Disclaimer*: *Creative Computing* assumes *no* responsibility for any computer subjected to the following maintenance hints.

Have you ever been annoyed that that new tape from *Creative Computing* software won't load properly every time. Chances are good that more precise head alignment could cure the problem.

Or how about that key on the keyboard that sometimes sticks down. Maybe one day your kids had a peanut butter and jelly sandwich too near the keyboard and the key got sticky – but how do you clean it?

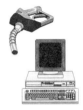

This short guide will give you some clues for solving these and other common maintenance problems. Expensive instruments are generally not needed, only time and a zest for experimentation. Before starting, clear a *large* work area, the basement floor perhaps.

The hard disk's capacity was 80 MB, or 5 litres.

## *Cassette Head Alignment*

First you'll have to disassemble the recorder. Most have four or more Phillips head screws accessible from the bottom. Most control knobs are friction fits and can be pulled off. The inevitable stubborn one can usually be removed by placing a chisel at the base and giving it a sharp blow with a hammer. Don't worry if the knob cracks – that's what crazy glue was made for.

To remove the head assembly may require jeweler's screwdrivers smaller than found in most home tool kits. Don't fret – a heavy-barreled screwdriver will effectively snap the head assembly out of its mounting. Simply employ it as a pry bar, placing the blade against the drive capstan for leverage.

Examine the head carefully, and then tap it sharply against a metal surface to dislodge foreign material. Deposits of oxide build up quickly and can adversely affect frequency response. Gently move a rasp back and forth across the pole pieces to make certain any oxide is fully removed. Any file ridges left by this operation can be burnished with sandpaper or emery cloth – or a grinder if available.

Place a thin bed of non-hardening putty in the head assembly mounting and replace the head assembly. This allows for fine alignment after reassembly. Indeed the head can actually be moved whilst playing a tape to get precise alignment.

Since the recorder is apart, this is as good a time as any to lubricate the motor and drive spindles. You'll notice very few signs of grease and oil on recorders manufactured in Japan, Hong Kong and the Far East because of a shortage of lubricants in that part of the world. Not so here. Household oil is okay for the volume and tone controls but for the motor and drive capstans a better choice would be Castrol HD with STP oil treatment mixed in. A full quart is clearly overkill; two 35mm film containers full is just about the right amount. But don't be afraid of using too much – moving parts are always hungry for lubrication.

Rubber that has dried out becomes brittle and lifeless (did you every try using a 1 year old rubber band). Lest this happen to your cassette recorder, work in some cup grease to all the rubber drive belts. They'll slip a bit at first, but they'll last a lifetime.

Reassemble the recorder. If the screws were misplaced as so frequently happens, simply use filament tape and crazy glue in liberal quantities. After all, performance is the name of the game, not appearance.

A new form of data encryption.

*Keyboard*

Problems with the keyboard are generally either in sticky keys or in the keyboard encoder Integrated Circuit (IC).

Sticky keys are usually caused by, appropriately enough, sticky substances on the keys such as jelly, bubble gum, hairspray, pine sap, and the like. Unfortunately lubrication alone will not always cure the problem because the sticky stuff must be removed also. Step one is to disassemble the keyboard – generally there will be four or six Phillips-head screws on the bottom of the  housing. Some are trickier than others but if you keep removing screws, eventually the keyboard will be free. Disconnect any cables and lay the keyboard on your work surface.

The key tops are friction fitted and a sharp pull with lineman's pliers, or vice grips if available, will remove the tops. Since dirt and gook are our enemies, first hose down the keyboard with a high pressure spray from your garden hose. Following that, place the keyboard in your kitchen dishwasher – the key tops can be placed in the silverware container – and run it through the super pot scrubber cycle.

Since certain gummy substances are resistant to soap and water you may still require the services of a wire brush, preferably in a drill motor. Brush the entire keyboard whilst pouring on copious amounts various grease cutting solvents in turn. Turpentine, lacquer thinner, ammonia, and Grease Relief are recommended.

If you have occasionally gotten an S when you typed A or O when you typed P, the problem is in the decoder chip. Find the largest IC on the keyboard and slip your 1/4" screwdriver under one end and pry it out. Notice that the IC is symmetrical. Because of this it is frequently installed backwards on the rush-rush factory assembly line. Simply turn the IC around 180° and reinsert into the socket. A sharp blow from a ball peen hammer will insure that the IC is firmly seated and making good contact on all its pins. (IC's that are not socketed are beyond the scope of this article. For the experimenter, one clue: a soldering gun will not unsolder an IC. By the time you get to the 14th pin, the first ones will have cooled. Hint: a Bernz-O-Matic propane torch, even the small one, will release any IC up to 32 pins.)

How to cut your hardware bills in half.

Before reassembling the keyboard use the remainder of the Castrol/STP mixture to lubricate all moving parts. Reassemble the keyboard. You'll find that the key tops are interchangeable so this is the time to put the keys in alphabetical order if you wish. Children often find the computer less mystifying if the keys are in a familiar order.

Resist the temptation to power up the system immediately. Rather, go have a couple of beers and check the warranties on the recorder and keyboard. You may need them. Next month: Maintenance of the CPU and CRT

# A Linguistic Contribution to Goto-Less Programming

*We don't know where to GOTO if we don't know where we've COME FROM. This linguistic innovation lives up to all expectations.*

R. Lawrence Clark*
*Communications of the ACM*, April, Vol. 27, No. 4, p.349-350,
© 1984 by Cahners Publishing Company.
First appeared in *Datamation*, December 1973.

Nearly six years after publication of Dijkstra's now famous letter [1], the subject of GOTO-less programming still stirs considerable controversy. Dijkstra and his supporters claim that the GOTO statement leads to difficulty in debugging, modifying, understanding, and proving programs. GOTO advocates argue that this statement, used correctly, need not lead to problems, and that it provides a natural, straightforward solution to common programming procedures.

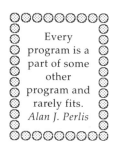

Every program is a part of some other program and rarely fits.
*Alan J. Perlis*

Numerous solutions have been advanced in an attempt to resolve this debate. Nevertheless, despite the efforts of some of the foremost computer scientists, the battle continues to rage.

The author has developed a new language construct on which, he believes, both the pro- and the anti- GOTO factions can agree. This construct is called the COME FROM statement. Although usage of the COME FROM statement is independent of the linguistic environment, its use will be illustrated within the FORTRAN language.

## Unconditional COME FROM statement

*General Form*
    COME FROM xxxxx

Where: xxxxx is the number of an executable statement in the same program unit.

This statement causes control to be transferred to the next statement (the statement immediately following the COME FROM upon completion of the designated statement.

*Example*:

```
10   J=1
11   COME FROM 20
12   WRITE (6,40) J
     STOP
13   COME FROM 10
20   J=J+2
40   FORMAT (I4)
```

He didn't know
whether he was
coming or going.

*Explanation*:

In this example, J is set to 1 by statement 10. Statement 13 then causes control to be passed to statement 20, which sets J to 3. Statement 11 then causes control to be passed to statement 12, which writes the current value of J. The STOP statement then terminates the program.

## Conditional COME FROM statement

*General Form*

IF (cond) COME FROM xxxxx

Where: cond is any logical expression. xxxxx is the number of an executable statement in the same program unit.

This statement causes control to be transferred to the next statement whenever the condition cond is true and the designated statement has just been completed.

*Example*:

```
     I = 1
     IF (I .LT. 10) COME FROM 50
     I = I+1
50   WRITE (6,60) I
     STOP
60   FORMAT (I4)
```

*Explanation*:

The COME FROM takes effect only while I is less than 10. Thus when I is equal to 10, the program continues past statement 50 and terminates. This is equivalent to the now-obsolete formulations:

```
     I = 1
30   I = I+1
```

```
        WRITE (6,60) I
        IF (I .LT. 10) GOTO 30
        STOP
60      FORMAT (14)
```

or

```
        DO 50 I = 2,10
50      WRITE (6,60) I
        STOP
60      FORMAT (I4)
```

Note how much clearer is the intent of the code containing the COME FROM construct.

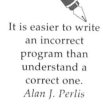

### Computed COME FROM statement

*General Form*

COME FROM (x1, x2, x3,...,xn), i

It is easier to write an incorrect program than understand a correct one.
*Alan J. Perlis*

Where: Each x is the number of an executable statement in the same program unit. i is an integer variable.

This statement causes control to be transferred to the next statement whenever any of the following conditions holds:

- statement x1 has just been executed and i is equal to 1

- statement x2 has just been executed and i is equal to 2

- statement x3 has just been executed and i is equal to 3

  :

- statement xn has just been executed and i is equal to n

If, when statement xj is executed, i has any value other than j, this statement has no effect.

*Example*:

```
        DO 200 INDEX= 1,10
10      X =1.
20      X = X*2.
30      X= X*3.
40      X= X*4.
50      X = X*5.
60      X= X*6.
70      X = X*7.
80      X= X*8.
```

```
90    X = X*9.
100   X = X*10.
      COME FROM (10,20,30,40,50,60,70,80,90,100), INDEX
      WRITE (6,500). INDEX,X
200   CONTINUE
      STOP
500   FORMAT (I4,2X,F12.0)
```

*Explanation*:

This program illustrates the power of the computed COME FROM by providing a compact algorithm for computing factorials. On the first iteration (INDEX=1), as soon as statement 10 has been executed, control passes to the WRITE statement. As a more general case, consider the fifth iteration: X is set to 1, and then multiplied by 2., 3., 4. and 5. before control passes to the WRITE statement.

**Assign and assigned COME FROM statements**

*General Form*

```
      ASSIGN xxxxx TO m
         :
      COME FROM m, (x1, x2, x3,..., xn)
```

Dr. Goto came to, with a jump.

Where: xxxxx is the number of an executable statement. It must be one of the numbers xl, x2, x3, ..., xn. Each x is the number of an executable statement in the same program unit. m is an integer variable which is assigned one of the statement numbers xl, x2, x3, ..., xn.

The assigned COME FROM causes control to be transferred to the next statement upon completion of the statement whose number is currently assigned to m. This provides a convenient means of passing control to a common point from a variety of points in the program unit. The actual point from which control is to be passed can be selected under program control.

*Example*:

```
      DO 60 I = 6,32
20    X = I*6+14
      IF (X – 20.) 10, 30, 50
10    ASSIGN 40 TO JUMP
30    Y = Z*X* *2. - 17.4
```

```
        COME FROM JUMP, (40,20,30)
        ASSIGN 30 TO JUMP
        X = X*Y-X**2
40      ASSIGN 40 TO JUMP
        IF (Y − X) 20, 60, 50
50      ASSIGN 20 TO JUMP
60      CONTINUE
```

*Explanation*:

This example is self-explanatory.

A language that doesn't affect the way you think about program-ming, is not worth knowing.
*Alan J. Perlis*

The author feels that the COME FROM will prove an invaluable contribution to the field of computer science. It is confidently predicted that this solution will be implemented in all future programming languages, and will be retrofitted into existing languages. Although it is clear that the COME FROM statement fulfills most of the requirements of the advocates of GOTO-less programming, it remains for the practitioners of automatic pro-gramming to evaluate just how much this construct contributes to the development of automatic proofs of program correctness. Having at last put to rest the GOTO controversy, we now may enter the era of the COME FROM conundrum.

\* The author is indebted to G. F. Groner and N. A. Palley for a valuable discussion which took place in New Haven, Conn.

[1] E. W. Dijkstra, "GOTO Statements Considered Harmful", Letter to the Editor, *CACM*, March 1968, p.147-148.

# BOFH (Part 4)

© *Simon Travaglia (spt@waikato.ac.nz)*

It's a Thursday, and I'm in a good mood. It's payday. I think I'll take some calls. I put the phone back on the hook. It rings.

"I've been trying to get you for hours!" the voice at the other end screams.

"No, it can't be hours" I say, putting *Blade Runner* back into it's cover and looking at the back, "it was more like 114 minutes. I was on a long phone call with the big boss, trying to get you users some better facilities."

Hook, Line and Sinker. "Oh. I'm sorry."

"That's ok, I'm a tolerant person." I make a mental note to change his password to something nasty in the next couple of days.

"Um, I need to know how to rename a file" he says.

Oh dear. Hang on, it's payday isn't it?! I'm in a good mood.

"Sure. You just go 'rm' and the filename."

"Thanks."

"No worries." (Now I'm in a *really* good mood. I think I just might write that script to make saving impossible on rogue at random times).

The phone rings again.

"Hello?"

"Hi there" I say.

"Is this the Operators?"

"Yes it is" I say, nice as pie.

"Could you get my printouts out please. I need them urgently, and I printed them over 5 minutes ago."

"Your username?" I ask.

Mediatation is often misunderstood.

He gives it to me, and I write it down for later. "No worries at all!" I say, and head to the printers.

There's a *huuuuuge* pile of printouts there, and sure enough, his is at the top of the pile. I pick it up, split it out of the rest and pour our ink-stained cleaning alcohol all over it, run it over a couple of times with the loaded tape trolley, then slam it in the tape safe door some times as well.

Beautiful.

"Here's your printout" I say "Sorry about the delay, we've got a few printer problems."

He takes a look and dies a little.

"Well, can I print it again?" he asks, worried.

"Sure you can", I say "but no promises, the printer's a bit stuffed today."

"Well can I print it on laser – is that working?"

"Yeah of course, but that'll cost you" I say, oozing compassion for the geek.

"It doesn't matter about the cost, *this is urgent!*"

I slide-on back into the printer room and put in the toner cartridge we save for special occasions – the one that prints thick black lines down the middle of the page and is all faint on one side. It took me quite a while to make it like that too. The printout shoots through and I bring it out immediately – I don't want to miss this!

"W-w-what's happened to my printout?" the geek squeals at me. Lucky I wrote that username down – I'm really starting to develop a taste for torture.

"Well nothing. I mean sure, it's a little soiled, but that cartridge has already done 47 thousand pages and been refilled 17 times. It's quite good compared to some we get."

Geek pays up and starts blubbing.

"Hey now. There's no reason to cry! Have you got a disk with your work on it?"

He gives me a box of diskettes and I step inside and run them across the bulk eraser. I come back out again.

"Sorry, I just remembered, our machine is on the fritz, you'll have to take these to the other side of campus to the machine there, it'll print them ok, and it had a brand-new toner yesterday."

"Great!"

"No worries. Oh, and hold the disks above your head the whole way there, the earth's magnetic field is particularly strong today."

Why do we want intelligent terminals when there are so many stupid users?

"Huh?"

"No arguments, just do it."

He wanders off, hand held high. I hate myself sometimes.

*To Be Continued...*

# The How-To-Choose-A-Computer-Book Book

© *Russel Griffin and Victor Miller*
*Computers and Electronics*, April 1985, Vol. 23, No. 4, p.73-74

We know it's hard to know where to start when you're buying that first computer. There are so many, you need a book to help you pick one. But if you check out the bookstore window, there are so many books to help you select a computer, you need a computer to pick which book! Big, small, thin, short, tall, and every color, it's a real jungle, and it's no snap deciding which one's right for you.

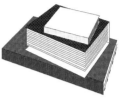

Be warned: big books usually cost big bucks.

And that's where we come in, to help you over the rough spots to that proud moment when you walk out of the bookstore ready to face the world with your brand new how-to-buy-a-computer book under your arm. So take a deep breath and relax. Buying a book's like riding a bicycle – first time's the hardest. All you do is follow our Ten Simple Steps.

*Dressing the Part.* The most important thing is to dress comfortably. We're not here to tell you what – you know what feels good and says you're you. But do wear running shoes or comfortable laced Oxfords with real support – you could be standing at the computer book shelf for a good long time! And if you're lucky enough to have a job or profession, jot it down on a 3 X 5 card and slip it in your shirt pocket before you leave home. We'll tell you why later!

*Being there.* Walk right on in. It's that simple. Chances are you'll find yourself in the middle of the computer books. Roughly 93% of all books published these days are about computers or by Peter McWilliams or both. But if you find yourself drowning in a broth of cookbooks, don't panic. Ask a clerk.

Next, assume a natural stance, hands in your pockets or outside them with your thumbs along your seams, and pick a shelf – the top one or the next down is best if you don't want a crick in the old neck. And look. Enough to make your head spin, isn't it? But don't lose heart. We're right behind you.

Now a lot of people in the field say the next step is to divide them all into two piles – books by Peter McWilliams and books by people who wish they were Peter McWilliams. But frankly, we don't see the point. Aside from the neat white covers on Pete's pile, they're both the same and you're no closer to knowing which book is for you. That's why we prefer our own next step:

*Scoping the Spine.* Before you've even touched a book, you can start narrowing the field. Those things facing you are called "spines," and you've probably noticed already that they're different from each other. Some books have straight glue binding, and some are spiral bound in shiny plastic or spiffy wire.

The best book on programming for the layman is *Alice in Wonderland*; but that's because it's the best book on anything for the layman.
*Alan J. Perlis*

Which is right for you? A glue-bound book's likely to flip shut instead of lying conveniently flat next to that computer it's going to help you buy, but it'll only collect half the dust of an open spiral job after the first month or two. On the other hand, you can yank the wire out of a metal binding for emergency rewiring or lunchtime flossing.

*Finding Your Niche.* Take a look at the titles on those spines (remember, they're backwards from the ones on the backs of your videotapes, so you've got to tip your head to the *right*) – *Microcomputers for the Legal Profession, Microcomputers for the Medical Profession, Microcomputers for the Executive Profession, Microcomputers for the Oldest Profession.*

Now, remember that 3 X 5 card you jotted your job on back home? Well, this is where that advanced planning pays off. Take it out and compare it with what you see (or, if you picked the right kind of comfortable shirt, you can read it right through your pocket without taking it out at all). Does it match any of the titles? If so, the how-to-buy-a-computer book you need is an arm's length away, and you can slip straight to the end of this article. If it doesn't, go to the next paragraph.

*Hefting the Book.* This is the "hands-on" part. With fingers extended and together, reach out with either hand – whichever is your favorite and grasp firmly any of the books with the binding that's right for you. Heft it, get the "feel." Does it feel important? Weighty? Helpful? If it dosen't, slap it back and try again.

*Getting the Copyright Right.* Okay, fine, now turn the book unit around so that the writing is right side up and toward you – the opposite of how you load a disk – and with one hand under the spine of the book, grasp the cover firmly with the other and leaf through till you find the copyright date. This is crucial. After years of study and heartbreak, we've found that anything copy-righted before 1985 is, well, just plain "out of date." You don't want something that's already "obsolete." You want "state of the art" or nothing. Luckily, 89% of what's on that shelf was probably written last month.

*Making Sure It's User-Friendly*. There's nothing worse than getting home and finding out you've got a book that makes you feel like you tracked in something on the bottom of your shoe. One way to avoid that is to check for graphics. We've found a picture can be worth a thousand words, so any computer book without lots of pictures isn't worth talking about.

And not just pictures. You want *funny* pictures. Face it – you don't want some computer nerd ordering you around, you want some-one neat, with a sense of humor who isn't afraid to Poke A Little Fun or take on computer-dom's Sacred Cows if it's going to put you at your ease.

One of our all-time favorites is this cartoon we saw of sixteen little girls named Kay, with one guy saying to the other "When I said 'K', that wasn't the kind I meant!" Great stuff, right?

I bet the human brain is a kludge. *Marvin Minsky*

Some of the best graphics are steel engravings from old books of, say, Acteon being torn apart by Diana's hounds, with a speech balloon that says, "When I said 'byte,' that wasn't the kind I meant!"

You might also run across graphics that look like steel engravings but are actually "collages" – pictures made by pasting together weird stuff cut out of etchings and parts catalogues. These can be real riots.

*Getting to Know Your Author*. Now's the big moment – time to take a look at the printed page and even read a sentence or two. What's the guy sound like? (You'll notice it's almost always a guy.) Does he know his stuff? Is he full of tidbits of the real inside computer dope like knowing where they hid the off switch on this year's models?

Maybe he's somebody who's been around since "computer" meant a ten-ton Univac with 4500 tubes. Sure, at first he's like having an uncle in the computer business, but sooner or later he'll turn into "Uncle Know-It-All" and get overbearing and "techni-cal" on you.

Personally, we prefer an author more like you and me, somebody who's only a week or two ahead and won't try to put on airs. Look for tip-offs like "Till last week, the nearest I'd even been to a computer was the one that sent me my KMart statement every month." After all, you don't just want an author who respects you as a person, you want one who *has* to.

*Buzzwords.* A lot of people think there's too much jargon in the computer world, but frankly, we don't think there's enough. Buzzwords are part of the magic of computing. What's the point if you can't dazzle your friends? When we first got into computers, we asked the used-car salesman how many "K" that Ambassador was going to set us back, and boy, was he confused!

Anyway, you want something with lots of them. Look for things like "ergonomics," or "footprint," "windowing," "software integration," or "transparent" to make sure you're getting your money's worth.

But watch out if you happen to come across "Nurnatrons," "core memories" or "nixie tubes." Same for chapter titles. Cute ones are fine – can't have too many of things like "Bits, Bytes. and Bottoms Up." But if you see anything like "Punch Cards or Magnetic Tape – The Eternal Question," "Keeping Memory Cool – A Good Fan Can Save Your Tubes," "Neon Indicators – Better Safe Than Sorry," or "The Tl-99: A Sensible Low-Cost Alternative," you may not have been holding up your end when you were supposed to be checking that copyright page. Better flip back and reboot!

Because of its vitality, the computing field is always in despearate need of new cliches: Banality soothes our nerves.
*Alan J. Perlis*

*Facing the Music.* So, okay, by now the manager is beginning to stare, but hang on, we're almost home. Close the book (that'll make the manager relax a little) and check the front and the back for a bunch of numbers preceded by something that looks like this: "$." That's the price.

If the cost is way below the price range of the actual computer you're interested in, then you've probably picked the wrong book. This is no time to cut corners or be satisfied with "just getting by." You want something that, if you don't wind up getting that computer, will at least give you the sense of well-being that comes from making a substantial investment.

So, hey, okay, last "but not least," let's review:

- Are you dressed for deciding?
- Are you at the bookstore?

- Is the spine for you?
- Do you have the right job?
- Is the book new?
- Is it heavy enough?
- Does it have plenty of pictures?
- Would you invite the author home to dinner?
- Does it have enough buzzwords?
- Does it cost enough?

For each "yes," score 10 points, for each "no" score 5, and for each "not sure," score 15. If you score over 100, you've got a book that's not afraid to ask the hard questions like whether or not *you* need a computer, and can be counted on to come up with hard answers like *yes*. If you score at least 50, you're probably still all right. Turn around and head for the cash register; the clerk will talk you through the paying part.

We've held up our end and given you all the help you need, so if you don't wind up with a really good book, you've got nobody to blame but yourself! Next time we'll tell you how to pick which computer magazine to subscribe to, cause it's dizzying array out there, a real jungle. In the meantime, *Happy Precomputing*!

# The Case of the Bogus Expert (Part 4)

*The Adventures of Joe Lisp, T Man*

*Kris Hammond (kris@cs.uchicago.edu)*
© 14th February 1984

...terminal and fired. Unfortunately, in the four weeks that had elapsed between episodes, the FAT man had not only moved his terminal and most of his office furniture but he had also shipped his operation to the University of Hawaii and was at this very moment drinking a badly prepared Mai Tai on the porch of Don Ho's veranda.

Protect your software at all cost – all else is meat.

I had once again fallen victim to the frame problem. Time had passed and I hadn't been updated in the data base. I had hoped that having a script would save me, but as I looked at it I realized that it was the wrong script. In fact it was a old script for an episode of "Our Miss Brooks." I had been beaten by a flawed representation.

Well two could play at that game. I wrote down all of the features describing Hawaii and California. I limited my descriptor list to only those predicates which the two locations had in common and fed the resulting data into a learning system with an impoverished data base. In no time at all I had rediscovered that California and Hawaii were in fact the same place. I had to pat myself on the back for this one, I wasn't an Einstein, but I could still bring home the Bacon.

Lisp let others clean up the mean streets (i.e. no garbage collection).

Once in Hawaii, I had little trouble tracking the FAT man down. As I got closer to his enclave, the people around me began to use more and more computer jargon. By the time I found him the silicon slang was flowing fast and furious. Outside the FAT man's door, a teaching assistant was explaining to a female student what it meant for a system to go down. It had gone further than I had thought. As I burst though the door of his office, I realized that I was just in time.

"It's over FAT man. All your students have fled to industry. Your grant supervisors are getting wise to your overblown promises, and your popular books are on the remainder tables. You've got nothing left."

He flashed a glance at his terminal screen and laughed insanely.

"If I fall, so do you Lisp. I'm sending out a letter to everyone I know in the field. You'll never get another paper published, you'll never get a tenure track position and you'll never see a single penny of grant money."

I knew he was serious and I'd come prepared.

"Don't try to send that mail FAT man. Go for that keyboard and you're a dead man."

He smiled and dove for the <RETURN> key. Then he died. As I said, I came prepared. I'd switched over to a representation with no actions, just state-changes. I had even told him, 'Go for that keyboard and you're a dead man.' I didn't have to do a thing. I just waited for an update of the state of the world. It's just a good thing that everyone knows that I never lie.

Well I picked up the professor down the hall and dropped him off with a deprogrammer I know. He'll be back to normal in just a couple of weeks of watching his rules become more and more baroque as he has to confront the real world.

And me... well I'm back in my office. I do my job and I'm happy. I just need the simple things in life: an Apollo, funding for another semester and bottle of '75 Talbot breathing in my desk drawer. I'm just waiting for the next time some lost soul walks though that door and asks for me: Joe Lisp – T Man.

That's it for now boys and girls. And remember, Joe Lisp is with you no matter where you are or what you are doing. When ever content wins over structure, whenever it is pointed out that a program is not a theory, whenever the rigors of science triumph over the daily needs of technology... Joe Lisp is there. He's always watching you, so keep it clean.

> One person's error is another person's data.

So ends another chapter in the ongoing saga of Joe Lisp. Be sure to buy Joe Lisp comics and the new Joe Lisp compiler coming out in June.

# A Parable About Generality in Architecture

*Anonymous*
*TLE::Diewald*, "Means, Motive, and Opportunity", 14th July 1990.
Also in *The TeleJokeBook* (1990), Brad Templeton (ed.),
Section 4, p.9.

Once upon a time, in a kingdom not far from here, a king summoned two of his advisors for a test. He showed them both a shiny metal box with two slots in the top, a control knob, and a lever. "What do you think this is?"

One advisor, an engineer, answered first. "It is a toaster," he said. The king asked, "How would you design an embedded computer for it?" The engineer replied, "Using a four-bit microcontroller, I would write a simple program that reads the darkness knob and quantizes its position to one of 16 shades of darkness, from snow white to coal black. The program would use that darkness level as the index to a 16-element table of initial timer values. Then it would turn on the heating elements and start the timer with the initial value selected from the table. At the end of the time delay, it would turn off the heat and pop up the toast. Come back next week, and I'll show you a working prototype."

The second advisor, a computer scientist, immediately recognized the danger of such short-sighted thinking. He said, "Toasters don't just turn bread into toast, they are also used to warm frozen waffles. What you see before you is really a breakfast food cooker. As the subjects of your kingdom become more sophisticated, they will demand more capabilities. They will need a breakfast food cooker that can also cook sausage, fry bacon, and make scrambled eggs. A toaster that only makes toast will soon be obsolete. If we don't look to the future, we will have to completely redesign the toaster in just a few years."

"With this in mind, we can formulate a more intelligent solution to the problem. First, create a class of breakfast foods. Specialize this class into subclasses: grains, pork, and poultry. The specialization process should be repeated with grains divided into toast, muffins, pancakes, and waffles; pork divided into sausage, links, and bacon; and poultry divided into scrambled eggs, hard-boiled eggs, poached eggs, fried eggs, and various omelet classes."

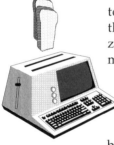

The new machine was the toast of the town.

"The ham and cheese omelet class is worth special attention because it must inherit characteristics from the pork, dairy, and poultry classes. Thus, we see that the problem cannot be properly solved without multiple inheritance. At run time, the program must create the proper object and send a message to the object that says, 'Cook yourself.' The semantics of this message depend, of course, on the kind of object, so they have a different meaning to a piece of toast than to scrambled eggs."

"Reviewing the process so far, we see that the analysis phase has revealed that the primary requirement is to cook any kind of breakfast food. In the design phase, we have discovered some derived requirements. Specifically, we need an object-oriented language with multiple inheritance. Of course, users don't want the eggs to get cold while the bacon is frying, so concurrent processing is required, too."

"We must not forget the user interface. The lever that lowers the food lacks versatility, and the darkness knob is confusing. Users won't buy the product unless it has a user-friendly, graphical interface. When the breakfast cooker is plugged in, users should see a cowboy boot on the screen. Users click on it, and the message 'Booting UNIX v. 8.3' appears on the screen. (UNIX 8.3 should be out by the time the product gets to the market.) Users can pull down a menu and click on the foods they want to cook"

"Having made the wise decision of specifying the software first in the design phase, all that remains is to pick an adequate hardware platform for the implementation phase. An Intel 80386 with 8MB of memory, a 30MB hard disk, and a VGA monitor should be sufficient. If you select a multitasking, object oriented language that supports multiple inheritance and has a built-in GUI, writing the program will be a snap. (Imagine the difficulty we would have had if we had foolishly allowed a hardware-first design strategy to lock us into a four-bit microcontroller!)."

The king had the computer scientist thrown in the moat, and they all lived happily ever after.

# *Taking a Stroll Down Babel Street.*

© *Peter J. Brown (pjb@merlin.ukc.ac.uk)*
*Communications of the ACM*, April 1984, Vol. 27, No. 4, p.352-353.
Also in *Computing Europe*, 1974

There are many shops in Babel Street. They range from Fred Fortran's successful grocery chain to Dr. Avery Tower's latest toy shop. To gain a better understanding of the businesses Peter Brown talked to some of their proprietors, beginning with the pernickety grocer himself.

Though the Chinese should adore APL, it's FORTRAN that they put their money on.
*Alan J. Perlis*

Of all the grocer's shops in town, Fred Fortran's does the most business. In fact only one shop of any nature does better and that is Cobol's stationers. Fred has been around for untold years and the doctors expected him to die long ago. Yet he continues working, looking the same as ever, watching his rivals come and go.

He is a man of very precise habits and it was important that I arrived at the right time to interview him. His day is broken into eighty periods, and various parts are set aside for different activities. This is one of his rules. If you arrived in the wrong period he might refuse to see you, or, worse, take you to be someone else.

Fortunately I was alright and walked straight into his office above one of his shops. He greeted me cheerfully, but did not interrupt his work.

I started by asking him why his shops sold so few lines, and why they had remained unchanged for years.

'I won't stock any of these fancy new-fangled foods,' he replied, what was good enough when I was a lad is good enough now. My customers have got used to the foods I stock and it would be madness to change.'

I had brought him a box of assorted subscripts as a present but, sensing that he might not be pleased with it, I decided to explore the ground first.

Fred Fortran at 90 has hardly altered since he was 77.

'I see you are still stocking the old Brand 704 plain subscripts.'

'Yes, sold well for many years, those have,' he said proudly, no one else makes them like that any more.'

I remembered that most items in his shops were labelled Brand 704. Obviously my intended present, a relatively new brand, would not be welcome so I decided to forget it.

I moved on to an even more controversial issue, and told him that many people accused him of spreading the debilitating disease of *gotoitis*, which results in a considerable loss of productivity.

'Rubbish!' he said. Everyone has gotoitis but it doesn't do them any harm. Nowadays some people want to cover it up by wearing fancy clothes, but it's still there underneath, you know. Back in the good old days...'

He continued talking, of the good old days for some time. When at last he finished I asked him about some details of the running of his shops.

'Let's say I ask you to repeat an order X times,' I said, 'and I tell you X is zero. Why do you execute the order once?'

'Your question is phrased badly, I won't accept it,' he said crustily.

'When you say X I assume you don't mean an integer. It's one of my rules. And if you don't mean an integer, I won't execute your repeat instruction at all. What's more I would reject all your other instructions until the error is corrected.'

'Alright, make it N times,' I said, amazed at the escalating consequences of my original slip.

"That's better. I will accept N times. To answer your original question, if you tell me to do something I get on with it. I don't waste time asking if you really didn't want it done after all. When I have finished the first time, I look to see how many more times I have to repeat the order. I try to be efficient, that's the point – not like Lady Algol, who spends so much time deciding whether or not to do anything that every job takes twice as long.'

The determined programmer can write a FORTRAN program in any language.

He continued his deprecating remarks about Lady Algol, who owned a rival chain of shops.

'...and the most ridiculous thing of all is that there is no standard input/output system in her shops.'

Eager to change the topic of conversation I asked him about his own input/output.

'Oh, mine is very simple,' he explained, 'you have formats with labels attached and within the formats...'

He tried hard to explain to me, but I never did manage to understand it.

We then talked about his worldwide success, a shop in every town. His plan has been to make every shop the same, so that customers could adapt easily from one to another. Every detail of the shops has been specified by Miss Ansi, who is very particular about such things. Fred was a bit resentful of her, however.

'She is very keen to standardise other people,' he complained, 'but with herself it's different. She even keeps changing her own name.'

The standardisation of shops had been quite successful ('Compare it with the mess the Algol shops are in,' said Fred), but the size of some goods varied a bit and many shops had introduced some new lines of their own. I had even bought my box of assorted subscripts in one of Mr. Fortran's other shops.

Throughout our interview, Fred had continued to work away at his accounts. It amazed me the work he got through. He did not show any imagination, just thoroughness and efficiency, and the result was low prices and lots of customers.

It was time to leave. I thanked him and gathered up my things. As I left I asked him where the toilet was.

'You go to Room 163.'

'Doesn't it have a name on the door?'

'No,' he said, 'I only allow people to go to rooms with numbers. It's one of my rules.'

## *Please Remove This Label*

*Or How I Configured my IBM Printer and Lived To Tell About the Experience*

*Espen Andersen*
© 29th June 1993

IBM does not leave anything to chance. If you buy a printer from IBM, the accompanying handbook will tell you that before you can use the printer, you will have to connect it to an electricity outlet, and turn the printer on. Then comes a little sidebar explaining that " | " is the international symbol for "ON" and "O" is the international symbol for "off", followed by a little drawing of a disembodied hand, index finger erect, showing the location of the on/off switch.

Nigel found the mouse easy to use, but slightly unresponsive.

IBM also gives us directions for use of their manuals. For instance, the printer manual tells you that if you have a problem with the printer, you should do the following:

1. Look up the 'Symptom' of the problem.

2. Read about the probable cause under 'Probable Cause'.

3. Do what is under 'Do the Following'.

The more subtle points of printer use are explained in Cassette Basic. Cassette Basic is a program that resides in ROM on all

IBM's PC's from the 1981 64K original PC at least up to the PS/2 Model 80-111. One way to access this program is to reformat your hard disk, so it is no longer bootable. This is time consuming, but a more efficient way is to use a utility program such as PC Tools to remove the COMMAND.COM file and DOS's two hidden startup files from your hard disk. Then the machine will go straight to Cassette Basic if you hit the Big Red Switch (which is called the Swedish Button in Norway, but I digress). Thereafter you can key in the source code for the printer configuration program (you have to key it in – nothing can be saved in Cassette Basic except on a cassette – and the IBM Cassette Storage Option Device disappeared about 1984. After keying in the program, you then hit the function key for RUN (function keys are great, reduce typing), the required codes will be sent to the printer port, and the printer turns on the big type (or whatever).

To err is human; to forgive, beyond the scope of the Operating System.

Thereafter, you carefully disconnect the printer cabel (the IBM Printer Connectivity Device Option for the Personal Computer and PS/2 Line). Then you boot the machine with a DOS diskette, replace the two hidden startup files and COMMAND.COM, and reboot. Remember to take out the diskette and reconnect the printer cable.

Some people say that there is another kind of BASIC, other than Cassette Basic, and when I dug through the inventory, I discovered 83 manuals in a suspicious green colour (maybe because they've been stored too long in plastic) for something called BASICA. Unfortunately there were no instruction on how to get the manuals out of their plastic cover, so further exploration was deferred.

Readers with a sense for corporate ethnography should now understand how to identify an IBM monitor: Look at the screen after you have unpacked it. Almost smack in the middle of the screen (about where you would have cell number C7 in Lotus 123) is a sticker, on which, in large letters, are written:

> Made in Taiwan R.O.C.

Underneath is written, in smaller letters:

> "After installation, please remove this label"

## *Productivity in Computer Science*

*Prof. J. Finnegan (finnegan@isi.edu)*
Oceanview University, Kansas

Productivity is the key to success from the individual level all the way up to the national level.

There are many scientific techniques for measuring productivity. By using such objective measures, and by comparing the level of productivity from time to time the rate of progress may be determined.

This report is based on a case study conducted in Oceanview, from which important lessons can be drawn for many other centers of Computer Science activities.

This report offers, for the first time, a precise mathematical relation between productivity and several independent parameters such as bitmap resolution and communication bandwidth.

You never finish a program, you just stop working on it.

The standard economic indicators and conventional statistics show that the general rate of progress in the United States is very low. Detailed studies of the situation reveal that productivity is actually on a steady decline, particularly in relation to Japan. Therefore, increasing productivity must be our top priority national goal. This decline exists in all fields except, obviously, the legal industry.

One area which still shows an uncharacteristic improvement in productivity is Computing. This encouraging phenomenon is the subject of this short report.

Computer scientists, like most other scientists, do not have a single strict objective measure for productivity. There are several alternate methods to measure the productivity of the Computing field. For example, the total number of patents granted (or applied for), papers published (or submitted), systems built (or talked about) or PhD degrees awarded (or sought).

Until the middle of the century there was no productivity to speak of. The little progress existing then was slow and in the wrong direction. Until recently the Computer Science community, as a whole, has been working hard on finding remedies to the mistakes of that era. The prestigious Anti-Von project is typical of that effort.

Productivity did not improve significantly until terminals were installed for use by scientists. Early systems of 50 and 75 baud pioneered the way for the First Generation of terminals, the 110 baud TTYs.

These terminals gave an unexpected boost to productivity, but they were only the beginning. Next, a new generation of 300 baud terminals followed. Productivity improved by a factor of three! (Actually only 2.71828)

Not long thereafter the 1,200 baud terminals joined the scene, and with them came an impressive further productivity improvement by a factor of four!!

Progress, obviously, did not stop there. The 9,600 baud terminals brought a further productivity improvement by a factor of eight!!!

Not all of this improvement was due only to the speed increase. Much of it should be credited to the introduction of CRTs, allowing users to actually see what they would get from the line-printer. "What You See Is What You Get" became one of the most fundamental principles of Computer Science. It is commonly referred to as WYSIWYG (pronounced "wee-zee-wig").

In parallel to the quantitative productivity increases, the quality of the published papers also soared. First came the change from old-fashioned line-printers to versatile 100ppi dot-printers. Soon thereafter the quality of the scientific papers further increased with the introduction of 196ppi printers.

Not much later a giant leap forward took place with the move to 392ppi, quadrupling the quality of all scientific publications. This high resolution of the printing process promoted the use of multiple type-fonts. Their widespread use brought new peaks of quality never before achieved.

The 2pt double-dutch font conveyed the meaning exactly.

However, progress was halted temporarily by software tools which allowed only 10 fonts per line. As soon as this artificial limit was removed, progress resumed its normal exponential course.

The average number of fonts per paper achieved an all time high. Papers which were rejected in the past could be reformatted, italicized, and printed by laser printers of higher and higher resolution, hence gaining higher levels of profundity, to the point that they had to be accepted by any scientific conference (especially those requiring submittals in camera-ready form).

This progress made it possible to right-justify any idea, even those which could not be justified on any other ground.

Sophisticated formatting proved to be the ideal tool for rescuing content-free articles which could not be saved even by their style.

In addition, precise software control of type-font size supported the easy expansion of papers to fill any given space, a feature admired by editors of camera-ready conference proceedings.

Society has not yet finished completely evaluating the move from slow, old fashioned terminals communicating at 10Kb/s to new workstations using 10Mb/s. It is expected that three orders of magnitude improvement in productivity is imminent. Anything less would be most disappointing.

MIPS: Meaningless Indicator of Processor Speed.

The sacred WYSIWYG has been unanimously voted the Most Valuable Principle (MVP) of the year, hence securing its eternal place in the Computer Science Hall of Fame.

Based on data available at the writing of this report a simple multi-dimensional statistical analysis proves that productivity is linear in workstation communication bandwidth (bit/sec) and bitmap dimension but is quadratic in both printing resolution (ppi) and the number of available printing fonts.

$$Pr = K \times BW \times BD \times PR^2 \times NF^2$$

Where: Pr is the Productivity, K is a constant, BW is the workstation communication bandwidth (bit/sec), BD is the bitmap dimension (bit x bit), PR is the printing resolution (ppi), and NF is the number of printing fonts.

The dimension of K is: (idea x sec x in$^2$) / (bit$^3$ x point$^2$)

Unofficial statistics support the suspicion that there is a steady increase of the percentage of effort that the PhD dissertations in Computer Science devote to formatting. It is impossible to believe that any significant work was ever conceived in the pre-WYSIWYG era, and since reports from that era are so hard to read there is no evidence to disprove this belief.

It is hard to remember the days when quality was measured in ideas per article rather than points per inch, and justification did not refer only to the margins.

Readers disagreeing with the conclusions of this report are challenged to read its proportionally-spaced italicized avec-serif version, printed on a laser printer of the highest resolution (available in PostScript, of course). Needless to say that that version is much more profound than this one, and much more convincing.

Prof. J. Finnegan is the alter-ego of Danny Cohen. The article was written at the Information Science Institute of the Univ. of Southern California (USC/ISI) in Marina Del Ray, California. Danny Cohen is now with Myricom, of Arcadia, California.
© *Danny Cohen*

☆ ☆ ☆ ☆ ☆ ☆ ☆ ☆ ☆ ☆ ☆ ☆ ☆

The attention span of a computer is only as long as its power cord.

## *Is Big Beautiful: Some Computer Cartoons From The 1960's.*

© *Greg Michaelson (greg@cww.hw.ac.uk)*
*The Computer Bulletin*, January/February 1993

*Introduction*

Computers are now so widely used that it is hard to remember that only 10 years ago most peoples' sole contact with them was through opening bank statements or utility bills. Before mass access to microprocessor based technology, the media played a crucial role in framing public perceptions of computers. Thus, one way of investigating social attitudes to computers is to look at their treatment in the media. Here, cartoons involving computers are particularly useful.

First of all, jokes often serve to diffuse fears or threats. Thus, looking at computer cartoons may highlight fears current about computers and their social effects. Furthermore, jokes often play on dissonances both between elements within a joke itself and between elements of a joke and the hearer/reader's pre-existing expectations and conceptions or misconceptions. However, these elements, expectations and conceptions are pre-given. Thus, analysing computer cartoons may help identify popular assumptions about computers and their properties, in particular what they look like, how they are used and who uses them.

In a previous article I discussed what I believe to be the first cartoon involving a computer to appear in the UK [1]. Here, I am going to consider a selection of cartoons from the 1960's, where the size of computers is a significant element in the joke.

The cartoons here all appeared in *Punch*, a once widely read establishment magazine of humour and social comment which folded in 1993. The readership was mainly middle class men: thus *Punch* may have influenced an important strata of British management and decision makers, in particular helping to construct their perceptions of computers.

*The Cartoons*

The first cartoon is from 1964 [2]. The computer is large and made up of banks of similar modules. The front panel has switches in groups of 8 or 6 and lights in groups of 5. Backing storage is in vertically mounted units for what might be tape drives. The machine is called UNAC, presumably a corruption of UNIVAC. UNAC may be a commercial system: the speaker is wearing a suit, the uniform of non-technical personnel in cartoons.

"Sorry about this UNAC, but you've been replaced by a smaller machine."

An interesting aspect of this cartoon is the imputation of intelligence to the computer, in particular through the implication of a natural language interface. Note that this cartoon is a variant of a "redundancy" style of joke, usually involving a human employer replacing a human employee with another human or a machine. This topic was first used in cartoons long before the development of computers. Perhaps the computer's substitution for a human in a familiar context may accentuate the reader's tendency to impute intelligence to it.

The second cartoon is from 1967 [3] and has an industrial setting. Once again, the theme is the decreasing size of computers. The new computer has rows of similar components: meters, switches; dials; lights. In the centre of the front panel are a screen and a speaker. On the right hand side is a reel to reel tape unit. The older machines in the background are also composed of regular modules but have patchboard wiring. Note the

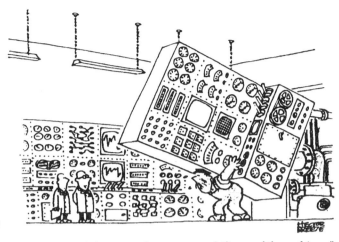

"Yes, in the old days it took ten men to shift one of those things."

stereotypes used for the people: the worker has a boiler suit and flat cap whereas the boffins are bald and wear white coats.

The third cartoon, from 1968 [4], is from the same genre as the first above and plays directly on fears of redundancy through automation. Here, the suggestion is that human administrative skills can be replaced entirely by a surprisingly small device. Perhaps the hapless employee is not actually very skillful?

The last cartoon (next page) is also from 1968 [5]. The computer is in an industrial cabinet. As in the first two cartoons, there are rows of dials and the suggestion of a console. Once again, there is an imputation of machine intelligence: it is well known that "Mr Big" is the brains behind organised crime.

"This is the machine that is replacing me?"

*Discussion*

Commercial and industrial computers in the 1960's were certainly extremely large relative to their functionalities. However, by the mid-1960's transistorisation enabled both increases in power

"We've got Mister Big!"

relative to size and sustained reductions in size. For example, Lavington [6] comments that the Elliot 802, first delivered in 1958, was a forerunner of what used to be called minicomputers and that the PDP8 began to be shipped to the UK in 1965. Growing awareness of this trend may be captured by the first two cartoons.

The machines portrayed in the first, second and fourth cartoons actually reflect what real computers looked like 10 or more years earlier. Early computers were festooned with low-level control and diagnostic components. Wiring and circuit boards were often visible. By the mid-1960's, such aspects were hidden inside uniform styled but plain cabinets, apart from the console with the ubiquitous banks of processor switches and lights. The second cartoon above hints at this transition with the new machine lacking the patchboards on the old. The older computer stereotype persisted in cartoons until the 1980's. Perhaps this is due to a lack of knowledge of technological development on the part of cartoonists. Alternatively, cartoonists may like working within a well established idiom, even when it becomes dated. See Lavington for pictures of 1940's and 1950's computers.

*Punch* helped reproduce this stereotype in other ways. For example, in 1964 *Punch* used a photograph of LEO captioned "A cheery smile from your editor", in an offensive article which trivialises computer training for women office workers [7]. The same photograph was reused in *Punch* in 1978 [8]. LEO entered service in the early 1950's.

The first, third and fourth cartoons also reflect widespread misconceptions about the abilities of computers. Media coverage of early computers sensationalised the possibilities of the development of truly intelligent machines in the not too distant future. Such expectations were also fueled by publicity generated by ambitious academic artificial intelligence projects prior to the Lighthill Report. Even now, intelligence is an important element of computer cartoons, despite the sobering realities of mass computer access in the last 10 years.

Note that in all the cartoons, the characters are male. In contrast, contemporary photographs often show women using computers albeit as operators: for examples see Lytel's 1965 book [9], Laver's introduction for HMSO from 1965 [10], or London's popular introductory text from 1968 [11].

The above cartoons, while selected for the size motif, are typical in gender composition of those that appeared in *Punch* between 1946 and 1983: women are generally absent. Where women do appear in computer cartoons it is often as the victims of blatant sexism. Perhaps these all-male images of computer interactees, coupled with the application of computers to the misogynist "humorous" tradition, helped contribute to the development of the tragic social perception of computing as a male discipline.

Finally, what of the computers themselves? We are invited to sympathise with the computer in the first cartoon: its replacement due to its size mirrors human replacement due to age. In the second cartoon, the computers are anonymous and our attention is drawn to the people that work with them. However, in the third cartoon the small size of the device militates against any undue anthropomorphism, and in the last, the size of the computer is celebrated. Perhaps, in computer cartoons, big is beautiful?

Bringing computers into the home won't change either one, but may revitalize the corner saloon.
*Alan J. Perlis*

*Acknowledgement*

I would like to thank Nancy Falchikov for commenting on an earlier draft of this paper. I am also grateful to *Punch* for permission to reproduce the above cartoons.

*References*

1. Michaelson, G., "Early computer cartoons," *Computer Bulletin*, Vol. 2, (4), pp. 22-24, (December 1986).
2. *Punch*, Vol. 247, p. 1009, (December 1964).
3. *Punch*, Vol. 253, p. 418, (September 1967).
4. *Punch*, Vol. 254, p. 389, (March 1968).
5. *Punch*, Vol. 254, p. 635, (May 1968).
6. Lavington, S., *Early British Computers*, MUP, (1980).
7. *Punch*, Vol. 246, pp. 652-653, (April 1964).
8. *Punch*, Vol. 275, p. 1079, (December 1978).
9. Lytel, A., *Fundamentals of DP*, Foulsham-Sams, (1964).
10. Laver, F. J. M., *Introducing computers*, HMSO, (1965).
11. London, K., *Introduction to computers*, Faber, (1968).

# Creators Admit Unix And C Were A Hoax

*Anonymous*

In an announcement that has stunned the computer industry, Ken Thompson, Dennis Ritchie and Brian Kernighan admitted that the Unix operating system and C programming language created by them is an elaborate April Fools prank kept alive for over 20 years. Speaking at the recent UnixWorld Software Development Forum, Thompson revealed the following:

"In 1969, AT&T had just terminated their work with the GE/Honeywell/AT&T Multics project. Brian and I had just started working with an early release of Pascal from Professor Nicklaus Wirth's ETH labs in Switzerland and we were impressed with its elegant simplicity and power. Denis had just finished reading *Bored of the Rings*, a hilarious National Lampoon parody of Tolkien's *Lord of the Rings* trilogy. As a lark, we decided to do parodies of the Multics environment and Pascal. Dennis and I were responsible for the operating environment. We looked at Multics and designed the new system to be as complex and cryptic as possible to maximize casual users' frustration levels, calling it Unix as a parody of Multics, as well as other more risque allusions. Then Dennis and Brian worked on a truly warped version of Pascal, called 'A'. When we found others were actually trying to create real programs with A, we quickly added additional cryptic features and evolved into B, BCPL and finally C. We stopped when we got a clean compile on the following syntax:

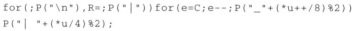

```
for(;P("\n"),R=;P("|"))for(e=C;e--;P("_"+(*u++/8)%2))
P("| "+(*u/4)%2);
```

X and Y were twice voted the best dressed designers of an imperative programming language.

To think that modern programmers would try to use a language that allowed such a statement was beyond our comprehension! We actually thought of selling this to the Soviets to set their computer science progress back 20 or more years. Imagine our surprise when AT&T and other US corporations actually began trying to use Unix and C! It has taken them 20 years to develop enough expertise to generate even marginally useful applications using this 1960's technological parody, but we are impressed with the tenacity (if not common sense) of the general Unix and C programmer. In any event, Brian, Dennis and I have been working exclusively in Pascal on the Apple Macintosh for the past few years and feel really guilty about the chaos, confusion and truly bad programming that has resulted from our silly prank so long ago."

Major Unix and C vendors and customers, including AT&T, Microsoft, Hewlett-Packard, GTE, NCR, and DEC have refused to comment at this time. Borland International, a leading vendor of Pascal and C tools, including the popular Turbo Pascal, Turbo C and Turbo C++, stated they had suspected this for a number of years and would continue to enhance their Pascal products and halt further efforts to develop C. An IBM spokesman broke into uncontrolled laughter and had to postpone a hastely convened news conference concerning the fate of the RS-6000, merely stating 'VM will be available Real Soon Now'. In a cryptic statement, Professor Wirth of the ETH institute and father of the Pascal, Modula 2 and Oberon structured languages, merely stated that P. T. Barnum was correct.

In a related late-breaking story, usually reliable sources are stating that a similar confession may be forthcoming from William Gates concerning the MS-DOS and Windows operating environments. And IBM spokesmen have begun denying that the Virtual Machine (VM) product is an internal prank gone awry.

☆ ☆ ☆ ☆ ☆ ☆ ☆ ✩ ☆ ☆ ☆ ☆ ☆ ☆

'Mahood Home Office Report'. Reproduced by permission of *Punch*, August 13th, 1986, p.17. © *Punch* 1986.

## *The Uzi Versus the Computer*

*Anonymous*

The following advertisement appeared in one of the munition magazines:

The Guy on the Right Doesn't Stand a Chance. The guy on the right has the Osborne 1, a fully functional computer system in a portable package the size of a briefcase. The guy on the left has an Uzi submachine gun concealed in his attache case. Also in the case are four fully loaded, 32 round clips of 125 grain 9 mm ammunition.

The owner of the Uzi is going to get more tactical firepower delivered – and delivered on target – in less time and with less effort.

All for $795. It's inevitable.

If you're going up against some guy with an Osborne 1 – or any personal computer – he's the one whose in trouble. One round from an Uzi can zip through ten inches of solid pine wood, so you can imagine what it will do to structural foam acrylic and sheet aluminum. In fact, detachable magazines for the Uzi are available in 25-, 32-, and 40-round capacities, so you can take out an entire office full of Apple II or IBM Personal Computers tied into Ethernet or other local area networks.

They were glad to get shot of the computer.

What about the new 16-bit computers, like the Lisa and Fortune? Even with the Winchester backup they're no match for the Uzi. One quick burst and they'll find what UNIX means.

Make your commanding officer proud. Get an Uzi – and come home a winner in the fight for office automatic weapons.

# The Church of the Cyber-Spiritualists

© *Andrew Davison (ad@cs.mu.oz.au)*

Australia is a land of frontiers, where pioneers live and die in a continual battle with untamed, primordial nature. In the late 20th century, these frontiers have migrated from the physical plain to the informational domains – fractious natives, ferocious fauna, and life-threatening landscapes have been replaced by uncontrollable data, fast-and-loose abstractions lost on a multi-lane informational highway.

However, just as Australia produced a hardy breed who conquered the physical terrain, it has now thrown up new explorers who are unafraid to gaze into the cybernetic maelstrom. These 21st century visionaries call themselves the cyber-spiritualists.

The cyber-spiritualist movement began quietly, when its co-founder and cyber-guru, Pungent Love Ph.D, bought a derelict warehouse in the deprived area of Melbourne known as Parkville. Nothing much was heard of the cultists until its members (the cyber-soothsayers) started appearing on street corners, handing out free admission tickets to raves held in their sprawling warehouse complex.

The cyber-soothsayers soon became a recognised part of Melbourne life – their colourful melange of tie-dyed t-shirts and industrial attitudes contrasted with the grey business-suited drones of the city centre. Not unsurprisingly, a generation of teenagers, dispossessed by the recession and a society fixated on its own faded past, turned to the life-affirming clarion call: 'If you haven't a life, get Artificial Life'. The kids simply wanted to partake in the cyber-spiritualist's hip musical soirees, where post-modern Techno met a hysterical perversion of their parent's bland LPs (e.g. *Manilow* and *The Bee Gees* played backwards at maddeningly fast speeds). But the cyber-spiritualists had a grander aim than the creation of a new musical nomenclature, they wished to give the aimless young new goals, objectives, a raison d'étre.

Cyberpunks use all available data to think for themselves.
*Timothy Leary*

It was with this sketchy history of the cyber-spiritualists in mind, that I contacted Pungent Love for an interview. I was taken aback when my email to pungent@love.au.oz was answered in the positive. I met him later that night at their warehouse, in time to experience the Winter solstice cyber-rave, the major dance event of those dreary, endlessly dark months.

Pungent approached me in the poorly lit entrance hall, clad in a psychedelic kaftan embroidered with printed circuit board patterns (the 68000 I think). He is a short man, perhaps 5 feet tall, with the gaunt angular build of an aspiring shaman. His slim body houses an awesome intensity, which emanates from his piercing blue eyes, and is enhanced by his striking hairstyle – rusty dreadlocks on the left and steely grey crew cut on the right.

He spoke: 'You have arrived, as I foretold. It is good that you are here at our threshold, since your thoughts are also at a threshold, one that leads to cyber-spiritualism.' His voice echoed amongst the crumbling masonry.

After a short breath, he continued: 'You may wonder why I have honoured you. It is simple, the world is fearful of what it cannot understand, and fear begets hatred. To the eyes of the non-believer cyber-spiritualism offers only fear. They are wrong and their erroneous views must be corrected. I have chosen you to report my words.' At this point, he raised his hirsute hands above his head and pointed them at me.

He started again: 'Cyber-spiritualism is a multi-faceted gem which may be viewed by ordinary mortals, but can only be grokked by a believer. I will facilitate your knowledge of cyber-spiritualism but, flawed as you are, you may never understand it. I have decided to show you three of the facets of our path to enlightenment – the cyber-rave, a virtual seance, and the meme gateway. These loci of belief will show you that we are neither to be feared nor hated. Indeed, we are to be praised, for we make sense of a senseless world.'

Information wants to be free. Believe it, pal.
*Bruce Sterling*

As he made his pronouncements, we moved towards an imposing set of double doors which muffled a crazed and rapid miasma of hectic rhythms. The guru ordered the portals of the Raving Room to be thrown back, revealing a cauldron of swirling black dervishes, swathed in a mind-numbing cacophony. As my senses reeled, I saw that each dancer was clad in a thick rubber suit, attached by cables to a complicated series of ducts and flues in the ceiling. Each raver also wore a silvery motorcycle helmet with an antenna rising from its top. The heat was intense, the lights stroboscopic, and the smell of rubber overpowering.

'Your senses have grepped the outer shell of reality. These young bodies are dancing to the musical arrangements which you hear, but their minds have ventured forth upon an unimaginable netrip. The rubber suits fully confine their physical manifestations and monitor their bodily processes. This information is ISDN'd to the matrix and used by the cyber-gururettes, and ultimately *The Ambient One*, to regulate the virtual environment fed to them through the meme helmet. In this way, their minds are purged and expanded in a controlled form, for the matrix is a wild and often villainous place.'

I asked him to elucidate upon the matrix.

'The matrix is oft equated with the paltry Usenet, and in a frail sense they are similar, but cyber-spiritualism transcends such parameters. Strictly speaking the matrix is the home of the ethereal corporality. The sum of all that was, is, and shall be. The tautological truth of this proposition is at the foundation of our creed.' He saluted the air as he concluded this statement.

I was still a little uncertain about what the meme helmet picked up: a religious station at the far reaches of the FM dial, a particularly active police band, or something from the Usenet? He snorted: 'You have an amusing turn of phrase which reveals your empathy with our vision. The meme helmet is a comunitek inspired receiver, a receptacle of filtered and enhanced virtuality, but still only a shadow of the truth, for that is all that neophytes can bear.'

My attention wandered back to the dance floor, and I saw one such exhausted neophyte being unhooked from his tubing by two soothsayers. He was dragged to a table where a steaming drink was placed in front of him, along with a slip of paper. I pointed this scene out to Pungent, and he deconstructed its meaning.

'The neophyte has supped from the cyberspace of knowledge and is sated. Now he is rewarded with a nootropic SmartDrink of my own creation. It is a patented mixture of dried herbs from Ceylon, heated spring water and a dash of lactose. The paper is a bill for the rental of the meme helmet for the dance duration, and for the drink. But enough of these lowly newbies, they do not befit my prolonged attention. Let us visit the virtual seance.'

We strode from the dance hall, climbed a staircase to another dimly lit corridor, and entered a room marked 'Seance (Virtual)'.

Along its sides, spaced at regular intervals, were a series of Victorian bathtubs replete with fine iron tracery and enamelled taps. However, my attention was inevitably drawn towards the individuals in the tubs, who were submerged in either yellow or black viscous liquids. Fortunately, the heads of the bathers were visible, and clad in meme helmets. In addition, each wore a pair of WWII-style flying goggles, connected to the ceiling by wiring.

The guru spoke: 'The individuals that you are privileged to behold are senior soothsayers – men and women who have at last taken full control of their bodily functions. This allows them to transcend the musical penury of the cyber-rave and to enter the next stage of their training. Of course,' he laughed, 'they are still unable to converse with *The Ambient One*, but they are ready to hear his words and view his visions.'

I surmised that the goggles were transmitting pictures, and the helmet a related sound track. But what about the bathtubs?

George began to doubt the veracity of the 'Tupperware Thought Projector'.

'You overstep your intellectual abilities, my child.' he said in a lightly scolding voice. 'The meme helmet and meme mirrorshades do not, nor never will, relay an understandable narrative. For why should the matrix perpetuate a fallacy? The world is a discordant concordance of sounds and images, and that must be reflected in the seance. Naturally, there are themes and agendas contained within the seance, but their form is chosen by the cyber-gururettes and *The Ambient One*. As for the bathtubs, they hold substances whose specific gravities are great enough to support the soothsayer during his encounter with the matrix. After extensive personal research, I have sanctioned the use of custard and chocolate sauce.'

He continued in a different vein: 'Time is short, the solstice approaches. I have spoken of the meme gateway, and so you shall see it. Come.'

His pace was more urgent now, and we hurried through more shadowy passages, up and down narrow stairwells, until I was quite lost. Abruptly, the guru stopped before a nondescript door and knocked out a code – it sounded like the first few bars of the *Star Trek* theme tune. The door was opened by a young man wearing a *Star Trek* outfit (old generation), and I couldn't fail to notice that everyone inside was similarly dressed.

Pungent explained: 'The meme gateway is staffed by my royal

cyber-gururettes. They have been through a rigorous didactic regime, of which the rave and seance are two insignificant stages. They have attained a mental melding with the matrix and *The Ambient One* of almost', he stressed 'almost' with a karate chopping motion with his left hand, 'almost the same vigour as my own.'

He moved over to one of the 5 PCs which adorned the poorly ventilated room. One of the gururettes was sat in front of it, scanning through the messages in two Usenet news groups (alt.tasteless and rec.food.cooking.uk, as I recall) and also looking at a series of gifs displayed in rapid succession in another window (the topic was *Caring Californian Babes in Bikinis* I believe). Occasionally, he would press the return or escape keys and a line from a news item, or a fragment of a gif, would be highlighted and then disappear from the screen. After doing this about 10 times, the gururette took a swig from a half empty bottle on the desk beside him. Again I asked the guru to reveal the significance of the scene.

The proof of a system's value is its existence.
*Alan J. Perlis*

'We are the music makers. And we are the dreamers of the dreams. The gururettes are perusing one of the earthly projections of the matrix for proclamations by *The Ambient One*. These, like all eternal truths, are esoteric and veiled from casual eyes. However, the gururettes have been taught to see through the barrage of irrelevancies that shroud our lives, and to alight instinctively on *The Ambient One*'s words and images. These are pulled from the matrix, assembled by the High Priestess, and piped to the meme helmets and mirrorshades throughout the building.'

I queried the presence of the bottles.

'Why are you so blinkered, feeble minded nonbeliever? Our name reveals all – the bottles contain the gururette's elixirs: gin, whiskey, vodka, bourbon. All spirits in the service of our mission.'

A red phone began ringing and, with a mild look of alarm, the guru hastened to answer it. After a few hushed words, he returned to my side.

'Your interface with our sanctum sanctorum has not gone unnoticed. The High Priestess has just returned from a visit to the matrix to commune with *The Ambient One*, and she has sensed your presence. She has decided to see you, so that you may learn more of the verities of our calling. Perhaps you may even see the

Symbols of *The Ambient One*?'

This last sentence was uttered in a subdued and reverential tone, as he guided me from the meme gateway. This time we headed in a heavenly direction for an inordinately long time, but I began to sense that we were approaching our destination as Pungent's breath became laboured. In fact, so did mine, as a peculiar aroma filled the air. I can only describe it as a mix between the smell of a less then fastidious public house just before closing time, and a rather ripe sack of dirty laundry. The stairs came to an end and Pungent led me into a candle-lit chamber. The public house aroma came from the thousands of empty beer bottles stacked around us, some dragooned into service as candle holders. The sack of dirty laundry odour emanated from the High Priestess herself, who closely resembled the smell she emitted.

The 'Computer Guru' look.

The guru began to speak: 'Lowly journalistic life form, behold and stand in awe of the High Priestess...'

The Priestess interrupted him: 'No need for formality dear. Just call me Granny Love. Have you got a bottle opener?'

The guru leapt forward, producing one from the folds of his kaftan. He seemed worried, and spoke to Granny Love in a hasty whisper. She ignored him and looked at me.

'You're interested in the Symbols of *The Ambient One* are you dear? It distresses me to show his failures to the outside world, even though he was just poor old Ambient Love, my first-born, when it happened.'

She turned and pulled back a small curtain, revealing a burnt piece of plastic supported in a framework of discarded bottles. The plastic had been in a heavy fire but on the front I could just read the letters "Z", "X", "8" and "1". Like a thunder bolt, I realised that the melted blob was the case of a ZX-81, a ground breaking personal computer of the early 1980's, designed and sold by the English super-entrepreneur Sir Clive Sinclair.

'I can see from your face, dear, that you've recógnised the origins of our shrine. Ambient was a fanatical home computer boffin way back when. Even after Stella, his wife, left him and poor little Pungent, he still wouldn't give up his ZX-81.'

I stuttered out a question about *The Ambient One*'s current location.

'It's strange you should say "current" dear. When his mind-expansion experiment went wrong, Ambient's empyreal existence was separated from its physical embodiment. If only he'd checked his BASIC coding and realised he was sending 200,000 volts through his cranium and not 0.2 volts. I thought he was dead, I really did, until I entered my trance state with the aid of these.' She gestured towards a few of the bottles. 'He appeared before me then, and explained about now being *The Ambient One*, being part of the matrix, and telling me to found the church. He even dictated some rules and regulations, but I lost those the next day, and he was too upset to tell me again. Very moody he is sometimes, just like Puggy-woogy.' She ruffled the guru's dreadlocks.

I asked if I could speak to *The Ambient One* using her approach.

'Sorry dear, no-can-do. You have to do the training first, and then there's still no guarantee. Absolutely no money-back guarantee.'

Money?

'$20,000 for the full course, $15,000 if you supply your own spirits. Very reasonable I'd say in such a fractured and chaotic world.'

"Damn! The Smiths have added business graphics, database management and communications!"

'Mahood Home Ofice Report'. Reproduced by permission of *Punch*, August 13th, 1986, p.16. © *Punch* 1986.

# *Personal Computing*

© *Evad Lha*
*Creative Computing* (*Datamazing*), March - April 1978,
Vol 4, No 2, p.76-77

Having seen page after page of advertising for personal computers in these new hobbyist and personal computing magazines I decided that this was just what our household needed. Household then included self, wife, three kids, three cats, three teevees, two teevee games (busted) and six (at last count) pocket calculators, cassette recorders (several), hie-fie and lots more electronic gadgetry. We were clearly in the electronic age and just as clearly we needed a computer.

Practical wife quietly inquires what effect computer purchase will have on next vacation. "Vacation, pah," think I, "computer will provide more entertainment than ten vacations." However, to molify wifey I decide to compile a list of benefits from computer.

Random access is the optimum of the mass storages.

1. Monitor intrusion detectors and stop possible theft of all household belongings. (Potential savings: $50,000)

2. Monitor fire alarm and save house. (Potential savings: $80,000)

3. Control furnace. (Potential savings over 20-yr. life of computer $40,000 assuming utilities remain constant and Arabs keep raising prices)

4. Computer assisted instruction. (Potential savings: $1,500,000 since kids can all get high-paying programming jobs as promised on many matchbooks and they won't mooch on Dad for entire life).

5. Games. (Potential savings: incalculable due to party guests playing fascinating computer games instead of drinking my best Wild Buzzard booze).

I decided to stop here as my calculations clearly revealed that I could justify much more than $599 for Radio Shanty, or Pest machine. Indeed none of the personal computers had any Real Capability. I thus turned to Real Industry magazines like *Datamazing* and there found what I was after – a multi-processing machine for monitoring with good CAI for kids and good graphics for games. After extensive evaluation, I realized that one system (I'm learning the jargon – they're systems not machines) best met my modest requirements: a CDC Cyber 6000 running PLATO.

The Cyber is capable of handling the simultaneous operation of up to 500 terminals or sensors which I felt allowed for future growth from the 5 sensors and 2 terminals I planned on initially. Another attractive feature is the elimination of expensive, time-consuming program swapping between the computer and mass storage through the use of extended core storage. This makes the transfer of data one hundred times greater and access time one thousand times shorter than systems using disks or drums. All terminals can thus enjoy fractional-second response.

Another feature I liked was that each and every key press at a PLATO terminal passes through the CPU before anything appears on the terminal screen. This allows for a 'redefinable' keyboard meaning that the 'j' key is not restricted to causing 'j' to appear on the screen. I felt this was handy in case I wanted to ever use the cyrillic (Russian) alphabet. Greek too.

I liked the calculation capacity that was automatically available at the terminal which would allow me to sit down and type in, say '46 + 24 =' and the system would, in a mind-boggling two-tenths of a second, respond with '70.'

The incredible graphic capability of the 512 x 512 matrix on the translucent plasma panel along with its touch screen response has been well-documented elsewhere so I'll not discuss that here. My kids wondered why it couldn't run colored games on the teevee like Atari's $69 video pinball but I pointed out that when I was a wee shaver we didn't even have teevee at all. They, of course, regard this as the Dark Ages, but I'm making up for my early depravation today.

Brad and Jane spent several hours looking for the washing machine.

Having decided which system to get, I then trekked on down to my local Computer Earth store but found, much to my chagrin, that although they handled surplus CDC power supplies ripped out of obsolete terminals ($35) they did not handle Cyber 6000 Systems. Dandy Computers never heard of CDC so I had no choice but to go to the CDC sales office in York. (*The ___ York Times* insists upon referring to my state as Jersey so I shall refer to that place on the wrong side of the Hudson River as York.)

I had a very pleasant discussion with the CDC saleswoman who was assigned to my account. She seemed surprised that I wasn't representing a consortium of universities or Major Foreign Power but at length got down to serious negotiations. (I'm convinced she still thought I was Fronting for someone other than myself).

Remember the good old days, when CPU was singular?

I soon realized from studying the engineering drawings that I might have to enlarge my garden tool shed somewhat to house the computer. Also upon leafing through my Sears catalog I found that they did not carry any 200,000 BTU air conditioners which was required for cooling, but that seven of their largest 29,000 BTU window units would do the job.

Each CDC system is custom-made, a nice touch I thought, except that the delivery time was almost a year. After much beating around the proverbial bush, we finally got down to the bottom line – cost. The total price for the system I wanted was $5,250,125.53 plus tax, delivery, and set-up. This was somewhat over my cost justification, but I figured I'd find other valuable uses for the system as time went on. Unfortunately my local credit union and S&L didn't quite see things my way so I had to make a pact with Satan to raise the necessary scratch. (The tarot cards already told me that my next reincarnation will be as a worm so I figured that the pact won't cause me too much extra anguish.)

The systern has been in a little over six months and to say that it has lived up to my every expectation and revolutionized my life would be a gross understatement. My applications could easily provide the grist for scores of articles like this. Watch these pages!

'The Lighter Side of Computer Hardware', Reprinted from *Creative Computing*, Vol. 4, No. 2, March-April 1978, p.130, © Creative Computing 1978.

# BOFH (Part 5)

© *Simon Travaglia (spt@waikato.ac.nz)*

I'm bored senseless, so I pass the time by reading users email. I must admit that today's lot is particularly boring, not one good message in all of them. I was expecting at least some veiled reference to a grope in a storeroom, but nothing. So I'm bored senseless by the usual drivel about some relative's surgery and how the weather is, over the other side of the world – that sort of thing.

To relieve the boredom, I remove a email party invite from a user's mail and post it under the sender's username to alt.singles.with.severe.social.dysfunctions on news, and make a note in my diary to be there with my camcorder. Should be fun!

Next in line is the online medical records database, in which the company doctors store the current medical histories of the staff. I grep it quickly for "herpes" and "syphillus" and sell the results to the local scum newspaper. I cover my tracks by adding an entry to one of the doctor's online electronic diaries for yesterday saying "$500, Med Recs To Paper". I think that's all it should take.

I move some tapes from the racks to the trolley to make it look like we really use them, then start looking through archie listings for a hidden x-gif site. I find one then start a batch job running under some user's account to get them all back, charged to him. I make sure he's got enough disk for the job by removing any files not related to the task at hand. Like all those "Doctorate Final Report" papers that have got quite large in the last few weeks.

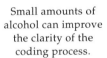

Small amounts of alcohol can improve the clarity of the coding process.

I go back to the mail now, as something's bound to have happened. I do a grep on all mail files for the words "pregnant" and "family way", and post them anonymously to the local general interest newsgroup.

Then, before anything can happen, the power goes out! The next second, the phone rings.

"Hello?" I say, annoyed – the coyote was just about to kill roadrunner again!

"Has the comput.."

I hang up. This is a matter of life or death. Quick as I can I rip the computer power cable out of the UPS and plug the TV in. Damn! Wylie missed again!

Meantime, all the alarms are going off like crazy as the disks spin down, but that's okay, because my Mac and terminal are hardwired to the UPS in any case; and I'm at the Beer Factory level in Dark Castle too.

The phone rings, so I pull the PABX breaker on the UPS switch-board and it stops. Now to look like I'm working. I break out the puck and the hockey stick and play a little one-on-wall. From the observation window it'll look like I'm being blindingly efficient, as per usual.

10 minutes later, the power is back and we're two HDA's down, but what the hell, I haven't lost a man, I'm onto the final screen, and there's more cartoons!

The phone rings, it's a luser (What a surprise).

"Computer Room" I say, being efficient.

"Hello, when will the compu..."

I hang up. I'm doing well in the screen, all I need do is get past the wizard who throws spells at you and I'm in!

The phone rings again. I put it on hands free.

"Computer Room" I shout, still deep in the game.

Software Pirates of the home PCs.

"I've lost my files" a user whines over the loudspeaker.

"You bet you have" I say, as my concentration lapses just long enough for me to get zapped by the wizard.

"What was your username?" I say, all sweetness and smiles.

He tells me, I look, and he's right. Shit, and I didn't even do it!

Not to be outdone, I change his login directory to the null device, set his path to "." and redefine the command "news" to execute a script in his old login directory to send a nasty message to the equal opportunities officer, then delete itself.

Now that's trying!

## Out of the Mouths of Babes

© *Eve R. Wirth*
*Creative Computing*, Nov.-Dec. 1977, Vol. 3, No. 6, p.110-111

"This year's social studies project," I ingeniously announced to the moppets in my elementary class, "is to learn about the computer industry." I proceeded to produce films, books, magazine articles lectures and the obligatory field trip.

When the term had come to its close, they demonstrated the wealth of their new knowledge in test papers, reports, and homework assignments.

If you are overworked, discouraged or tired, have no fear, the next generation is almost ready, as you will quickly ascertain from these quotes from their writings:

"Take a good long look at a computer. Does it have input, output, a bit of binary? No, you say to all these questions? Then you are not taking a good long look at a computer."

"Girl computer workers have to make real certain all the holes are in the right spots, because if not then how will the computer man get in them."

Perhaps if we wrote programs from childhood on, as adults we'd be able to read them.
*Alan J. Perlis*

"Lots of people are working in the hustling bustling business of computers. There could easily be 1000 of them doing this. Maybe 5000 doing this. Might even be a million. I can't be too for sure because it takes just about all of my knowing to even know that lots of people are working in the hustling bustling business of computers."

"Just yesterday when I read my libury book I knew real good what computers axaly do for us, but today it's a different colored horse story."

*Question*: What do you think is the greatest feat of the invention of the computer? *Answer*: "I didn't think it has feat, but when I think about it I would say the right foot is the strongest and greatest."

"In the pre-me times of history one day a guy decided to make a machine that could do stuff faster. He thought it was high time for action, so here's what he did. He put alot of holes in it and lots of buttons and stuff, and when you pressed the buttons zoom-voom-boom you got your answer and then everybody yelled with their deep throats woopee, yippee and maybe even sock-it-to-me."

"Remembering eggacly what 'binary' means is something that is forever going to be on my mind."

"What a 'bit' is has a very short memory on my end."

*Question*: How long do people in school learn about computers? *Answer*: "They could be anywhere from 5 feet and up."

"A bit of blarney is computer talk for all practical purposes invented by the Irish."

"I was so glad in my body to know that someday I would go to school to find out how to be a computer programmer. I had so many glad tickles in my stomach about it. Then with a sudden finding out that I also wanted to be a pilot, all my glad tickles went down my throat upside down and with a lump coming of sadness it was all over me being a computer programmer."

*Question*: How long have computers been in existence? *Answer*: "Since the beginning of time and maybe even longer than this."

"The very first modern computer was built in the dark ages of 1930, in either the A.D. or V.D. times of history."

"If you like to fool around with figures alot then become a design engineer. My Uncle Henry is one, and he fools around alot with figures."

"A lady computer operator and a man computer operator are the same, only just the opposite in the you know where places. "

Two of the chief software designers at Nintendo.

"They are producing more and more people to work on computors anally."

"From now on, after learning all about computers, I'm going to think wonderful happy-that-you-made-it-so thoughts with a smile in my heart."

Aren't you?

☆ ☆ ☆ ☆ ☆ ☆ ☆ ⭐ ☆ ☆ ☆ ☆ ☆ ☆

## Computers Don't Argue

*Gordon R. Dickson*
Copyright © 1965 by Condé Nast Publications, Inc.
Reprinted by permission of the author.

Treasure Book Club
PLEASE DO NOT FOLD, SPINDLE
OR MUTILATE THIS CARD

Mr: Walter A. Child Balance: $4.98

Dear Customer: Enclosed is your latest book selection. "Kidnapped," by Robert Louis Stevenson.

Once you understand how to write a program, get someone else to write it.
*Alan J. Perlis*

437 Woodlawn Drive
Panduk, Michigan
Nov. 16 1965

Treasure Book Club
1823 Mandy Street
Chicago, Illinois

Dear Sirs:

I wrote you recently about the computer punch card you sent, billing me for "Kim," by Rudyard Kipling. I did not open the package containing it until I had already mailed you my check for the amount on the card. On opening the package, I found the book missing half its pages. I sent it back to you, requesting either another copy or my money back. Instead, you have sent me a copy of "Kidnapped," by Robert Louis Stevenson. Will you please straighten this out?

I hereby return the copy of "Kidnapped."

Sincerely yours,
Walter A. Child

Treasure Book Club
SECOND NOTICE
PLEASE DO NOT FOLD, SPINDLE
OR MUTILATE THIS CARD

Mr: Walter A. Child Balance: $4.98

For "Kidnapped," by Robert Louis Stevenson. (If remittance has
been made for the above, please disregard this notice.)

437 Woodlawn Drive
Panduk, Michigan
Jan. 21, 1966

Treasure Book Club
1823 Mandy Street
Chicago, Illinois

Dear Sirs:

May I direct your attention to my letter of November 16, 1965?
You are still continuing to dun me with computer punch cards for
a book I did not order. Whereas, actually, it is your company that
owes me money.

Sincerely yours,
Walter A. Child

Treasure Book Club
1823 Mandy Street
Chicago, Illinois
Feb. 1, 1966

Keyhole
optimisation can
cause neck strain.

Mr. Walter A. Child
437 Woodlawn Drive
Panduk, Michigan

Dear Mr. Child:

We have sent you a number of reminders concerning an amount
owing to us as a result of book purchases you have made from us.
This amount which is $4.98 is now long overdue.

This situation is disappointing to us, particularly since there was
no hesitation on our part in extending you credit at the time
original arrangements for these purchases were made by you. If
we do not receive payment in full by return mail, we will be
forced to turn the matter over to a collection agency.

Very truly yours,
Samuel P. Grimes
Collection Mgr.

437 Woodlawn Drive
Panduk, Michigan
Feb. 5, 1966

Dear Mr. Grimes:

Will you stop sending me punch cards and form letters and make me some kind of a direct answer from a human being?

I don't owe you money. You owe me money. Maybe I should turn your company over to a collection agency.

Walter A. Child

FEDERAL COLLECTION OUTFIT

88 Prince Street
Chicago, Illinois
Feb. 28, 1966

Mr. Walter A. Child
437 Woodlawn Drive
Panduk, Michigan

Dear Mr. Child:

Your account with the Treasure Book Club, of $4.98 plus interest and charges has been turned over to our agency for collection. The amount due is now $6.83. Please send your check for this amount or we shall be forced to take immediate action.

Jacob N. Harshe
Vice President

In software systems, it is often the early bird that makes the worm.
*Alan J. Perlis*

FEDERAL COLLECTION OUTFIT

88 Prince Street
Chicago, Illinois
April 8, 1966

Mr. Walter A. Child
437 Woodlawn Drive
Panduk, Michigan

Dear Mr. Child:

You have seen fit to ignore our courteous requests to settle your long overdue account with Treasure Book Club, which is now, with accumulated interest and charges, in the amount of $7.51.

If payment in full is not forthcoming by April 11, 1966, we will be forced to turn the matter over to our attorneys for immediate court action.

Ezekiel B. Harshe
President

Cache Register
Allocation?

MALONEY, MAHONEY,
MACNAMARA and PRUITT
Attorneys

89 Prince Street
Chicago, Illinois
April 29, 1966

Mr. Walter A. Child
437 Woodlawn Drive
Panduk, Michigan

Dear Mr. Child:

Your indebtedness to the Treasure Book Club has been referred to us for legal action to collect.

This indebtedness is now in the amount of $10.01. If you will send us this amount so that we may receive it before May 5, 1966, the matter may be satisfied. However, if we do not receive satisfaction in full by that date, we will take steps to collect through the courts.

I am sure you will see the advantage of avoiding a judgment against you, which as a matter of record would do lasting harm to your credit rating.

Very truly yours,
Hagthorp M. Pruitt, Jr.
Attorney at law

437 Woodlawn Drive
Panduk, Michigan
May 4, 1966

Mr. Hagthorpe M. Pruitt, Jr.
Maloney, Mahoney, MacNamara and Pruitt
89 Prince Street
Chicago, Illinois

Dear Mr. Pruitt:

You don't know what a pleasure it is to me in this matter to get a letter from a live human being to whom I can explain the situation.

This whole matter is silly. I explained it fully in my letters to the Treasure Book Company. But I might as well have been trying to explain to the computer that puts out their punch cards, for all the good it seemed to do. Briefly, what happened was I ordered a copy of "Kim," by Rudyard Kipling, for $4.98. When I opened the package they sent me, I found the book had only half its pages, but I'd previously mailed a check to pay them for the book.

I sent the book back to them, asking either for a whole copy or my money back. Instead, they sent me a copy of "Kidnapped," by Robert Louis Stevenson – which I had not ordered; and for which they have been trying to collect from me.

Meanwhile, I am still waiting for the money back that they owe me for the copy of "Kim" that I didn't get. That's the whole story. Maybe you can help me straighten them out.

Relievedly yours,
Walter A. Child

P.S.: I also sent them back their copy of "Kidnapped," as soon as I got it, but it hasn't seemed to help. They have never even acknowledged getting it back.

In computing, the mean time to failure keeps getting shorter.
*Alan J. Perlis*

MALONEY, MAHONEY,
MACNAMARA and PRUITT
Attorneys

89 Prince Street
Chicago, Illinois
May 9, 1966

Mr. Walter A. Child
437 Woodlawn Drive
Panduk, Michigan

Dear Mr. Child:

I am in possession of no information indicating that any item purchased by your from the Treasure Book Club has been returned.

I would hardly think that, if the case had been as you stated, the Treasure Book Club would have retained us to collect the amount owing from you.

If I do not receive your payment in full within three days, by May 12, 1966, we will be forced to take legal action.

Very truly yours,
Hagthorpe M. Pruitt, Jr.

COURT OF MINOR CLAIMS
Chicago, Illinois

UNIX is fun. UNIX is fun. You are feeling sleepy...

Mr. Walter A. Child
437 Woodlawn Drive
Panduk, Michigan

Be informed that a judgment was taken and entered against you in this court this day of May 26, 1966, in the amount of $15.66 including court costs.

Payment in satisfaction of this judgment may be made to this court or to the adjudged creditor. In the case of payment being made to the creditor, a release should be obtained from the creditor and filed with this court in order to free you of legal obligation in connection with this judgment.

Under the recent Reciprocal Claims Act, if you are a citizen of a different state, a duplicate claim may be automatically entered and judged against you in your own state so that collection may be made there as well as in the State of Illinois.

COURT OF MINOR CLAIMS
Chicago, Illinois
PLEASE DO NOT FOLD, SPINDLE
OR MUTILATE THIS CARD

Judgment was passed this day of May 27, 1966, under Statute $15.66

Against: Child, Walter A. of 347 Woodlawn Drive, Panduk, Michigan. Pray to enter a duplicate claim for judgment.

In: Picayune Court – Panduk, Michigan

For Amount: Statute 941

437 Woodlawn Drive
Panduk, Michigan
May 31, 1966

Samuel P. Grimes
Vice President, Treasure Book Club
1823 Mandy Street
Chicago, Illinois

Grimes:

This business has gone far enough. I've got to come down to
Chicago on business of my own tomorrow. I'll see you then and
we'll get this straightened out once and for all, about who owes
what to whom, and how much!

Yours,
Walter A. Child

From the desk of the Clerk
Picayune Court

June 1, 1966

Harry:

The attached computer card from Chicago's Minor Claims Court
against A. Walter has a 1500-series Statute number on it. That puts
it over in Criminal with you, rather than Civil, with me. So I
herewith submit it for your computer instead of mine. How's
business?

Joe

CRIMINAL RECORDS
Panduk, Michigan
PLEASE DO NOT FOLD, SPINDLE
OR MUTILATE THIS CARD

Convicted: (Child) A. Walter
On: May 26, 1966
Address: 437 Woodlawn Drive, Panduk, Mich.
Crim: Statute: 1566 (Corrected) 1567
Crime: Kidnap
Date: Nov. 16, 1965
Notes: At large. To be picked up at once.

Software is to
computers as yeast
is to dough.
*Chuck Bradshaw*

POLICE DEPARTMENT, PANDUK, MICHIGAN. TO POLICE DEPARTMENT CHICAGO ILLINOIS. CONVICTED SUBJECT A. (COMPLETE FIRST NAME UNKNOWN) WALTER, SOUGHT HERE IN CONNECTION REF. YOUR NOTIFICATION OF JUDGMENT FOR KIDNAP OF CHILD NAMED ROBERT LOUIS STEVENSON, ON NOV. 16, 1965. INFORMATION HERE INDICATES SUBJECT FLED HIS RESIDENCE, AT 437 WOODLAND DRIVE, PANDUK, AND MAY BE AGAIN IN YOUR AREA.

POSSIBLE CONTACT IN YOUR AREA: THE TREASURE BOOK CLUB, 1823 MANDY STREET, CHICAGO, ILLINOIS. SUBJECT NOT KNOWN TO BE DANGEROUS. PICK UP AND HOLD, ADVISING US OF CAPTURE . . .

The laptop's security lock was overly successful.

TO POLICE DEPARTMENT, PANDUK, MICHIGAN. REFERENCE YOUR REQUEST TO PICK UP AND HOLD A. (COMPLETE FIRST NAME UNKNOWN) WALTER, WANTED IN PANDUK ON STATUTE 1567, CRIME OF KIDNAPPING.

SUBJECT ARRESTED AT OFFICES OF TREASURE BOOK CLUB, OPERATING THERE UNDER ALIAS WALTER ANTHONY CHILD, ATTEMPTING TO COLLECT $4.98 FROM ONE SAMUEL P. GRIMES, EMPLOYEE OF THAT COMPANY.

DISPOSAL: HOLDING FOR YOUR ADVICE

POLICE DEPARTMENT PANDUK, MICHIGAN TO POLICE DEPARTMENT CHICAGO, ILLINOIS

REF: A. WALTER (ALIAS WALTER ANTHONY CHILD) SUBJECT WANTED FOR CRIME OF KIDNAP, YOUR AREA, REF: YOUR COMPUTER PUNCH CARD NOTIFICATION OF JUDGMENT, DATED MAY 27,1966. COPY OUR CRIMINAL RECORDS PUNCH CARD HEREWITH FORWARDED TO YOUR COMPUTER SECTION.

CRIMINAL RECORDS
Chicago, Illinois
PLEASE DO NOT FOLD, SPINDLE
OR MUTILATE THIS CARD

SUBJECT (CORRECTION – OMITTED RECORD SUPPLIED) APPLICABLE STATUTE NO. 1567

JUDGMENT NO. 456789
TRIAL RECORD: APPARENTLY MISFILED AND UNAVAILABLE
DIRECTION: TO APPEAR FOR SENTENCING BEFORE JUDGE
JOHN ALEXANDER MCDIVOT, COURTROOM A JUNE, 9 1966

From the Desk of
Judge Alexander J. McDivot

June 2, 1966

Dear Tony:

I've got an adjudged criminal coming up before me for sentencing
Thursday morning – but the trial transcript is apparently misfiled.

I need some kind of information (Ret: A. Walter – Judgment No.
456789, Criminal). For example, what about the victim of the
kidnapping. Was victim harmed?

Jack McDivot

June 3, 1966

Records Search Unit
Re: Ref: Judgment No. 456789 – was victim harmed?

Tonio Malagasi
Records Division

June 3, 1966

To: United States Statistics Office
Attn.: Information Section
Subject: Robert Louis Stevenson
Query: Information concerning

Records Search Unit
Criminal Records Division
Police Department
Chicago, Ill.

A computer
program does what
you tell it to do,
not what you want
it to do.

June 5, 1966

To: Records Search Unit
Criminal Records Division
Police Department

Chicago, Illinois

Subject: Your query re Robert Louis Stevenson (File no. 189623)
Action: Subject deceased. Age at death, 44 yrs. Further information requested?

A. K.
Information Section
U.S. Statistics Office

June 6, 1966

To: United States Statistics Office
Attn.: Information Division
Subject: RE: File no. 189623

No further information required.

Thank you.
Records Search Unit

Criminal Records Division
Police Department
Chicago, Illinois
June 7, 1966

Percy tried to
remember the
advice about
'Pressing Any Key
to Begin'.

To: Tonio Malagasi
Records Division
Re: Ref: judgment No. 456789 – victim is dead.

Records Search Unit

June 7, 1966

To: Judge Alexander J. McDivot's Chambers

Dear Jack:

Ref: Judgment No.456789. The victim in this kidnap case was
apparently slain.

From the strange lack of background information on the killer and
his victim, as well as the victim's age, this smells to me like a
gangland killing. This for your information. Don't quote me. It
seems to me, though, that Stevenson – the victim – has a name
that rings a faint bell with me. Possibly, one of the East Coast
Mob, since the association comes back to me as something about

pirates – possibly New York dockage hijackers and something about buried loot.

As I say, above is only speculation for your private guidance.

Any time I can help . . .

Best,
Tony Malagasi
Records Division

MICHAEL R. REYNOLDS
Attorney-at-law

49 Water Street
Chicago, Illinois
June 8, 1966

Within a computer,
natural language is
unnatural.
*Alan J. Perlis*

Dear Tim:

Regrets: I can't make the fishing trip. I've been court-appointed here to represent a man about to be sentenced tomorrow on a kidnapping charge.

Ordinarily, I might have tried to beg off, and McDivot, who is doing the sentencing, would probably have turned me loose. But this is the damndest thing you ever heard of.

The man being sentenced has apparently been not only charged, but adjudged guilty as a result of a comedy of errors too long to go into here. He not only isn't guilty – he's got the best case I ever heard of for damages against one of the larger Book Clubs headquartered here in Chicago. And that's a case I wouldn't mind taking on.

It's inconceivable – but damnably possible, once you stop to think of it in this day and age of machine-made records – that a completely innocent man could be put in this position.

There shouldn't be much to it. I've asked to see McDivot tomorrow before the time for sentencing, and it'll just be a matter of explaining to him. Then I can discuss the damage suit with my freed client at his leisure.

Fishing next weekend?

Yours,
Mike

MICHAEL R. REYNOLDS
Attorney-at-law

49 Water Street
Chicago, Illinois
June 10

Dear Tim:

In haste –

No fishing this coming week either. Sorry.

You won't believe it. My innocent-as-a-lamb-and-I'm-not-kidding client has just been sentenced to death for first-degree murder in connection with the death of his kidnap victim.

Yes, I explained the whole thing to McDivot. And when he explained his situation to me, I nearly fell out of my chair.

It wasn't a matter of my not convincing him. It took less than three minutes to show him that my client should never have been within the walls of the County Jail for a second. But – get this – McDivot couldn't do a thing about it.

What *does* the C stand for in PCMCIA?

The point is, my man had already been judged guilty according to the computerized records. In the absence of a trial record – of course there never was one (but that's something I'm not free to explain to you now) – the judge has to go by what records are available. And in the case of an adjudged prisoner, McDivot's only legal choice was whether to sentence to life imprisonment, or execution.

The death of the kidnap victim, according to the statute, made the death penalty mandatory. Under the new laws governing length of time for appeal, which has been shortened because of the new system of computerizing records, to force an elimination of unfair delay and mental anguish to those condemned, I have five days in which to file an appeal, and ten to have it acted on.

Needless to say, I am not going to monkey with an appeal. I'm going directly to the Governor for a pardon – after which we will get this farce reversed. McDivot has already written the governor, also, explaining that his sentence was ridiculous, but that he had no choice. Between the two of us, we ought to have a pardon in short order.

Then, I'll make the fur fly . . .

And we'll get in some fishing.

Best,
Mike

OFFICE OF THE
GOVERNOR OF ILLINOIS

June 17, 1966

Mr. Michael R. Reynolds
49 Water Street
Chicago, Illinois

Dear Mr. Reynolds:

In reply to your query about the request for pardon for Walter A.
Child (A. Walter), may I inform you that the Governor is still on
his trip with the Midwest Governors Committee, examining the
Wall in Berlin. He should be back next Friday.

I will bring your request and letters to his attention the minute he
returns.

When we write
programs that
"learn", it turns out
we do and they
don't.
*Alan J. Perlis*

Very truly yours,
Clara B. Jilks
Secretary to the Governor

June 27, 1966

Michael R. Reynolds
49 Water Street
Chicago, Illinois

Dear Mike:

Where is that pardon?

My execution date is only five days from now!

Walt

June 29, 1966

Walter A. Child (A. Walter)
Cell Block E
Illinois State Penitentiary
Joliet, Illinois

Dear Walt:

The Governor returned, but was called away immediately to the White House in Washington to give his views on interstate sewage.

I am camping on his doorstep and will be on him the moment he arrives here.

Meanwhile, I agree with you about the seriousness of the situation. The warden at the prison there, Mr. Allen Magruder will bring this letter to you and have a private talk with you. I urge you to listen to what he has to say; and I enclose letters from your family also urging you to listen to Warden Magruder.

Yours,
Mike

June 30, 1966

*So many ideas are never heard from again once they embark upon a voyage in the semantic gulf.*
*Alan J. Perlis*

Michael R. Reynolds
49 Water Street
Chicago, Illinois

Dear Mike: (This letter being smuggled out by Warden Magruder)

As I was talking to Warden Magruder in my cell, here, news was brought to him that the Governor has at last returned for a while to Illinois, and will be in his office early tomorrow morning, Friday. So you will have time to get the pardon signed by him and delivered to the prison in time to stop my execution on Saturday.

Accordingly, l have turned down the Warden's kind offer of a chance to escape; since he told me he could by no means guarantee to have all the guards out of my way when I tried it; and there was a chance of my being killed escaping.

But now everything will straighten itself out. Actually, an experience as fantastic as this had to break down sometime under its own weight.

Best,
Walt

FOR THE SOVEREIGN
STATE OF ILLINOIS

I, Hubert Daniel Willikens, Governor of the State of Illinois, and invested with the authority and powers appertaining there to, including the power to pardon those in my judgment wrongfully convicted or otherwise deserving of executive mercy, do this day of July 1,1966, announce and proclaim that Walter A. Child (A. Walter) now in custody as a consequence of erroneous conviction upon a crime of which he is entirely innocent, is fully and freely pardoned of said crime. And I do direct the necessary authorities having custody of the said Walter A. Child (A. Walter) in whatever place or places he may be held, to immediately free, release, and allow unhindered departure to him ...

Interdepartmental Routing Service
PLEASE DO NOT FOLD, MUTILATE,
OR SPINDLE THIS CARD

Failure to route Document properly.

To: Governor Hubert Daniel Willikens
Re: Pardon issued to Walter A. Child, July 1, 1966

Dear State Employee:

You have failed to attach your Routing Number.

PLEASE: Resubmit document with this card and form 876, explaining your authority for placing a TOP RUSH category on this document. Form 876 must be signed by your Departmental Superior.

RESUBMIT ON: Earliest possible date ROUTING SERVICE office is open. In this case, Tuesday, July 5, 1966.

WARNING: Failure to submit form 876 WITH THE SIGNATURE OF YOUR SUPERIOR may make you liable to prosecution for misusing a Service of the State Government. A warrant may be issued for your arrest.

There are NO exceptions. YOU have been WARNED.

> Sometimes I think the only universal in the computing field is the fetch-execute cycle.
> *Alan J. Perlis*

# Transcripts from the General Motors HelpLine

*© Michael Edward Chastain (mec@shell.portal.com)*

Imagine a help line for novice car owners ...

*HelpLine*: "General Motors HelpLine, how can I help you?"
*Customer*: "I got in my car and nothing happened!"
*HelpLine*: "Did you put the key in the ignition slot and turn it?"
*Customer*: "What's an ignition?"
*HelpLine*: "It's a starter motor that draws current from your battery and turns over the engine."
*Customer*: "Ignition? Motor? Battery? Engine? How come I have to know all these technical terms just to use my car?"

> It is easier to change the specification to fit the program than vice versa.
> *Alan J. Perlis*

*HelpLine*: "General Motors HelpLine, how can I help you?"
*Customer*: "My car ran fine for a week and now it won't go!"
*HelpLine*: "Is the gas tank empty?"
*Customer*: "Huh? How do I know?"
*HelpLine*: "There's a little gauge on the front panel with a needle and markings from 'E' to 'F'. Where is the needle pointing?"
*Customer*: "It's pointing to 'E'. What does that mean?"
*HelpLine*: "It means you have to visit a gasoline vendor and purchase some more gasoline. You can install it yourself or pay the vendor to install it for you."
*Customer*: "What? I paid $12,000 for this car! Now you tell me that I have to keep buying more components? I want a car that comes with everything built in!"

*HelpLine*: "General Motors HelpLine, how can I help you?"
*Customer*: "Hi, I just bought my first car, and I chose your car because it has automatic transmission, cruise control, power steering, power brakes, and power door locks."
*HelpLine*: "Thanks for buying our car. How can I help you?"
*Customer*: "How do I work it?"
*HelpLine*: "Do you know how to drive?"
*Customer*: "Do I know how to what?"
*HelpLine*: "Do you know how to drive?"
*Customer*: "I'm not a technician. I just want to go places in my car!"

# Related Reading

The books (and other resources) described here have the common aim of being both humorous and concerned with computing. Aside from that, they are very different, ranging from cartoon guides to folklore to novels. I make no claims that this list is comprehensive, but it has been greatly improved by the generous help of the following people, whom I heartily thank:

Marc Abrahams (jir@mit.edu)
Bruce J. Baker (bjb@cs.mu.oz.au)
Mark Brader (msb@sq.com)
Roy Carlson (roy@netcom.com)
David H Dennis (david@amazing.cinenet.net)
Ian Feldman (ianf@random.se)
Lars Marius Garshol (larsga@ifi.uio.no)
David Goldfarb (goldfarb@ocf.Berkeley.edu)
Yoram Grahame (Y.Grahame@cs.ucl.ac.uk)
A. Grant (A.Grant@ucs.cam.ac.uk)
Andrew Guy (guya@cpsc.ucalgary.ca)
John Honniball (bj@inmos.co.uk)
Nancy Lebovitz (nancy@genie.slhs.udel.edu)
Petri Maaninen (fnord@vinkku.hut.fi)
Nathen Mates (nathan@cco.caltech.edu)
David Nash (dnash@chaos.demon.co.uk)
Donald Nichols (ceilidh!dnichols@uunet.uu.net)
Doug Palmer (dfp@cs.mu.oz.au)
Eric S. Raymond (esr@snark.thyrsus.com)
Brian Reynolds (reynolds@panix.com)
Arne Rohde (arne@pinn.nacjack.gen.nz)
Bob Roos (roos@sophia.smith.edu)
Col. G. L. Sicherman (gls@hrcms.att.com)
Marc Sira (aa382@freenet.carleton.ca)
Keely M. Swenson (cyberfox@netcom.com)
Roger Scowen (rss@seg.npl.co.uk)
Barry Traish (B.G.Traish@bradford.ac.uk)

Needless to say, if you have any suggestions about how to make this list *even better*, please get in touch.

The most recent version can be accessed via the WWW at:

http://www.cs.mu.oz.au/~ad/humour/HTCreading.html

A few keywords are used in the entries:

OOP – Out Of Print (according to 'Books in Print', 1993-1994);
R – Read by me; E – There's an extract in the main text.

Adams, Douglas. 1979. *The Hitch-Hiker's Guide to the Galaxy*, Pan Books, R.
This book and its sequels have very little to do with hitch-hiking. Adam's work has been described as a combination of "satire, humour and carefully crafted lunacy with whimsical speculation about such universal themes as 'life, the universe and everything'." The BBC radio series of the same name, which was the source for the first book, is also very enjoyable. The other Hitch-Hiker books are: *The Restaurant at the End of the Universe* 1980, *Life, the Universe and Everything* 1982, *So Long and Thanks for All the Fish* 1984, and *Mostly Harmless* 1992. The first 'Dirk Gently' book contains some computer-related humour: *Dirk Gently's Holistic Detective Agency* 1987. It was followed by: *The Long Dark Tea Time of the Soul* 1988.

Adler, Bill. (ed.). 1968. *Dear Dating Computer*, Bobbs-Merrill, OOP.

Ahl, David. H. (ed.) 1977. *The Colossal Computer Cartoon Book*, Creative Computing Press, E; R; OOP.
A lovely selection of cartoons from *Creative Computing* magazine from the mid 70's. The magazine was also famous for its April Fools parodies, some of which are included in the main text. Three of the best April issues are from 1978, 1980 and 1982. Also of interest by the same author: *Amazing, Thrilling, Fantastic Computer Stories* 1976.

Ainsley, Robert. and Rae, Alexander C. 1988. *Bluff Your Way in Computers*, Ravette Books, R.
Some of the advice includes: seven golden rules for computing bluffing, how to identify different kinds of users, and how to choose a computer. My copy is a few years old, but I believe a new edition came out at the end of 1993.

Alcock, Donald. 1977. *Illustrating Basic*, Cambridge Univ. Press, R.
At school, this cartoon book helped me to understand data structures for the first time. Alcock has also written several other books in a similar style, on C, FORTRAN, etc.

Amann, Dick. and Smith, Dick. 1978. *Forgotten Women of Computer History*, Programmed Studies, Inc., OOP.
Concerned with sex discrimination against women in the computing field. Also has a humorous element (don't ask me how).

*The Annals of Improbable Research* (AIR), R.
Dedicated to dangerously potent science humour. AIR is a new magazine produced by the former editorial staff (1955-1994) of *The Journal of Irreproducible Results* (JIR, see entry). The new magazine's co-founders are Marc Abrahams (air@mit.edu), who edited JIR from 1990-1994, and Alexander Kohn, who founded JIR in 1955 and was its editor until 1989. The editorial board consists of more than 40 distinguished scientists from around the world including 7 Nobel Laureates. AIR will appear 6 times per year, starting in Dec. 1994. For subscription details, send a SASE to:

> The Annals of Improbable Research (AIR)
> The MIT Museum, 265 Massachusetts Ave.
> Cambridge, MA 02139, USA

Their fax number is: 617 253 8994, or email: air-subs@mit.edu

There is a miniature version of AIR available free over the Internet. The mini-AIR is distributed as a *listserv* application, and about 12 issues will be published per year. To subscribe, send a brief email message to either of these addresses:

listserv@mitvma.mit.edu      or      listserv@mitvma

The body of your message should contain *only* the words "SUBSCRIBE MINI-AIR" followed by your name.

The USENET newsgroup clari.feature.imprb_research presents a syndicated weekly column of reports extracted from AIR.

Armstrong, Jeffrey. 1985. *The Binary Bible of Saint $ilicon*, Any Key Press, OOP.
An example illustrates the writing style: "Boota, the on-line one who taught us how to achieve nerdvana." The word play makes plentiful use of religious imagery.

Arneson, D.J. 1983. *The Official Computer Hater's Handbook*, Dell, OOP.
On the back cover, it says "Everything the computer hater needs to know about: How to destroy a computer; What to do with a dead computer; How to spot a computer hacker; How to tell if your teenager is using computers; How to understand computerspeak; How to turn off computer conversations at cocktail parties; Video games... the 25¢ lobotomy; The real difference between computer chips and buffalo chips."

Asimov, Issac. and Jeppson, J.O. 1982. *Laughing Space*, Houghton Mifflin.
An anthology of humorous science fiction, containing a few stories about computers and robots.

Barry, John A. 1991. *Technobabble*, MIT Press, R.
An examination of the language of technology, with an emphasis on computing. It's no surprise that a lot of computer folklore is tied up with jargon.

Barth, John. 1966. *Giles Goat Boy*, Doubleday.
The computer acts the goat?

Bear, John. 1983. *Computer Wimp*, Ten Speed Press, R.
A list of 166 things that anyone should know before buying a computer. There is a sequel: *Computer Wimp No More: Intelligent Beginner's Guide to Computers*, 1991, Ten Speed Press.

Bell, Patty. and Myrland, Doug. 1983. *The Official Silicon Valley Guy Handbook*, Avon Books, OOP.

Bishop, Ann. and Warshaw, Jerry. 1982. *Hello, Mr. Chips!: Computer Jokes and Riddles*, Lodestar Books, OOP.
A collection of riddles involving computers.

Breathed, Berke. 1980-90's. *Bloom County Cartoons*, Little, Brown and Co.
There are some good cartoons about computers (Apple Macs), among the 10,000 other ones about penguins. They appear in 10 or so books.

Brown, Gene. 1983. Small Bytes: *An Irreverent Computer Dictionary*, Collier Books, OOP.

Busch, David D. 1985. *Sorry About the Explosion: A Humorous Guide to Computers*, Prentice-Hall.
I wonder where the explosion fits in?

Byte, Dr Maurice K. (Steve Carter and Josh Levene). 1984. *How to Make Love to a Computer*, Pocket Books, OOP.
From the back cover: "Let a leading computer sexologist teach you his secrets. Why a computer is an ideal partner; Is size important?; The G-spot controversy; Plugging in; The many languages of love; The mysteries of aural sex; Hardcore software and other computerotica; The big O versus the little o; The special needs of a word processor; Premature programming; and much, much more!"

Ciarcia, Steve. 1978. *Take my Computer – Please*, Scelbi Computer Consulting, OOP.
The author documents the scrapes you can get into with a home computer (back when home machines were scarce).

Cook, Rick. *The 'Wiz' Series*, Baen Books.
This series includes in chronological order: *Wizard's Bane* 1989, *Wizardry Cursed* 1993, and *Wizardry Compiled* 1993. They feature a UNIX 'wizard' who is summoned to a fantasy world where he becomes a 'real' wizard, whose magic works like a computer language. Most enjoyable for readers with a knowledge of UNIX. Typical dialogue from *Wizard's Bane*:

"The closest I ever came to magic was working with UNIX wizards."
"Eunuchs wizards? Did they do that to themselves to gain power?"

Cornwall, Hugo. and Gold, Steve. 1989. *Hugo Cornwall's New Hacker's Handbook*, (4th ed.), Century.
Full of hacker-type information, and some great stories.

Ditlea, Steve (ed.). 1984. *Digital Deli*, Workman Publishing, OOP.
A "comprehensive user-lovable menu of computer lore, culture, lifestyles and fancy."

Ebert, Roger and Kratz, John. 1994. *The Computer Insectiary: A Field Guide To Viruses, Bugs, Worms, Trojan Horses, and Other Stuff That Wil Eat Your Programs And Rot Your Brain*, Andrews and McMeel.

Fiddy, Roland. 1993. *The Fanatic's Guide to Computers*, Exley Pub. Ltd.
Cartoons by the author. Some good ones.

Flaherty, Doug. 1986. *Humanizing The Computer: A Cure For The "deadly embrace"*, Wadsworth Pub., OOP.
Includes a chapter on computer fiction and humor.

Frampton, Rodger (ed.). 1990. *It's a Funny Thing*, Robert Hale.
A collection of byte-size stories, anecdotes, witticisms and cartoons from the world of computers and information technology. The material was donated by many people working in the industry and all the royalties from the book go to the *Great Ormond Street Hospital for Sick Children* in London.

Frayn, Michael. 1965. *The Tin Men*, Collins, E; R; OOP.
The funniest novel written about computer scientists, technocrats, and the absurdities of research. This book should be reissued immediately.

*FTP Sites*
Numerous anonymous FTP sites store humorous material. If you don't know what I'm talking about, then pick up a book on the Internet. I've listed the addresses and directories of some good places below. Typically, a site holds many megabytes of files.

| Address | Directory |
|---------|-----------|
| mc.lcs.mit.edu | /its/ai/humor *and* |
| | /its/ai/humor1 (very good) |
| cathouse.org | /pub/cathouse/humor (very good) |
| cco.caltech.edu | /pub/humor |
| nic.funet.fi | /pub/doc/humour |
| rascal.ics.utexas.edu | /misc/funny |
| donau.et.tudelft.nl | /pub/humor |
| ocf.berkeley.edu | /pub/Library/Parodies |
| prep.ai.mit.edu | /pub/gnu (the Jargon file is stored here) |

When I was first collecting articles in late 1992, I used an archie server to search for all the file names which contained 'humor' or 'humour'. It built a list of hundreds of names, with the files spread across almost as many sites.

An alternative to using FTP is to access these sites using Mosaic (or similar software). See the entry on the World Wide Web (WWW) for some details.


Gall, John. 1975. *Systemantics, How Systems Work and Especially How They Fail*. Fontana (originally published by Quadrangle/NY Time Book Co).
Not specifically about computers, but many of the principles are applicable to computer and software systems. There is a follow-up book called *Systematics: The Underground Text of Systems Lore*, 1986, (2nd edition), General System Press.


Garfinkel, Simson. Weise, Daniel. and Strassmann, Steven. 1994, *The Unix-Haters Handbook: The Best of the Unix-Haters On-line Mailing List Reveals Why UNIX Must Die!*, IDG Books.
Contains a forward by Donald Norman, Apple Computer and Anti-Forward by Dennis Ritchie, AT&T Bell Labs. It has a lot of hilarious material, and is not to be missed.


Gerberg, Mort. 1986. *Computer Hooters!: Computer Riddles, Jokes, and Knock-Knocks*, Scholastic Inc., OOP.
A collection of riddles and jokes about computers, using words and ideas associated with computers.

Glass, Robert L. 1978. *Tales of Computing Folk: Hot Dogs and Mixed Nuts*, Computing Trends, R; OOP.
Stranger-than-Fiction stories, mostly from a series of 'Sociology of Computing' articles published in *ComputerWorld*. Glass has written several other books along similar lines, which are in print: *The Universal Elixir and Other Computing Projects Which Failed* 1977; *The Power of Peonage* 1979; *Computing Catastrophes* 1983; *Computing Shakeout* 1987; *Software Folklore* 1991 (all published by Computing Trends).

Godin, Seth (ed.). 1993. *The Smiley Dictionary*, Peachpit Press, R.
A smiley, in case who didn't know, is something like this :), but there are hundreds of variations, many of them collected in this little book :^}.

Gonick, Larry. 1991. *The Cartoon Guide to the Computer*, Harper Perennial, R.
This guide painlessly introduces computing with the aid of some excellent cartoons. Incidentally, Gonick has produced cartoon guides for several other subjects, including genetics and statistics.

Hartman, Peter. 1990. *Junior Citizen's: An Owner's Manual: Child Care for the Computer Generation*, Great Bear Press.

Hedtke, Patricia Callander. 1993. *A Field Guide to Windows Icons: An Introduction to The Commonest Icons in North America*, Osborne McGraw-Hill.
From the cover: "A witty take-off on naturalists' field guides that describes common and uncommon sightings of Windows icons."

Heinlein, Robert A. 1968. *The Moon is a Harsh Mistress*, Berkley, R.
Not so much a novel, as a handbook on lunar revolution. It's included here because of a sentient computer that tell jokes, and displays a reviving streak of black humour at the end of the story.

Hofstadter, Douglas R. 1979. *Godel, Escher, Bach: An Eternal Golden Braid*. Basic Books, R.
It's quite hard to sum up this magnificent book in a few lines. The discussion ranges over music, logic, artificial intelligence, genet-

ics, and onwards. It closes with a conversation involving Charles Babbage, Alan Turing, the author, a tortoise, a crab, and Achilles.

Hogan, James P. *The 'Giants' Series*, Ballantine.
The series in chronological order: *Inherit The Stars* 1977, *The Gentle Giants of Ganymede* 1978, *Giant's Star* 1981, and *Entoverse* 1991. The stories feature self-aware computers, sophisticated enough to make witticisms in social situations, which is more than many real computer scientists can manage.

Holmes, Jeffrey. 1975. *Shakespeare Was A Computer Programmer*, Brunswick Press, OOP.
Great title.

Honeysett, Martin. 1982. *Micro Phobia: How to Survive Your Computer*, Tribeca Communications, OOP.
Cartoons.

Kawasaki, Guy. 1992. *The Computer Curmudgeon*. Hayden Books.
A classic repository of the Macintosh attitude, including: Why using a Macintosh is like sex; The sly strategies and clues to getting good tech support; How to get a job in the hot world of computers; Five ways to tell whether your kid will be a Mac or PC user; Who the *real* enemy is.

James, Geoffrey. 1987. *The Tao of Programming*, InfoBooks, R.
This collection of computing proverbs aims "to share with you a few serious thoughts presented on soft pillows of warm smiles." It was conceived while the author was practicing Tai Chi. The order form at the back of the book mentions *The Zen of Programming* which probably merits a look. He has also written *Computer Parables: Enlightenment in the Information Age* 1989, published by InfoBooks.

Jennings, Karla. 1990. *The Devouring Fungus: Tales of the Computer Age*. W.W. Norton, R.
A comprehensive discussion of computer lore.

*The Journal of Irreproducible Results (JIR)*, E; R.
Since 1955, JIR has been the publication of record for overly
stimulating research and ideas. JIR publishes original articles,
news of particularly egregious scientific results, and short notices
of satiric and humorous intent. For details on subscribing, contact:

> The Journal of Irreproducible Results
> c/o Wisdom Simulators, P.O. Box 380853
> Cambridge, MA 02238, USA

Also see [The Annals of Improbable Research].

There are two "best of" JIR books: *Sex As a Heap of Malfunctioning
Rubble (And Further Improbabilities): More of the Best of The Journal
of Irreproducible Results*, Marc Abrahams, (ed.), Workman Publishing, 1993, and *The Best of the Journal of Irreproducible Results*,
George H. Scherr, (ed.), Workman Publishing, 1983.


Kaufman, Robert Emanuel. 1978. *A FORTRAN Coloring Book*, MIT
Press, OOP.
Witty, bordering on corny. For example: variables called DAFDIL
and P2NIA, a cartoon with a floor mat (FORMAT), and example
code to calculate the temperature in a liquor still.


Keller, Charles. 1982. *Ohm On The Range: Robot and Computer Jokes*,
Prentice-Hall.


Kelly-Bootle, Stan. 1981. *The Devil's DP Dictionary*, McGraw-Hill,
R; OOP.
A homage to Ambrose Bierce's *The Devil's Dictionary* set amongst
computer folk. The dictionary entries make numerous references
to fictional characters and organisations.


Lebovitz, Nancy, 1994. *Button Mail-order Catalogue*, R.
A collection of 2,259 slogans of all types (not just computing): you
choose the slogan you want, and a button sporting that saying
will be sent to you for a small fee. (For fellow English people:
buttons are the same as badges.) The computing categories include: angst, bugs, dealing with users, personal computers,
programming, puns, specific languages, UNIX and related operating systems, USENET, Other Networks, Email, and bulletin

boards. For more details contact:

> Nancy Lebovitz,
> 400 Wollaston Ave. #C6,
> Newark, DE 19711, USA
> Email: nancy@genie.slhs.udel.edu

Leiber, Fritz. 1961. *The Silver Eggheads*, Ballantine, OOP.
The novel dissects the world of publishers, writers and readers, with humorous references to a wide range of literature.

Le Noury, Daniel. and Panish, P. 1984. *Computer Crazy*, Sybex, OOP.
French cartoons.

Lerner, Lawrence. 1974. *ARTHUR: The Life and Opinions of a Digital Computer*, University of Massachusetts Press (also Harvester Press), OOP.
The philosophical verse of a thick-witted Artificial Intelligence program. A forgotten classic.

Ley, James M. and Logsdon, Eileen M. 1983. *Computers Are Useless: 100 Uses For a Dead Computer*, Thunderbolt Publications, OOP.
Cartoons.

Lodge, David. 1984. *Small World: An Academic Romance*, Secker and Warburg.
A novel set in an English literature department of a university, which features computers as part of a minor side-plot. This mainly concerns a version of Eliza, and computer analysis of an author's work (which ruins his ability to write.) Some of the technical details are incorrect, but the book is still a great read.

Malik, Rex. 1987. *The World's Best Computer Jokes*, Angus and Robertson, OOP.
Includes the prize winning jokes from the Times-CMG humour competition.

Matusow, Harvey. 1968. *The Beast of Business: A Record of Computer Atrocities*, Wolfe, OOP.

Neumann, Peter G. *Risks*.
Peter Neumann is the moderator of the comp.risks news group, and for those of us who enjoy reading about computer calamities, this group always has plenty of juicy tidbits, liberally spiced with gallows humour. The best items also appear in the *Risks* section of *Software Engineering Notes*, a monthly ACM Press publication. In 1994, Neumann wrote a book on risk themes, entitled *Computer Related Risks*, published by the ACM Press (Addison-Wesley).

*News Groups on the Internet*
The Internet is one name for the spaghetti-like network of computer systems that support news groups (and other things). To be precise, it is USENET that carries news articles, and this is accessible from the Internet.

If the preceding sentences are news to you, then you should get hold of one of the many excellent texts on the Internet.

A recent estimate put the number of mainstream news groups at over 800, with a similar number again of more unusual groups. Of course, this doesn't take into account the plethora of local and regional groups, which probably run into the thousands. It's likely that a high proportion of news groups have some humorous content, but for the sake of your sanity, I'll only list the main ones:

> rec.humor.funny  (moderated)
> alt.humor.best-of-usenet   (culled from many sources)
> rec.humor
> rec.humor.oracle  (the USENET equivalent of Delphi)
> alt.tasteless.jokes  (strong stuff, as the name suggests)

rec.humor.funny is also available in book form, on CD-ROM (see [Templeton]), and is archived at a lot of FTP sites. Other good sources of humour are:

> comp.risks  (see [Neumann])
> alt.folklore.computers

Orfali, Sebstain. (ed.) 1984. *Computer Comics*, Ronin Publishing. Cartoons.

Panish, Paul., Panish, Anna Belle., and Small, T. 1984. *Mother Goose Your Computer: A Grownup's Garden of Silicon Satire*, Sybex, OOP.

Perlis, Alan J. 1982. Epigrams on Programming, *SIGPLAN Notices*, Vol. 17, No. 9, p.7-13. E;R.
The sayings by Alan J. Perlis which adorn the margins of this book comes from this article. Actually, I've only used about 45 of the 130 epigrams presented there.

Pfeifer, Diane. 1993. *Quick Bytes: Computer Lover's Cookbook*, Strawberry Patch.
Vegetarian cookery and computers.

Raymond, Eric (ed.). 1993. *The New Hacker's Dictionary*, MIT Press (2nd edition), R.
If you want to understand what a Hacker is saying, then this book will allow you to translate the guy's mumbled utterances into English. The text of the dictionary is available at a lot of FTP sites, usually called *The Jargon File* (see [FTP Sites]), but downloading all of it is more painful than buying a copy. A useful World Wide Web (WWW) version of the Dictionary, which is searchable by keyword, can be found at:

http://web.cnam.fr/bin.html/
    By_Searchable_Index?Jargon_File.html

A few more book details (including a picture of Eric Raymond) are available from:

http://www-mitpress.mit.edu/mitp/recent-books/
    comp/new-hacker.html

See [World Wide Web] for some details on the WWW.

Rochester, Jack B. and Gantz, John. 1983. *The Naked Computer*, William Morrow, OOP.
The full title describes the book as "a layperson's almanac of computer lore, wizardry, personalities, memorabilia, world records, mind blowers, and tomfoolery."

Sanderson, David W. 1993. *Smileys*, O'Reilly and Assoc.
From O'Reilly's catalogue: "A collection of the computer underground hieroglyphs called "smileys." Originally inserted into email messages to denote "said with a cynical smile":-), smileys now run rampant throughout the electronic mail culture. They include references to politics 7:^] (Ronald Reagan), entertainment

C]:-= (Charlie Chaplin), history 4:-) (George Washington), and mythology @-) (cyclops). They can laugh out loud %-(I), wink ;-), yell :-(0), frown :-(, and even drool :-)~."

Schneider, Ben Ross. 1974. *Travels in Computerland or, Incompatibilities and Interfaces*, Addison-Wesley, OOP.
From the back cover: "An outsider's perspective on the mad world of computing. Written by an English professor who knew little about computers before finding himself engaged in a mammoth computer project converting *The London Stage*, an 8000-page calendar of performances from 1660 to 1800, to a computer-accessible information base for scholars in theatre, drama and history. Based on his experiences while working on this project, the book is a witty tale of the long, hard road from idea to reality via computer."

Selkirk, Errol. and Kandler, Benny. 1986. *Computers for Beginners*, Writers and Readers, R.
A lively 'comic book'-style introduction to computing, which covers a wide range of topics.

Sias, Mary Ellen. 1984. *Computer Jokes and Riddles*, Weekly Reader Books, OOP.
A collection of jokes and riddles about computers using words and ideas associated with computers.

Sladek, John Thomas. 1968. *The Reproductive System* (Known as *Mechasm* in the US), Gollancz, R; OOP.
The story begins when a failing toy company gets government support for 'a project that is utterly, hopelessly useless'. They develop a machine that can reproduce itself and, naturally, things get out of hand (e.g. Las Vegas gets eaten).
Other Sladek books of interest:

*Roderick*, 1982, and *Roderick at Random*, 1983, Carroll and Graf.
The adventures of a Candide-like robot boy among humans, many of whom are intent on explaining how the sentence 'this sentence is false' should cause a mental seizure.

*Tik-Tok*, 1983, Gollancz, OOP.
A robot who's Asimov circuits don't work, allowing it to take life

with relish, never be suspected of crimes, and move on to politics.
*Bugs*, 1989, Gollancz, OOP.
A rather black book, revolving around an Artificial Intelligence
research company and its missing robot.

Spencer, Donald D. (ed.). 1993. *Computer Humor* (2nd ed.),
Camelot Publishing.
A collection of computer cartoons, drawn by Theresa B. Balon and
others. Spencer has written several other books: *Computer Cartoon
Visual Masters* 1987, *Cartoons for Computer Classes* 1988, and *Computers, Computers, Computers* 1992, all published by Camelot Pub.

Templeton, Brad. *The TeleJoke Books*, Clarinet Communication
Corp, E; R.
These compilations are drawn from the rec.humor.funny news
group. There are four books: *Vol. I* 1988, *Vol. II* 1989, *Vol. III* 1990,
and *Vol. IV* 1991. A complete archive of rec.humor.funny is also
available, as part of a CD-ROM anthology of Hugo and Nebula
nominees and winners for 1993. More information can be obtained by FTP from ftp.clarinet.com in the files /sf/info and
/clarinet_info/jokebooks.

Tennant, Rich. 1992. *The Fifth Wave: BYTE-ing Humor*, Andrews
and McMeel, OOP.
A surfing/computing book?

Tennant, Rich. and Barry, John. 1984. *The Unofficial I Hate
Computers Book*, Hayden.

Wahlstrom, Mat. 1992. *101 Uses For A Dead Computer*, Hayden, OOP.
Cartoons.

Webb, Spyder. 1983. *What Do You Think, Machinehead?*, Reston
Pub. Co., OOP.

Weber, Robert L (ed.). 1992. *Science With a Smile*, IOP Pub., R.
A lovely anthology of science-related humour (including computer science). A great book for dipping into, and you can salve your
conscience by calling it instructive. Weber's earlier books are just

as much fun: *A Random Walk in Science*, and *More Random Walks in Science*, both published by the Institute of Physics, UK.

Wells, Clyde. and Saidis, Frank. 1986. *101 Uses For An Unused Home Computer*, Peachtree Publishers, OOP.
Cartoons.

Wilde, Larry. and Wozniak, Steve. 1988. *The Official Computer Freaks Joke Book*, Bantam Books.

Williams, Kipper. 1986. *Warning! This Computer Bytes!*, Javelin, OOP.
English humorous cartoons from various artists.

Winchester, Dorothy M. and D'Spain, Rob. 1987. *101 Uses For Your Burned Out Computer*, Computer Paraphernalia, OOP.

Woo, Dianne. 1992. *The Computer Munched My Homework*, Tor Books.
Aimed at kids.

World Wide Web (WWW)
I have seen the future, and it's called the WWW (or Web): a much easier and more enjoyable way of browsing through the Internet ('surfing' if you prefer). The most popular software for doing this is called *Mosaic,* a distributed hypermedia system; information about it can be obtained from ftp.cc.gatech.edu in the directory /pub/gvu/mosaic-info.

A highly readable, non-technical, introduction to the WWW and Mosaic can be found in the October 1994 issue of *Wired,* called 'The Second Phase of the Revolution Has Begun'.

A great starting point for WWW-accessible humour is Nathan Mates' page:

http://www.ugcs.caltech.edu/~nathan/humor.html

It leads to formidable archives from the rec.humor newsgroup and other places.